THE ROAD TO PASSCHENDAELE

THE ROAD TO PASSCHENDAELE

The Heroic Year in Soldiers'
own Words and Photographs

Richard van Emden

Pen & Sword
MILITARY

First published in Great Britain in 2017 by
Pen & Sword Military
an imprint of
Pen & Sword Books Ltd
47 Church Street
Barnsley
South Yorkshire
S70 2AS

ISBN 978 1 47389 190 6

Typeset in Ehrhardt by
Mac Style Ltd, Bridlington, East Yorkshire
Printed and bound in Malta by Gutenberg Press Ltd.

Pen & Sword Books Ltd incorporates the imprints of Pen & Sword Archaeology, Atlas, Aviation, Battleground, Discovery, Family History, History, Maritime, Military, Naval, Politics, Railways, Select, Transport, True Crime, and Fiction, Frontline Books, Leo Cooper, Praetorian Press, Seaforth Publishing and Wharncliffe.

For a complete list of Pen & Sword titles please contact
PEN & SWORD BOOKS LIMITED
47 Church Street, Barnsley, South Yorkshire, S70 2AS, England
E-mail: enquiries@pen-and-sword.co.uk
Website: www.pen-and-sword.co.uk

Title Page: *A private of the 3rd Worcestershire Regiment stares at the camera during the Battle of Messines, June 1917.*

Frontispiece: Shell explosions during fighting, January 1917.

To
Linne Matthews

CONTENTS

Opposite: *A piper of the 1/4th Seaforth Highlanders plays during a roadside break, July 1917.*

Introduction

'I was woken by a heavy trench bombardment and got
up to see what it was.… It turned out to be a half-hour's
strafe by the enemy of the brigade on our left, but as it
was nothing to do with me I turned in again and finished
my sleep.'

Major Rowland Feilding, 6th The Connaught Rangers

Back in the 1970s, Great War veteran Lieutenant Patrick Koekkoek was interviewed for a book on the Battle of the Somme. After publication, the author sent Koekkoek a complimentary copy but, after reading it, he remarked to his daughter that he did not like it. 'It wasn't like that,' he said. This anecdote, recalled forty years later, was intriguing.

In any popular campaign history, the author is understandably inclined to flit from one part of the battlefield to another, to follow, in effect, the action: why dwell where nothing was happening? The technique is entirely valid and normally vivid, but the effect can be, albeit unintentionally, to give a skewed impression of carnage without end, of death and horror as a daily staple diet for men in the midst of a battle. That was what this former officer had objected to, not the veracity of assembled veteran recollections or the manner in which they were turned to prose. Koekkoek's memories were more nuanced than the collected wisdom of scores of men asked specific questions of a battle.

Mentally, men simply could not have survived without periodic lulls in the fighting. They needed rest in the line as much as out of it, even if that rest was continually interrupted. So, although engaged in a general offensive, if the fighting raged 2 or 3 miles away, soldiers learnt to switch off, at least in part. As the officer quoted at top of the page wrote to his wife from the trenches, in 1917, 'as it was nothing to do with me I turned in again and finished my sleep.'

Opposite: *Stretcher-bearers and runners of the 3rd Worcestershire Regiment in a trench, Messines, June 1917.*

And although the fighting ranged over many miles, sucking in hundreds of thousands of men, the majority of men serving on the Western Front were not directly involved. When the British Army numbered 2 million men in France and Flanders, the majority of them were in other, quieter parts of the line, perhaps recuperating and largely ignorant of an offensive elsewhere even though it might be audible. While writing this book about 1917, I have reminded myself not to forget the 'elsewhere'.

Captain James Pollock VC, 5th Cameron Highlanders, near Ypres, July 1917.

Unlike 1916, a year during which British and Empire troops were involved in one campaign, 1917 was a year of four distinct offensives, two of significant duration: Arras (early April to mid-May) and Third Ypres (July through to November) and two short: Messines (June) and Cambrai

(late November to early December). Given the number of offensives, it is surprising that the fighting of 1917 lasted, in total, just twenty-five days longer than that of the previous year's Battle of the Somme.

Nevertheless, and with the benefit of hindsight, 1917 does appear to be a year of unparalleled misery on both sides of the line: an end to the war was nowhere near in sight, and popular enthusiasm for the struggle had long since eroded. There were high points for the British and Empire troops in 1917: the seizing of the Messines Ridge was an attack of extraordinary cunning and brilliant execution. The storming of Vimy Ridge by the Canadians on the first day of the Arras offensive was another notable moment, as too were the opening hours of the Ypres offensive on 31 July and the first days of the fighting at Cambrai when, in late November, long-silent church bells in Britain were rung in premature jubilation at success. But these 'moments' did not lead to wider tactical success but rather to stalemate of one form or another. Vimy Ridge, for example, was the prelude to a further thirty-eight days of escalating attritional wretchedness in which British and Empire troops suffered 159,000 casualties, or 4,000 casualties on average a day – by comparison, a third higher than those suffered on the Somme.

Interestingly, the casualties for the offensives of 1916 and 1917 are not radically different: 415,000 on the Somme, 475,000 for the combined attacks of 1917. What was different was the mindset of the men who undertook them. In the lead up to the Somme, even during the battle, there were still the vestiges of spirited optimism that a decisive blow would bring the war to an end, a view held by the Commander-in-Chief, General Sir Douglas Haig, for some considerable time during the offensive. By contrast, the struggles of 1917, particularly at Arras and Ypres, were characterized by a grim resignation to the necessity of attrition and gradual battlefield predominance in men and arms. British troops did not lack morale and most fully expected to win, but not by a stroke of battlefield mastery. All in all, 1917 completed the transition to the 'wearing out' war. And, perhaps for the first time, the soldiers began to question the competence of their most senior commanding officers, as one long-serving company quarter master sergeant wrote of the fighting at Ypres in September 1917:

There was a growing conviction that the High Command was incompetent. I did not think so myself. I disliked the sort of journalism which was always talking of duds in high places. [But] it was natural that the poor devils in the slime, driven to the extreme of misery, should begin to doubt their commander just as they doubted God.

Where artillery fire was at its greatest concentration, the battlefields became featureless and, to the casual eye, life-abandoned, save for the men hunkered down in battered trenches. This landscape was an alien world in which easy orientation was nigh impossible: villages were obliterated and woods stripped back to petrified trunks. The contrast with the ground just a few miles away was stark, and the unbridled joy of troops out on rest, proper rest, 20 miles or more from the fighting, was intense. They had to get there from the trenches, of course. As they left the forward area, they had no energy for shows of gratitude or elation. As one of the last Great War veterans, Henry Allingham, described to me:

They [the infantry] were at the end of their tether. They were worn out, absolutely done up. They could hardly put one foot before the other, they were gone, depleted, finished, all they wanted to do was sleep, sleep, sleep.

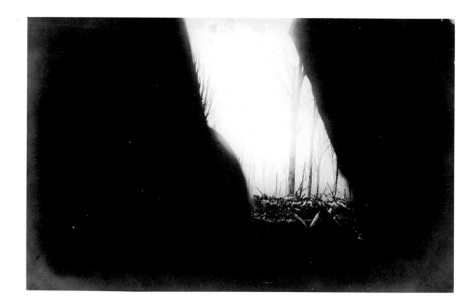

A small aperture in a front line trench with a view across no-man's-land.

But after sleep, after hot food, the lives of these men would be temporarily transformed. In building a picture of 1917, it would be remiss of me not to reflect that 'other' world, away from the line where fields were green and undamaged and there was time and space to think about home and family.

Passchendaele is the next in a series of books using the soldiers' own words and photographs to tell the story of the war, as opposed to the images taken by official photographers and the words of generals and politicians. These battlefield photographs, snapped on illegally held cameras, have, in the main, never been published before and have given us a new appreciation and understanding of the war as captured by men who had the presence of mind to stop whatever they were doing in order to peer momentarily through the camera's viewfinder, set the aperture and shutter speed and … snap: it is the war as they wished to record it. These men were taking a serious risk. Possession of cameras had been made illegal in December 1914 by the British Army, alarmed by the number of men selling images to the British press back home for publication in newspapers, newspapers that were almost entirely starved of front line photographs. The British Army had not appreciated the need of official photographers until 1916, when the first two were sanctioned for service on the Western Front.

In trying to quash the private use of cameras, the army threatened severe retribution, and a court martial awaited those unwise enough to disobey and then get caught. Nevertheless, a number of men did keep their cameras, mostly, but not exclusively, officers, who might be able to rely on their commanding officer's blind eye. Even so, the number of cameras

Left: *Officers of the Queen's Bays with cameras more sophisticated than most taken overseas.*

Right: *The ubiquitous Vest Pocket Kodak, by far the most common used camera by both officers and men.*

on the Western Front declined steeply as time passed. Army threats had removed most by the end of 1915, but the shortage of film stock also took its toll. But the decline in the use of cameras in France and Belgium also reflected a general wane in enthusiasm for the war. Gone was the thrill of adventure and in its place came the eviscerating reality of industrialized warfare. It is relatively easy to source soldiers' photographs taken in 1914 and 1915, significantly less easy to find images taken in 1916, and very hard to find soldiers' photography dating from 1917 or 1918. Photographs snapped overseas in the last twelve months of the war were typically taken by officers and men who had had no earlier experience of the reality of war.

Writing a book on 1917 introduces a new set of challenges. Artillery predominated: the number and weight of guns was far in excess of anything seen on the battlefield just two years before. The murdered earth, ground where lip-to-lip shell holes were the visual norm and trenches oozed with mud, does not immediately lend itself to images of great variation. My recent book on the Somme was able to offer greater scope in that sense. The troops had arrived on the Somme, a relative backwater, and for the first few months the land was in full bloom before it declined, slowly at first, into an abyss, culminating in and gripped by the extraordinarily hard winter of 1916/17. The battles of 1917 do not offer such a transition in soldiers' photography, and so to bring frequent relief to the pages of this book, I have sought to utilize images of the back areas, of men out on rest, of men preparing for the worst, while enjoying the best that life out of the line could bring.

One year: four offensives: this book does not set out to tell the detailed and convoluted story of these battles for it would be of inordinate length, and both repetitive and morbidly violent. Like my other books, *The Road To Passchendaele* does not offer the reader a slugfest of the minutiae of battles described to destruction, in which every morsel of ground taken is noted and quoted; rather, this book is about atmosphere.

What was it like to serve on the Western Front in 1917? What was so different about that year compared to what had happened before and what was to come? How did old soldiers appreciate the changes that had taken place since they had embarked for France and how did newcomers adapt to a ferociously violent front where the expenditure of munitions was prodigious and far greater that two years before? I wish to explore the attitude of the men who served and to question the view that because the men underwent untold miseries that they must also have lacked morale or questioned the war's purpose or validity. While it would be impossible to tell the story of that momentous year without addressing the Allies' offensives, this in not the focus here. Rather, this book is about reflecting as much on the men out of battle as in it, a war as Patrick Koekkoek, the individual soldier, wished to remember it.

Richard van Emden
March 2017

Overleaf:
*January 1917,
near Combles
village. The frozen
wasteland of
the Somme
Battlefield.*

1 Winter Wonderland

'We are not ashamed of being afraid, as we often are not afraid of any definite thing, but just afraid of being afraid; when the time for action comes there is little time for fear. In warfare only cowards are the really brave men, for they have to force themselves to do things that brave men do instinctively.'

Lieutenant George Brown, 9th The Suffolk Regiment

———

As each year of conflict ended and a new one began, there was an opportunity for a pause, a traditional festive moment of reflection when men could look back upon the year that was and forward to what might be. The war had not been brought to a successful conclusion, clearly, but surely the New Year would bring victory? These were thoughts common to troops of every nationality, resolutely optimistic that they would prevail. British and Empire troops, feet stamping in draughty camps and freezing trenches, held a conviction as strong as anyone of victory, not necessarily straightaway, but at some point during the forthcoming calendar year. Back in January 1915 it mattered little that there was physical evidence to the contrary – the enemy's predominance in men and munitions – rather, the manifest virtue of Britain's cause and her conspicuous power built on Empire would provide the impetus for success. Princess Mary had included that presumption in her festive gift, her present of 1914, given to all soldiers on the Western Front. Tucked under the packets of tobacco and cigarettes – a slab of acid drop in paper for non-smokers – was a small envelope: inside, her picture and her message wishing all a happy Christmas 'and a Victorious New Year'.

Twelve months later, many soldiers again expected success, as was made apparent in letters and diaries. There were more tangible reasons for hope by 1916. The British Secretary of State for War, Lord Kitchener, had recruited his New Army of civilians-turned-soldiers on the outbreak of war, and they were now pouring into France. These men were taking much of the strain so courageously borne by Regular and Territorial troops that had held the German Army in check. Now

Opposite: A direct hit: a house made uninhabitable by shellfire.

anyone who had been abroad twelve months or more could hardly fail to notice the exponential growth in troop numbers or the near parity between British and German arms – no more scandalous rationing of artillery shells to the Royal Field Artillery, as had happened in early 1915. 'Old sweats', as these soldiers liked to see themselves, could compare and contrast not only the ebb and flow of the fighting but its changing nature too. The Battle of the Somme in 1916 had ushered in a profound change. The 'Big Push', as it was known, was fully fledged industrial warfare and of an entirely different order from anything the British Army had been involved in … ever. Artillery bombardments were frequently of stupefying length and intensity, and tanks, that ingenious product of focused war minds, had made their debut, a very visceral and visual addition to the panoply of new battlefield weapons. On the defensive, the German Army fought with tenacity, and British troops could not but grudgingly acknowledge the enemy's stubbornness and resolve. In four and a half months, the Germans relinquished slivers of tortured ground and showed no signs of military collapse. It was now a foolhardy man who blithely predicted Allied victory in 1917, and those who spoke of the future were circumspect in what they said. Lieutenant Paul Jones took a moment for reflection on 1 January 1917 when he wrote home to his family. He had been in France eighteen months:

> Hearty wishes for a happy New Year, wishes which always seem to me more serious than the greetings that pass at Christmas time. With most people Christmas is a purely festive season, but with the end of the old year comes the necessity of looking forward to a new period – perhaps to be joyful, perhaps otherwise; anyway, a period on which it is necessary to enter as far as possible with confidence. From the general point of view that is not an easy matter as things stand. I am bound to say I am getting pessimistic about the war. The chief trouble is the total lack of action that characterizes it. This grovelling in ditches is a rotten, foolish business in many ways.

Ditch grovelling had been the war's chief characteristic since autumn 1914, when entrenching was the only sensible reaction to machine guns and artillery fire that made unprotected exposure to their combined power lethal. Since then, the ground into which men had hunkered gradually altered from fields that looked agricultural to something otherworldly, more moonscape than landscape. Only concerted action brought large numbers of men out into the open, but time and again the 'defensive' trumped the 'offensive' and no-man's-land would resume its wasteland characteristics, observed through the infantryman's trench periscope or, looking down, viewed from the pilot's cockpit.

The Battle of Verdun, launched by the Germans against the French in February 1916, and the Allied Somme offensive, launched in July, were supreme tests of man's endurance. Numerically, the Germans lost more troops on the Western Front than any other single country and resolved, out of tactical necessity, to alter the situation. The Battle of the Somme had been fought within a large and, with the benefit of hindsight, rather unwieldy bulge in the German lines. This 'bulge' meant more German troops were deployed to occupy the front line than would otherwise be the case had it been straighter. For the first time in the war, circumstances forced the Germans to value lives more highly than holding land, so a decision was taken to withdraw to a newly constructed, intensely defended trench system. The Germans named it the Siegfried Stellung; to the Allies it was the Hindenburg Line.

When the Germans began to pull back to this new position in March 1917, British troops wondered whether the withdrawal might adversely affect the enemy's morale: but after all the disappointments of the last two years, many nebulously 'hoped' the war might end soon but fewer extrapolated further. Nevertheless, the Germans' withdrawal from land they had fought so hard to hold was suggestive of weakness rather than strength. The current was turning against the Germans and should have given the Allies cause for quiet optimism. On the Western Front, the balance of physical power was slowly, irresistibly and perceptibly moving in favour of the Allies, while elsewhere, diplomatically, the Germans had been the first to put out tentative feelers for a negotiated peace. These first moves came to nothing, but it suggested that the enemy was no longer confident of ultimate victory.

1917 would be a hateful year. The German launch of unrestricted submarine warfare was their attempt to starve Britain into submission, just as the Allies were attempting the same to the Germans by their use of a maritime blockade. On the Western Front, the year would be characterized by perhaps the bitterest fighting of the war, an unprecedented slugfest. The niceties of war were consigned to the past: any idea of a Christmas Truce, as had so famously occurred in 1914 and to a lesser extent in 1915, belonged to another world. War was a serious business and best business practice required results without sympathy, unnecessary inefficiency or delay. The Germans, the Allies decided, would be harried at every possible turn.

Whereas the battles of 1916 had been fought in the main by Kitchener's Army, war in 1917 would be prosecuted by increasing numbers of conscripted men, men who did not want to be in France a moment longer than necessary. Those who

January 1917: Tank C16 abandoned between Leuze Wood and Combles on the Somme. It was knocked out by a British shell falling short, 15 September 1916.

fought did so with grim determination to see the war to its conclusion, reluctantly resigned to whatever fate had in store. This attitude percolated down to French and Belgian civilians too, who had grown used to enemy shelling and displayed an astonishing level of sangfroid while clinging to their towns and villages within the war zone. But while the Germans were the greatest enemy, in the first months of 1917 soldiers and civilians alike would be challenged by another formidable adversary: the winter weather, the bitterest in living memory.

Lieutenant Colonel Rowland Feilding, 6th The Connaught Rangers, Cooker Farm, facing Messines-Wytschaete Ridge, near Ypres

25 December 1916: Though this is Christmas Day, things have not been as quiet as they might have been, though we have not suffered. I fancy the battalion on our right has done so to some extent. In fact, as I passed along their fire trench, I saw them at work, digging some poor fellows out who had been buried by a trench mortar bomb.

   This evening since dark, for a couple of hours, the Germans have been bombarding some place behind us with heavy shells. The battery from which the fire is coming is so far away that I cannot even faintly hear the report of the guns while I am in the open trench, though, from the dugout from which I now write, I can just distinguish it, transmitted through the medium of the ground. I can hear the shells at a great altitude overhead rushing through the air. …

I went round and wished the men – scarcely a Merry Christmas, but good luck in the New Year, and may they never have to spend another Christmas in the front line! This meant much repetition on my part.

I have a good many recruits just now. Some of them went into the line for the first time last night. I visited them at their posts soon after they had reached the fire trench, and asked them how they liked it. They are just boys feeling their way. They wore a rather bewildered look.

30 December: Today, the battalion being out of the trenches, we celebrated Christmas in a sort of way; that is to say, the men had turkey and plum-pudding, and French beer for dinner, and a holiday from 'fatigues'.

I hope they enjoyed it. The extras – over and above those contributed by friends at home (whose presents had been very liberal) – cost the battalion funds around £90. But when I went round and saw the dinners I must confess I was disappointed. Our surroundings do not lend themselves to this kind of entertainment; and, as to appliances – tables, plates, cutlery, etc. – well, we have none. The turkeys had to be cut into shreds and dished up in the mess tins. Beer had to be ladled out of buckets (or rather dixies) later, into the same mess tins; out of which also the plum pudding was taken, the men sitting herded about on the floors of dark huts. …

Although well within range of the daily shellfire, there is a woman with a baby living in the farm where I and my headquarter officers' mess. There have, during the past few days, been some heavy bombardments, directed at our batteries in the immediate neighbourhood, in fact in the adjacent fields, some of which are sprinkled like pepper pots with shell holes. There is a hole through the roof of the hut in which I live, made by shrapnel, and I admit that the thought of the battalion with nothing but galvanized roofing and thick wooden walls between it and the enemy, is at times depressing. The place is indeed most unsuited for a 'Rest' Camp, which it is supposed to be, and still less for a nursery.

Still, the woman with the baby clings to her home. I wonder at these women with their babies. They must be possessed of boundless faith. There seems to be a sort of fatalism, and, as a matter of fact, they seldom get injured.

31 December (midnight): It is midnight. As I write, all the heavies we possess are loosing off their New Year's 'Joy' to the Germans, making my hut vibrate. The men in their huts are cheering and singing *Old Lang Syne*.

The rumpus started at five minutes to twelve. Now, as it strikes the hour, all has stopped, including the singing as suddenly as it began. The guns awakened the men, who clearly approved. The enemy has not replied with a single shot in this direction.

1 January 1917: We heard Mass again this – New Year's – morning; our third Sunday in three days! The first *our* Christmas Day; the second yesterday, the real Sunday when Monseigneur Ryan, from Tipperary, preached; the third, today.

In spite of the heavy calls for working parties for the front line each day and night, the men off duty toll up always, and march behind the drums to wherever the service may be – in small parties, of course, owing to the proximity of the firing line.

Pray for them as hard as you possibly can.

9 January [facing Messines-Wytschaete Ridge]: After a peaceful day yesterday the enemy is at it again very vicious (I suppose auxiliary to his peace negotiations), and is plastering the place with thousands of trench mortar bombs and shells; doing precious little harm; – like a naughty child breaking its toys out of spite, but necessitating a good deal of repair work on our part. We give him back a good deal more than we get, and it must all be very expensive. The whole place is a sea of mud and misery, but I must not grumble at the mud. It saves many thousands of lives by localizing the shell bursts, and by muffling those very nasty German trench mortar bombs.

14 January: We came out of the trenches last night. I could not describe them if I tried, but they are more wretched looking than any I have seen since I came to the war.

The most imaginative mind could not conceive an adequate picture of the frail and battered wall of shredded sandbags without actually seeing it, nor the heroic manner in which the men who hold it face its dangers and discomforts; – the mud and the slush and the snow; often knee-deep, and deeper still, in water. The foulest of weather; four days and nights (sometimes five) without moving from one spot; pounded incessantly with what the soldiers call 'rum-jars' – great canisters of high explosive, fired from wooden mortars, making monstrous explosions; and often in addition going through an hour or two during the day or night – sometimes two or three times during the twenty-four hours – of intense bombardment by these things as well as by every other sort of atrocity the enemy knows how to use. …

From the front line, after eight days, the battalion goes into Brigade Reserve. Even from there the men go up to the front line most nights on working parties, and are pounded again. Then eight days in the front line once more.

I suppose men now going about in short frocks will thrill thirty years hence as they read of our adventures – of charging over the dead littered no-man's-land against the battered German lines, or running hell for leather through a barrage of shells, or bringing in wounded under fire. These readers will envy us our romances of danger. They will hardly realize how dull and dirty war really is, what a fight we have against lousiness and trench inertia. How thoroughly 'fed-up with the whole issue' every soldier is, save, perhaps, a few young gentlemen who, previously aimless, now find responsibility, the exercise of command and caste exclusiveness, much to their liking. … For myself I dislike this life, not so much because it is dull and unprofitable. The censor has pretty well stifled the journalistic me – it is the people at home who are writing most of the war stuff. But we must go on and not lose heart. We had to fight this war, and we must win it. We must not be disloyal to our dead.

CQMS William Andrews, 1/4th The Black Watch (Royal Highlanders)

14 February: After a break of two days it has started freezing here again, and we are once more back in the somewhat sub-arctic state of affairs to which we had become accustomed. It just thawed enough to make

Second Lieutenant Harold Parry, 17th The King's Royal Rifle Corps

everything muddy on the top, and whatever progress one made was rendered precarious by the fact that one never quite knew what either foot was doing at a specified moment. One foot might be planted with Horatian firmness on an obvious and non-treacherous spot, the other would glide down into a welter of mud and water and snow ice, such as one becomes especially and reluctantly conversant with out here. However, now that it has frozen again, now that the roads are glassy and the fields icebound, we do know where we are and can go on sliding till further notice. This state of affairs is, on the whole, infinitely preferable to that which existed during the brief thaw. Then you earnestly desired to keep upright and dignified (to fall meant to get intolerably wet and muddy), and one was in a constantly preoccupied and strained state of mind in futile endeavours to avoid the inevitable. Now one can fall down without loss of dignity, and sympathy (hitherto absent) is forthcoming from other and like unfortunates. ...

To remain cheery under depressing circumstances is a necessity to the average mortal out here. The other thing has one ending only – lunacy. Of course, one does meet not infrequently pessimists of the darkest sort and grousers of the most complete equipment out here, but if one were to enquire closely into their antecedents, one would inevitably find that in civil life they were the same. Their pessimism is their lifeblood. They do not lack cheeriness or humour – they seriously believe that pessimism is most exquisite wit – and use it as a balm and salve to all their ills and misfortunes. ...

I'm glad to hear that everyone at home is feeling better. War, lack of fitness and abominably cold weather must have conduced to a violent attack of the dumps. Keep tolerably fit and you can keep tolerably happy. As for myself, I'm still jogging along horribly fed up with the war, but immeasurably more fed up with the Boches as a nation. Germany, to say the least of it, is a bitter disappointment to her sister nations. That Kultur should end in the avowed intention of sinking hospital ships is more than lamentable. It brands Germany with the devil's mark, and the war must go on until there is never, never again any chance of such a Kultur with such an ending. Though war is so inhuman, especially in its utter severance of a man from everything for which he cares, it is infinitely preferable to peace while yet the devil has not been cast out of Germany. Still, even so, it can't

Sporadic fighting continued on the Somme into the New Year. A German officer is taken across the frozen duckboard track.

go on much longer, and then will come the real and vital part of the conflict – the aftermath. I often wonder on what lines the world will be reconstructed, and seek for assurances which often times are terribly hard to discover, and when discovered they are where one would last look for them – close alongside in the trenches – Bill Smith on gas guard or John Thomas on the Lewis gun. These are just a few thoughts and impressions I've gained, a very few out of a grand and imposing incoherence.

My sponge and shaving brush, except when in use and despite the fire, were permanently frozen solid on their shelf; for it was a time of intense cold and of snow. The wide sweeps of the Somme were transformed by the mantling snow. Leagues and leagues of duckboard tracks like filigree upon the whitened surface, traced paths across this undulating country. Although no more than five years have gone, I cannot recapture the magic there then. The whole picture effortlessly comes to mind; yet something at the heart of the magic eludes me. I am left with a vivid pattern of feeling which is too esoteric to share. It teases me, it balks me and is not of the least importance as I do not suppose that anyone wishes, or ever will wish to share it. Awhile I will talk to myself, so to say; and hum to myself that haunting period piece *There's a Long, Long Trail*. It was apt to my mood then. Easily, always it awakens those moods. It spreads out that landscape as nothing else can, spreads it out before me: the wide, white almost silent Somme landscape and the track which wound itself to the top of the rise then ran a straighter course down to Martinpuich and beyond. Daily I tramped along it, humming the tune as I went, often returning late in the afternoon, facing the setting sun, leaving behind the darkening country where the enemy was. It was just the air of the chorus which affected and still affects me.

Captain Lawrence Gameson, RAMC attd. / 1st Brigade, Royal Field Artillery

The frozen covering snow was crisp. It shone. The terrible countryside, of filth and of sorrows that could never be counted, glittered. The shining snow temporarily hid all scars. The transformation was heartening. Movement was reduced for movement left traces. Fixed battery positions in the surrounding whiteness could scarcely fail to be seen from the air; and gun flashes melted the snow in front of them; so perhaps guns shot less, I do not remember. Be that as it may, peace of a sort came to this shining country; even to the infantry, even to the Jocks – many of whom were restless folk ever itching for offensive action.

In the gloriously fresh air and the intensely cold weather, one was quickly rid of the debilitating effects of my longish bout of tonsillitis. Journeys to batteries were physically exhilarating. The air was icy. Often when moving along the duckboard track I had to step off and crouch in a shell hole to warm up my ears. My handkerchief, if left in an outside pocket, was always frozen stiff as I walked. The tracks were very slippery, needing the nimble footwork of a young goat rather than that of feet shod with studded boots. All the tracks were known to the enemy, as our own air photographs clearly proved. He seldom shot at the one to Martinpuich, except at the end near the village. Here the track was often disordered, splotched at each side with thrown-up soil and sometimes with blood.

Lieutenant Alan Thomas, 6th (Queen's Own) Royal West Kent Regiment

In January we had been up to Arras for a spell. A queer experience that – an amazing blend of civilization and desolation. For billets we used maisonettes and sometimes wealthy looking mansions: only there was no glass in any of the windows and as often as not the walls and ceilings were gashed with ugly rents. Such furniture as had been left was usually of the solid, immovable kind: a vast mahogany table would be in position in the dining salon, and placed round it for the evening meal would be not chairs, but packing cases. In the bedrooms splendid bedsteads appeared ready to receive us – but it was impossible to lie in them because they had no springs or slats. But the oddest thing of all about Arras was the change that came on the city when darkness fell. By day Arras was a city of the dead. No one was allowed out except on duty, and even then you were expected to go about singly and to hug the walls instead of walking in the middle of the pavement or the road. But after sunset the whole place would spring to life. The streets would be crowded and the shops would open up. The cheap jewellers in the rue Gambetta must have done a roaring trade selling trinkets to the troops. The theatre, too, would be open and here the various divisional concert parties would rival one another in giving 'all-star' performances to crowded houses.

Another strange feature of our stay in Arras that January was our situation in the line. The trenches we occupied were in the suburb of Blangy. A few houses were still standing and our company headquarters occupied one of them – a pleasant little villa with a bowl of goldfish in the drawing room and a nude statue of Venus at the bottom of the garden (the statue was chipped about a bit as it served as a target for revolver practice). The trenches themselves were just across the road: good bricked-up trenches they were, running north to the banks of the river Scarpe: and your footsteps could easily be heard as you walked along them. So could those of the German sentries as they paced along *their* trenches, which in this small section of the line were no more than 10 or 15 yards away from ours. The closeness of the two lines was a good insurance against strafing on either side. The mildest exchange of hand grenades or bombs, still more of Minenwerfers, would have made life quite intolerable.

Most of the inhabitants had been driven from their homes to take but one. I had learned something of them and the manner of their going. Entirely without specious sentiments, actually it hit you at every turn, one could not help imaginatively looking backwards from time to time. When, for example, I walked through the station and saw the damaged clock halted at 3.55, I found it impossible to evade effortless daydreaming about what that dead piece of machinery had once meant to hundreds of hurrying passengers straining their heart in efforts to catch the trains. The lines were grown over with grass now. Great tufts of greenstuff grew rank on the platforms between broken flagstones. There was chaos in the waiting room's arid booking hall. On a morning's wandering to batteries, I remember adding fuel to futility by playing a lone game in the booking hall. I uncovered a shelf of local tickets and a thing for punching, then booked myself to places I knew from the map to be in enemy country. It seemed a reasonable step towards getting there – although hardly the infantry's method.

Captain Lawrence Gameson, RAMC attd. 71st Brigade, Royal Field Artillery

Those unused tickets were only a tiny part of things left behind. The silent town was bestrewn throughout with things made for use, but unused. It was bestrewn, too, more plentifully, more poignantly, with handled and abandoned things.

My leisure time was mostly spent strolling around alone. I made my way into houses, climbed to attics, went down cellars, peeped into rooms and got fleeting glimpses as if peeping in on a party when the guests had gone, seeing there the empty chairs and how the guests had grouped them, hazarding guesses.

Often I wandered out of my way along the older, narrow streets; streets for so long without human warmth, uncannily quiet, shuttered, eyeless, lost and rather frightening, yet sometimes opening quite unexpectedly upon the width of spacious, sunlit, strangely quiet squares. Such a one was the Petite Place, a charming open space that had fared badly in 1914. The graceful Hotel de Ville was flat with the ground. Only the belfry's stump stood up. I remember a metal top hat, still in position there, which marked the shaken premises of a departed hatter. In early 1917, the Hun wasted no ammunition on the Petite Place. It was a quiet, though woefully battered square. . . .

Near the station we saw a house which had been neatly bisected like a doll's house with the front removed, but not an exact simile. One side of the kitchen was in perfect order: unbroken plates in their racks, this and that and the other hanging on hooks in precise alignment. The opposite side had vanished, deftly removed as if cut off by a knife. And the same upstairs; a bed remained on half a floor along with intimate appurtenances common to human nests. The front of the house was boarded up. I wriggled inside while Topsy kept watch without. When searching for a token, I am undeterred by the strict rules against even minor looting. Topsy suddenly hissed that a Frenchman was upon us and I had to wriggle back tokenless. My conscience, so one imagines, is tolerably clear in this matter of picking up trifles, yet there is always the possibility that my trifle may turn out to be somebody's treasure. However, considering the things I take and the circumstances in which I find them, this is very doubtful.

Civilians cling to their homes despite the danger of shellfire. These women are washing clothes in a ruined house on the outskirts of Arras.

In Achicourt, a village about half a mile from the Germans' front line, a few civilians were still living. The troops would buy eggs, butter, bread, vegetables, and such like articles from these French residents. Another man and I used to make a practice of going down to the house of a French carpenter's wife and having the usual meal of omelette, 'petit pois' or 'haricot vert' and café au lait. She was a wonderful cook, as most of the French women are, and seemed to find a good deal of amusement in our attempts at conversation with her. Like many other French women still living in their homes close to the line, shelling did not bother her much. We used to have our meals in her kitchen. The room adjoining, the parlour, had been entirely destroyed by a shell, and several bullets had gone through the window of the kitchen. Shells would often land in the road outside and in the garden at the back while we were at meals there. Madam B. would immediately order her young son, aged about twelve, and her daughter, about eighteen, to light a lamp and go down to the cellar while the shelling continued.

Her husband was serving with the French Army at Verdun and returned on a week's 'permission' (leave) during the time we were in

Second Lieutenant Harry Trounce, 181 Tunnelling Company, Royal Engineers this village. It amused the Tommies very much to think that any soldier would care to spend his leave in a village so close to the line. We were constantly advising the civilians to move back to a safer area, particularly the women, but the poor people had not much choice. The British Army authorities I understand offered to move them all, together with their portable belongings, but they were evidently afraid of having their houses destroyed and their little farms or gardens torn up. Their love of home was stronger than their fear of death, or else they couldn't understand.

Second Lieutenant Harry Trounce was surprised, just as Lieutenant Colonel Feilding had been, at seeing civilians living so close to the front line. In January, his unit of the Royal Engineers was moved from the Somme battlefield to Arras, where he was charged 'with the construction of forward underground galleries under no-man's-land' as well as deep dugouts in Arras 'and the villages and trenches to the south'. There was good reason for such special industry.

Although the Somme offensive had been officially shut down, British troops continued to take small bites out of the German lines, partly to keep up pressure on the enemy, but also to take ground advantageous to troops relaunching an offensive in the spring. A joint Anglo-French venture had been planned, though not cheek by jowl as on the Somme. Rather, the British would attack between the Somme and Arras, the French, on the Aisne to the south.

The Somme battle still raged when the decision to launch an offensive was taken. It was pencilled in for February 1917 but political and military machinations had altered the outlook, most notably when the French Army's Commander-in-Chief, General Joseph Joffre, was sacked in December, to be replaced by General Robert Nivelle.

Nivelle's reputation was riding high after success at Verdun when his troops counter-attacked in October, seizing in a matter of hours much of the ground lost to the Germans earlier that year. With overweening confidence, inflated by public adulation, Nivelle dispensed with the plans of attack as agreed between Joffre and the British Commander-in-Chief, predicting instead that his tactics would rupture overnight the stalemate on the Western Front. Field Marshal Haig, whose primary ambitions lay in the Ypres Salient, was reluctantly persuaded by the British Prime Minister, Lloyd George, to cooperate, including, to Haig's consternation, placing the British Expeditionary Force temporarily under French control.

Nivelle's forces would spearhead the push against the Germans, with a major subsidiary attack conducted by the British to draw off enemy reserves. Haig agreed to Nivelle's robust plans, though he predicted 'heavy losses, and no possibility of a showy success' for his own troops. Haig was also uneasy about attacking before he felt fully prepared, but then, before a final date was settled, the enemy threw Allied plans into a state of flux by their sudden withdrawal to the Hindenburg Line, German soldiers laying waste to the land vacated and leaving a plethora of booby traps in dugouts and houses to catch unsuspecting and curious Tommies.

That winter's sporadic fighting on the Somme was a departure from corresponding periods in 1914 and 1915. Then opposing sides had engaged in a weather-enforced truce, the fighting petering out as the High Command assessed the forces at their disposal and made plans for the following year. For experienced soldiers such as CQMS William Andrews, the radical changes he had witnessed over two years' service in France gave him reason for reflection.

Sometimes, when I tramped with speckless boots along the duckboards of a neatly ruled trench, 1917 pattern, the mood of the Ancient Inhabitant came upon me. Like the village crony who has seen some streets grow out into the leafy countryside, and remembers the tumbledown cottages standing where now a merchant has his mansion, I thought with a certain satisfaction, mingled with a little regret, of changed days. ...

When I did my first turn of sentry in the front line, we thought of trench life as the stagnation of warfare. Then we saw it change in form and spirit, most notably in the development of the continuous offensive – the raids, the multiplication of trench mortars and rifle grenades, and the exchange of fire at all hours. Very different was that watchful waiting of 1914–15 days, when you might eat and drink and sleep the round of the clock and hear not a dozen shots.

The chief trench occupation in the first war winter was, normally, nothing deadlier than tea making. We made tea for breakfast, tea for dinner, tea at teatime, tea for supper. There was no tinned milk, and rarely sugar, but plum and apple jam was abundant, and was mixed with the boiling water. Biscuits and bully were rarely short. Such a luxury as stew in the front line was never thought of. But now hot meals were cooked in well-protected kitchens behind the line, and taken up in containers. They

CQMS William Andrews, 1/4th The Black Watch (Royal Highlanders)

were much more varied, too. About the time we went to the front, 'the best-fed army in history' was an ironical phrase of great popularity among the troops. Few of us could dispute its sober accuracy now.

If our feeding was makeshift then, in comparison with 1917, much more so was the shelter the trenches afforded. The trench was usually shallow and always muddy. If it was raining (it generally was) you rigged up your waterproof sheet with bayonets across a corner of the trench bay, and sat under it on the firing step to snatch what sleep you could.

The dugout at first was a hole in the parapet, or the parados, with a sheet or a door across the top. Gradually men became more ambitious and carved dugouts big enough to shelter the whole body.... None foresaw the succession of fruitful improvements destined to make the dugout the underground fortress it became.

Soldiering was a simple affair of endurance when the battalion went out to France. After a few weeks in the trenches, and our experiences in the battle of Neuve Chapelle, we considered – we gallant fellows of the Territorial first line – that we were by no means novices in the art of war, by no manner of means. None of us had thrown a bomb, gas was a horror veiled in the future, and about the only specialists we had, in the army sense, were cooks and signallers.

But now it seemed that fighting required a long apprenticeship. The drafts came up with heads chock-full of instructions and muscles trained to their tasks like prizefighters. Schools of instruction had become an immense business in the great world of the army. Every man was a specialist, in addition to being trained in musketry. This development had beneficial results both directly and indirectly. A man who went to school and came back a certified first-class bomber fought with increased self-respect.

The greatest change seen in the trenches since 1914, so far as the ordinary infantryman's ordinary experiences were concerned, was the introduction of cloud gas fighting. There was an alertness, a tenseness, in the trenches we never knew in the old days. Gas was a hideous stimulant to our trench garrisons. The use of it by the Germans in the agony of the fight for Ypres, in which we first learned its diabolical nature, was considered the unforgivable sin. If the private soldier had been permitted to choose the form of punishment for the author of the war, he would have suggested a whiff of gas.

Opposite: *New weapons of war: thermite shell explosions in early 1917. The shells' contents burnt at an extremely high temperature, turning the snow into columns of steam.*

Under such radically altered conditions, Andrews was acutely aware of the pressure new men were under in France. The changing nature of the war meant there were far fewer options for a soft introduction to front line life.

CQMS William
Andrews, 1/4th
The Black
Watch (Royal
Highlanders)

We were getting many conscripts from home, and I was intensely sorry for them. Many were middle-aged, with wives and families, and to be put straight into action, as many of them were, was beyond all question a far greater trial than we veterans had to begin with. Yet for the most part they made a good show. One day I went up to the line to see an oldish man, who had just come out to us and cheer him up if possible. To my amazement I found him quite happy in a shell hole, drying his stockings on the feet of a German who had been blown up and landed head first in the mud, and whose legs alone were now to be seen.

By comparison to the Somme offensive, the relative lull in fighting afforded men some time to rest from the extraordinary demands that had been made of them. It also gave the army the opportunity to reward exemplary behaviour and courage, and parades were held and medals pinned on swelling chests. Such ceremonies were good for morale. In February, during a particularly arctic period of winter weather, Lieutenant Colonel Rowland Feilding composed a letter to his wife in which he reflected on the award of decorations.

Lieutenant
Colonel
Rowland
Feilding, 6th
The Connaught
Rangers

A certain very charming and gallant general, who sometimes visits us, is fond of making little speeches to any group of men he may find drilling, or in the huts when we are out of the line. He also – very properly – likes to take an opportunity to shake hands with any man who has been rewarded or mentioned for having performed a gallant action: and he has a way on such occasions of turning suddenly to the senior officer present and asking 'What were the details of the act for which this man was recommended?'

Among so many stirring events, that is not always easy to recall at a moment's notice, especially when some period has elapsed since the recommendation was made.

Some little time ago, I was told to put forward the name of an NCO or man for a certain foreign decoration. In parenthesis, I may say that I am often called upon to do this, but the recommendation so rarely materializes that the pastime is a dull one. On the occasion in question it had been stipulated, as usual, that the recommendation should be for a 'specific act'. It so happened at the moment that there was no 'specific act' outstanding. However, I decided to give the chance to the Lewis gunners, who I thought had not been recognized as well as they might have been.

The Lewis gun officer either did not take sufficient interest in the matter or did not feel himself equal to the task of 'writing the necessary story'; at any rate, he said he had nobody to recommend. Immediately, one of the company commanders who happened to be in the room, more alert, said to me: 'Why not put forward Sergeant R___? He has done excellent work since the battalion came to France, and has got nothing.'

This was very true, and no other man being forthcoming, I asked, 'What is the specific act?'

The Company Commander said: 'Well, I don't quite know about that.'

I said: 'Think it over, and if you can recommend Sergeant R. for a specific act, I shall be glad to put his name forward.'

The Company Commander went away, and later in the evening I received his recommendation, couched in the glowing 'paint the lily' style, which is required if these efforts are to be successful. I sent it forward and, not long afterwards, Sergeant R. was awarded the Military Medal – a better decoration than that for which he had been recommended. Clearly, the Company Commander's word picture of the 'specific act' had been well thought of by the Powers who decided these things. Incidentally, Sergeant R. had received what he richly deserved, though perhaps would never have had but for the circumstances I have mentioned.

Weeks passed. I went away on a course. Many exciting incidents intervened, and I confess that the nature of Sergeant R.'s 'specific act' had entirely escaped my memory, when the General arrived on the scene while Sergeant R.'s company was at exercise.

He first made the men a little speech. Then, having finished, he turned to me and asked: 'Is there anyone in the company who has received any decoration lately?'

I said: 'Yes, Sir, Sergeant R. has received the Military Medal.'

He went on: 'What was the act for which Sergeant R. received the Military Medal?'

As I have said, the literary effusion which had secured the well-merited award had gone completely out of my head. I looked towards the Company Commander. He, too, for a moment, was nonplussed. Then he butted boldly forward, and in glowing language described how one night when the enemy had demolished part of our breastwork, Sergeant R. had collected six bombers and without any orders had taken up a position in the battered breach etc., etc., etc.

The General then called Sergeant R. out in front of the company, and shaking him by the hand said: 'I am glad to have this opportunity of congratulating Sergeant R. for this gallant act on the night of the _____, when in the middle of a heavy trench mortar bombardment he collected six bombers, etc., etc.' – then, turning to the Company Commander, he asked: 'And what were the names of the six bombers? I should like to congratulate them, too.'

This time the Company Commander really was defeated. But the most amusing part of the episode was the look of modest surprise which mounted into the face of Sergeant R. as he heard his 'specific act' recounted. He stood like a solid block, his eyebrows rising higher and higher, while the company gazed in amazement at their hero.

I fancy the General, who is very wide awake, saw through it: but he was far too wise to show the fact.

The first tangible signs of a German withdrawal occurred in mid-February when British soldiers discovered some of the enemy's forward outposts and trenches abandoned, including, later that month, villages such as Pys, Serre Miraumont and Eaucourt, ground bitterly fought over in the latter parts of the Somme battle and now relinquished for free. This was not a general retirement; the Hindenburg Line was still under construction and the Germans were not prepared to leave the Somme just yet.

Captain Graham Greenwell, 1/4th The Oxfordshire and Buckinghamshire Light Infantry

We live in daily expectation of a Hun retirement, and this hope is strengthened by the numerous large fires seen behind their lines in a large town in front of us. Every time a new fire is sighted, the generals for miles around leap out of bed and begin babbling of pursuit, open warfare and cavalry manoeuvres. But after upsetting the well-earned rest of all the battalions in their immediate neighbourhood, they once more subside and content themselves with the lengthy pow-wows on what to do when the Germans do start recrossing the Rhine, and how best to run a subaltern's platoon for him from a chateau 15 miles behind the line. But it doesn't make much difference, as one can and does run one's own show when in the trenches without much interference save over the telephone wires, and they, thank God, are often cut.

Then, in mid-March, the move came suddenly. On the Somme, Captain Graham Greenwell had been ordered to take part in a small raid on the enemy trenches.

I am bursting with news, but dead tired; physical infirmity is doing battle with the spirit. … On the night before last at practically a moment's notice I was ordered to carry out [a] raid at 1.30 am. Motor lorries would start at 7.00 pm to take us to the trenches. We were *not* to return but to hang on, as in the opinion of our general, the Boche was almost certainly preparing to retreat.

> Captain Graham Greenwell, 1/4th The Oxfordshire and Buckinghamshire Light Infantry

We went up, but owing to the short notice we had been given, everything was a ghastly muddle. No guides were provided to take us to the front line and it was pretty dark. As we moved forward the Germans started putting up lights all the way along their front trenches almost without intermission; and as soon as they saw us coming along they began a bit of harmless firing. At 2.20 am I was still not in position to kick off, and the time for starting had carefully been put off from 1.30 until I reported that I was ready.

However, just as I was making my way to the CO to get him to put off the artillery bombardment till 3.00 am, the show began. There was a ghastly racket and a Boche bombardment descended promptly on our front and second lines, cutting me off from my men. I was furious and thought the whole business had been irretrievably muddled and that we should never even start. I rushed into the CO's dugout and told him he must stop the artillery and put the show off, but he said it was impossible and that I must push on.

I came out of the dugout into the trench feeling that the best thing I could do was to get hit as quickly as possible, and when I saw the Boche 'barrage' on the very trench I was in I realized it would be murder to take the men through it over the open [ground].

So, risking court martial, I stayed where I was until the row had died down a bit. Then I ran down to our front line and found my company mostly intact and all together, with my best subaltern – a dear boy, Pearson – knocked out.

I then got into touch with the two companies of Gloucesters on the right and found that they were all in confusion, but that some of them had got over to the German line. I therefore sent over at once my remaining officer with a platoon. I got a message back to say that he was in, that the Boche were gone and that he had a prisoner. So I came over with two more platoons at once, and sent back for the other company, which also came over. We pushed on to the second line and then to the third line. I got my telephone going and telephoned through to the CO to say that I could take a fourth line, too, if required, and that we had patrols out all round searching for the Boche.

Second Lieutenant Harry Trounce was just to the south of Arras but at the very northern corner of the German retirement. His tunnelling company had made great physical efforts to prepare dugouts for a spring offensive. Suddenly, all the work was put in jeopardy.

Second Lieutenant Harry Trounce, 181 Tunnelling Company, Royal Engineers

For a week previous to 18 March we had noticed many fires in the enemy lines and heard numerous explosions in the villages behind their trenches. Everything seemed to indicate that the enemy was preparing to retire along the trenches opposite us, as they had been doing to the south. Our own plans for an offensive were nipped in the bud by this untimely retreat of the Boche. It came earlier than was anticipated by the British Staff. For our part we had nearly finished the construction of a large number of dugouts close up which were to be used as assembly shelters for large attacking forces. On 18 March they evacuated the trenches at Beaurains, a village in the enemy lines across from us at Achicourt. Evidently they had abandoned these lines on the night of the 17th. On the morning of the 18th our infantry reported that there were no Germans in the trenches opposite.

View of BEAURAINS from trenches
North of Achicourt Road.

In the afternoon another man and I crossed over to Beaurains to investigate any dugouts which might have been left there. We only found two or three which had not been destroyed. These were all very deep and were strengthened at the entrance from the trench with heavily reinforced concrete, and in most cases there was a concrete wall also on the parados side of the trench opposite the entrance. As they were shelling the village heavily with 8-inch shells as they retreated, we did not tarry longer than necessary. The next day we went across again and followed up the retreating Huns until we came within rifle range. Our infantry had pursued them as hard as they could, but they were considerably handicapped on account of the fact that no supplies except what they could carry in their packs could be brought forward. The infantry had a hard time. The destruction of the road made it impossible for them to use their transport. It was very difficult for them to carry up sufficient rifle and machine-gun ammunition, much less adequate rations and water. I saw

Below: Bapaume abandoned by the Germans in March 1917.

many poor chaps drinking from the muddy shell holes, and they lived for several days on much-reduced 'iron rations'. Everywhere along the area of their retreat the Germans had blown big craters in the roads, craters from 30 to 100 feet deep and from 50 to 200 feet wide. These were blown at all crossroads, and in addition, at every quarter-of-a-mile interval on the roads. Their work of destruction everywhere was most thorough. All buildings and walls had been destroyed. Those alongside roads were felled across the latter – anything to tie up traffic. We seldom found a wall left which was over 3 feet in height.

Captain Graham Greenwell, 1/4th The Oxfordshire and Buckinghamshire Light Infantry

So trench warfare is over just here. We are miles away and cannot hear a gun – it seems absolutely extraordinary. I personally think the Huns will fall right back onto the enormously strong Hindenburg Line, and that we shall not dig in in front of them, which would be suicidal madness, but simply keep in touch by cavalry patrols.

March 19: Here we are still. We have not yet started in pursuit, as there is such a lot to do in the way of road making and bridging. But we shall be off very soon now. It will be strange to do open warfare for a bit, and rather exciting.... The Huns did certainly put arsenic in the wells at Baisleux, and they have left all sorts of little booby traps behind them. I quite forgot to look for them the other night when I got into their trenches, until the CO sent me up two sappers the next morning to examine the captured dugouts.

The cunning dogs half sawed through some bridges across the Somme, and put bombs underneath, which promptly blew up. They have left stoves in the dugouts all ready for lighting, which also blew up – in fact, they have done this retreat as thoroughly as they do everything else, and in spite of all that the papers say they have had very few casualties and have lost an extraordinarily small number of guns: Of course, they fired Péronne and Bapaume so as to get rid of military stores and to destroy billeting accommodation [for the advancing British troops].

Cellars, dugouts, and shelters of any description were obliterated or their entrances had been closed by firing charges of high explosives. The dugouts and ruins in many places were still on fire or smouldering. All trees were sawn off within a foot to 18 inches of their base, this work having evidently been done with small gasolene saws. Large trees were everywhere felled and left lying squarely across the roads. All wells were either blown up or had been poisoned by chemicals. The latter course must have involved the use of very large quantities of chemicals. The work assigned to us later was to unearth and withdraw all mines left in dugout entrances and elsewhere, and pick up all bomb traps and devilish contrivances of a similar nature.

Second Lieutenant Harry Trounce, 181 Tunnelling Company, Royal Engineers

This kept us very busy. Thousands of these had been laid. All railroads were undermined; the first train going over near us at Achiet-le-Grand was destroyed. Contact mines were left under the roads in many places, especially at crossroads, and these would be fired when any heavy vehicle or gun crossed them. In other places they had placed mines with delay action fuses. A large brigade dugout headquarters near us went up in smoke about ten days after being occupied. Most of the dugout mines were placed about halfway down the entrances on the right or left side, and

Opposite:
A destroyed
canal bridge at
Manancourt:
the Germans
adopted a
scorched earth
policy as they
withdrew to the
Hindenburg Line.

these had been tamped with sandbags, detonators connected with leads which were fastened to the wooden steps, and these would be fired as men walked down. It required a careful eye to detect them. We would notice some slight change in the timber at these places and invariably carefully withdraw this and the sandbag tamping and take out the detonators and the high explosives. Running short of high explosives, the Germans often threw in bombs, trench mortars, etc., to add to the charges.

In the barbed wire on top of the trenches we would find the German hairbrush bombs tied by their fuses to the wire, with the latter looped in a half circle so that as a soldier walked along he would catch his foot in the loop and fire the bomb. In the trenches we found thousands of the German egg bombs connected to and underneath the duckboards or trench boards laid on the floor of all their trenches. These would be fired by anyone stepping on the duckboard, and as there was no other place to step in the trench, it was a case of Hobson's choice. It afforded us much amusement to explode these by throwing bricks on them from behind cover. In such dugouts as were left we would find attractive souvenirs hung up; to most of these, bombs would be attached. Some poor chap would see a good-looking German helmet hung on a nail in the dugout, attempt to remove it and fire the bomb attached. We decided to go pretty carefully and gingerly about this work and were lucky enough to get through with only ten casualties in our company.

Captain Victor
Erberle, 475th
Field Company,
Royal Engineers

One of our young subalterns, Harry Lambert, [was] killed instantly by a German booby trap mine. He had gone on one of two German light bridges across the river to their bridgehead. They had been partly demolished and preliminary reconnaissance indicated that they might be mined. After warning two sappers with him he passed a plank cross a wide gap in the centre of the bridge. Directly he stepped on it a mine in the water exploded and two others, one on each side of the gap. The two sappers were blown into the water. They were rescued by an NCO diving into the river, but one had to suffer the loss of an arm by subsequent amputation.

We were billeted in the village of Blairville, a short distance south. Here we occupied an old ruin, which had evidently been the quarters of some German officers before we arrived. From the cellars of this house we could walk back to their old front line trenches in underground galleries for over half a mile without once coming on top. In fact, one could go through the entire village underground in this way. The day after our arrival I noticed a French woman coming out of a garden nearby. She was carrying something in a yellow scarf and looking very pleased with herself. In answer to my inquiry, she informed me that she had just dug up from her old garden the savings of a lifetime – several thousand francs.

Second Lieutenant Harry Trounce, 181 Tunnelling Company, Royal Engineers

The Boche had occupied the village for nearly three years, but had failed to unearth her little fortune. Many old residents had adopted the same means of secreting their money and recovered it after the German retreat. The relief of the French civilians at the retreating Hun was very marked. As one French girl rather curiously expressed it to me: 'Boche *partir* finish wind up now.' Everywhere possible they started to rebuild their roofs and walls, and emerged from their partial cellar life with great satisfaction.

The London Rifle was marching down to Arras from trenches further north. After their exertions on the Somme the previous year, they had longed for a good rest but by the direction they were taking, rest appeared to be the least likely option.

Driver Aubrey Smith, 1/5th (City of London) Battalion, London Rifle Brigade

The thought that every pace you take carries you a pace farther from danger is a great incentive to march on and on, regardless of fatigue. The LRB knew that they had a few days' tramp before them when they left Levantie, but the long trek was worthwhile, as they had been led to expect a period of rest and longed to be in some peaceful spot similar to the training areas of the preceding spring. We spent the first night at Vieille-Chapelle, not far from Neuve Chapelle, and another day's march brought us to St Venant. The third night saw us at Tangry and on the fourth we reached Fillièvres. These names convey nothing to the reader and precious little to the writer. One day's tramp was like another.

While daily route marches might encourage a feeling of déjà vu, there was another aspect of life that did change, and not for the better. The further south Aubrey Smith's battalion marched, the more hostile local civilians became. Smith mused whether passing close to the old medieval battlefields of Cressy and Agincourt, where the British trounced the French in 1346 and 1415 respectively, might have something to do with it, but apparently not. Through biting winds and snow, the London Rifle Brigade marched and found the same miserable attitude to their appearance. British soldiers might not spell trouble but they meant nuisance and disruption and civilians were getting fed up with the war and, by extension, soldiers. The battalion's transport was headed for the village of Simencourt, just outside Arras and an uncertain welcome.

17 March: I have often written to you about mud and there is no need to enlarge much on that subject. In this village it is of the watery, clayish variety and is most abundant in the streets and round the water troughs. There are endless queues of horses on the way to water and they give all passers-by a free mud spray. Officers glare, privates grouse and civilians screech – positively screech. The inhabitants here are not so friendly as we usually find them. Perhaps the village of mud into which the British Army has transformed their once peaceful surroundings has made them a trifle short-tempered. Hardly anyone will serve you with a café and at one farm they tapped at the window, shouting 'No! No!' before ever I had reached the door.

There are a few wells available, but most people put them out of order or lock them up. By dint of a few pleasant remarks and a feeble attempt at wit, I persuaded one old French woman to unlock her well and let me use it on occasions, as a special favour. I had only been there a few times when a Scotch chap came up to draw water just as I had finished and, instead of lowering the bucket gently, let go the handle! There was a terrible shaking and jolting as the bucket sped downwards at about 60 miles an hour.

My first billet at SIMENCOURT.

Driver Aubrey Smith, 1/5th (City of London) Battalion, London Rifle Brigade

Simencourt: civilians in the village had grown increasingly tired of soldiers' presence by early 1917.

That roused the whole household. The old woman croaked and swore, while an old man rushed up, seized a bucket of water and hurled it at ME! Fortunately I was not drowned and I was laughing too much to mind. At any rate the Scotch chap didn't get his water and the well is locked up once more.

I had a wordy argument today with a Frenchman who tried to hit my horse because he imagined he was being forced into the mud beside the road. I also had trouble with a fat old wench who swore at me. One of her fowls flew through the mud, spraying my face with slosh: as I was in a bad temper I gave vent to my wrath by chasing the offending chicken up the road. The owner happened to see the chase and ran after me, jabbering away nineteen to the dozen and shaking her fist, which led to retorts in equally strong language conveying, however, nothing to her unreceptive mind.

The first day we came here, a few of us arrived after midnight and I learnt that my party were in a billet half a mile away. It was no easy matter to find it in the darkness, but after looking in a dozen barns, I struck the right one at last, finding that the beds were arranged in tiers, one above the other, like bunks on a ship. They were made of wire netting and the third 'storey' was close to the roof, so that those on the top floor had a difficulty in climbing up and down: my party had reserved me a place in the middle storey and that was bad enough to scramble into. You have to keep all your equipment, blankets, overcoat, etc., on the 'bed' and clamber up in muddy boots whenever you need a plate or mug. You eat your meals standing in the passageway, resting your plates on the middle tier, and imagine you're at Pimms'. But if you're just passing along the gangway and someone climbs backwards out of his bed, sticking his foot in your face, you are rudely disillusioned.

Another disadvantage of this system is that all the dust and odds and ends from the kit of the man above descend on you, on account of the wire netting! Last night I found an avalanche of bits of straw coming through: it was only the 'man upstairs' getting into bed. The most unfortunate occurrence was when I spilt some tea on my bed. Poor Williams underneath was so annoyed that he promptly shifted his quarters and no one else will come to take his place, knowing my reputation. Whenever I want to get something from my bed, Figg insists on getting it for me to prevent half of the kit being kicked on the floor and the other half covered with mud.

While Aubrey Smith and his friends got to grips with his complex billeting arrangements, south of Arras and to the west, the Germans were continuing to pull back, leaving little undamaged that might be profitably used by advancing British troops

30 March, Tincourt: We are now billeted in leaky cellars and ruined barns quite close up and are preparing to 'dig trenches'. Isn't it too ghastly? But the Staff is nothing if not cautious, and the Boche is developing a certain power of resistance.

Captain Graham Greenwell, 1/4th The Oxfordshire and Buckinghamshire Light Infantry

We marched in here last night in pouring rain, and on arrival found practically no accommodation – bivouac sheets and a few tents – otherwise mud and wet and filth. But within two or three hours the men had got themselves in somehow, had cleared out the filthiest-looking cellars covered with debris and had got great fires going. They are never depressed by mere appearances and are always prepared to make the best of everything.

We are having great difficulties with the commissariat, as transport is difficult and there are only about two bridges over the Somme. Two or three REs stand by them night and day with hammers and tin tacks, and every time a wagon passes over they rush forward, put in a few extra nails and let the next one go over. I hear that a whole gunner limber – six mules – careered over the side the other day and went right in. It contained all the officers' mess stuff, and for days afterwards their servants were to be seen angling for lost tins of salmon and bottles of whisky, to the joy of the spectators.

March 22: The Hun rearguards are now well beyond _____ [Bapaume]. I knew the place so intimately from photographs, and from high up in the air, that a view of it from terra firma promised to be quite interesting. So with great eagerness, some sandwiches, and the faithful sketchbook,

Lieutenant Keith Henderson, Royal Flying Corps

I sallied forth. Harry came, too. A glorious day of brilliant sun and brief snowstorms.

From the aerodrome through all this devastated country, past wrecked villages, orchards laid waste, dugout camps, bivouac camps, RE dumps, light railways, battered trolleys lying on their sides, and all the ugly confusion of old wire rusted a red-hot colour, bits of corrugated iron, bits of netting screens, more wire, dead horses, dead men in all stages of decomposition, legs, hands, heads scattered anywhere, dead trees, mud, broken rifles, gas bags, tin helmets, bully beef tins, derelict trenches, derelict telephone wires, grenades, aerial torpedoes, all the toys of war, broken and useless. . . .

Péronne: a view from the window of the town's Citadel.

The ground becomes more and more like boiling porridge as you approach no-man's-land. Of no-man's-land itself, perhaps, the less said the better. No-beast's-land – call it that rather. And yet men have been very brave, very tender, in no-man's-land. Next we come to those Hun trenches that I have peered at from a distance so long and mapped so often. It all seems rather futile now.

Past the support trenches. Past the second line. Damn it! How much larger and deeper that old emplacement is than I thought! The country is less pitted, too. Of course, it hasn't been fought over like our back areas. Why, here are trees scarcely knocked about at all. A recognizable field there. How real that stream looks! And, oh Jemima! a blue tit.

A little distance farther. Over that gentle rise, and there behold surely one of the loveliest towns [Péronne] in France, on its low hill surrounded by the quiet waters of the Somme. From a distance it looks all right; though somehow, the smoke still ascending from it doesn't look natural. As you approach you realize that what looks so charming is just empty, shelled, charred, and broken. The Huns have destroyed every single house, all the bridges, and the cathedral, too. The cathedral that once crowned the town now stands a pale crushed ghost in the deserted marketplace.

Some of the streets are almost amusing. Imagine Rye with the pretty alleys so encumbered and piled up with roofs, sofas, the contents of wardrobes, dormer windows, smashed mirrors, rubble, and dust, that it's quite impossible to proceed.

Go into the houses, and there it's just as it is in the streets. Everything crushed to atoms. Images of saints have been hurled out onto garbage heaps, and in the cathedral huge pillars are lying about in clumsy confusion amongst chairs, organ pipes, and gilded flowers. On a huge noticeboard in the Grande Place the Hun has written:

NICHT ARGERN: NUR WUNDERN!

(Don't argue: only wonder! We the Huns did this. Why discuss what we have done? We have destroyed your city. Gape and stare, stupid fools! What does it matter to us? We took your precious town from you, because we wanted it. Now we don't want it any more. Here it is back again. With our love.) Some merry soldier wrote that up, I suppose. It was a pity …

Another odd sight was a tub full of water, with a little dog trying to get out. But the little dog was dead. A crump evidently landed somewhere near, and just petrified him, as it were. You often see men like that, struck dead in the middle of some act. Men are usually turned a dull purplish or greenish black. So was this little dog. We ate a delicious lunch on the battlements, our legs dangling 50 feet above the reedy water. Lots of moorhen and coot swimming about.

The sun was warm. We enjoyed ourselves immensely. What a heavenly world it is!

The British troops followed up the German retirement with curiosity at their new surroundings but also with understandable caution. It was only a matter of time before they would bump into the Hindenburg Line and the war proper would begin again. Sergeant Read, serving with the Leicestershire Regiment, found himself peering across a valley at the enemy's new, formidable defences that were still undergoing last-minute improvements.

Sergeant I.L. (Dick) Read, 8th The Leicestershire Regiment

Very early the following morning we moved up in artillery formation across more fields in a thick mist. We proceeded slowly, therefore, but reaching a road, our officers checked on their maps, and as they appeared satisfied, we crossed it at right angles, making our way in a clearing mist up a long gradual slope, culminating in a definite ridge. Here we extended and were ordered to get down in the wet grass until our officers, having again checked our position, waved us forward again. Rising to our feet, we saw at the bottom of the long slope of fields perhaps a thousand yards distant, a dark brown band many yards in depth, threading its way as far as we could see it on either side of the front. Three hundred yards or so in the rear of this, we could see another band of staggering thickness, running approximately parallel with it. We came upon three khaki bodies lying about 20 yards apart. By their appearance they had not been there long, and were lads of the 6th Brigade of our division. They had been caught by an unlucky burst of machine-gun fire.

As we slowly picked our way forward, we made out the brown bands to be belts of rusty wire defences of terrific strength, and hoped fervently that we would not be called upon to surmount these obstacles that morning. Between the belts of wire we could make out the piles of sandbags and turned-up earth of a trench system, and we were expecting to be fired on when a single machine gun opened up, the bullets whistling high over our heads. We lay down under orders, and now advanced in short rushes of 50 yards or so by sections, between whiles eagerly examining the landscape before us, which stretched for several miles up a gentle slope behind the German trenches, dotted here and there with villages untouched as yet by shellfire. We wondered how much nearer that wire we were expected to go, and speculation among us became intense. Then we saw that those in front were dropping into a half-hidden cart track, and within seconds we had joined them in a final rush, considerably out of breath, with the machine guns opposite still firing bursts.

As we crouched there, about 350 yards from the first wire belt, we were told to dig in – and to put our backs into it. We needed no second bidding, expecting the shells to start dropping at any moment, and wishing that we had brought up twice as many shovels. Still, our entrenching tools were quite useful. Occasionally we would look over the top of our excavations and saw that parties of Germans were working in the approaches to the nearest village behind the reserve trench system. They had a concrete-mixing machine, and were trundling wheelbarrows of cement to and fro with a will. We wished that we had some of it, and many jokes were made as the lads dug. Through field glasses, it seemed that the Germans were joking also; some certainly appeared to be singing. They were about 900 yards away, and we thought of turning a Lewis gun on them, but just then we were too busy getting our own house in order. By nightfall we possessed a tolerably deep trench, with funk holes dug into the side, and in the gathering dusk we saw that the German party had knocked off for the day, but their wheelbarrows, cement sacks and the various etceteras were still there. Perhaps we would interrupt them in the morning. But, truth to tell, we could not escape a real feeling of uneasiness, difficult to define, but sensing the calm before the storm.

Overleaf: The advance to the Hindenburg Line, March 1917. Officers of the 2nd Queen's Royal West Surrey Regiment resting close to the village of Bullecourt.

Driver Aubrey Smith could not only sense the build-up, he could see it. Transport vehicles passed down all the roads leading to Arras, while troops were wending their way forwards to the trenches, and heavy guns, forced to move owing to the German retirement, came out of gun pits, causing further congestion. Overhead, aircraft reconnaissance was imperative for both sides, and battle for aerial supremacy raged as both sides fought for control of the skies.

Driver Aubrey
Smith, 1/5th
(City of London)
Battalion, London
Rifle Brigade

I was on water cart duty and spent hours on my own trying to find the battalion, for I took a wrong fork road by the railway bridge beyond Achicourt and, of course, roamed completely beyond the 56th Divisional area. In the end an officer gave me my bearings and I retraced my steps. On that trip I noticed what a concentration of artillery there was on this front. … After months of preparation of gun pits, etc., most of it was now compelled to move forward in view of the German retirement, but no doubt all would be ranged onto the new targets by the time the Arras attack was desired. How cold it was! The wind drove through whatever clothes one put on, and the long waits owing to traffic blocks caused many drivers' noses to take on a permanent purple hue.

The following morning, while we were in our barn eating biscuits and bacon for breakfast, listening to the sound of anti-aircraft guns and the whirring of aeroplanes, which did not in the ordinary way excite us, we heard a 'pop-pop-pop-pop-pop-pop-pop!', whereupon there was a precipitate rush for the door. Kicking over my mug of tea and seizing Figg's biscuit in my haste, I joined the crowd – some forty in number – who were all trying to get through the door at once.

'Pop-pop-pop-pop-pop!'

Having kicked my way near the front and squeezed through the opening, I followed the rushing figures over a neighbouring cabbage patch and gazed upwards. Three aeroplanes were circling around, flying low down just over our heads – one German and two British. We were just in time to see one of the British ones, which was evidently winged, break away from the fight and make off to the rear; meanwhile, the German turned its attention to the other machine. How anxiously we watched the duel! We shouted in our excitement, in our anxiety to see the other man avenged, and worked ourselves into a frenzy as we realized the German machine was the faster. They were still flying around, firing machine guns just above our heads. Then we saw a heart-rending thing. A bullet had hit the British petrol tank, which had caught fire; from a little spurt of flame it grew into a regular blaze and, as the machine turned circles, we could see the two men quite distinctly. After some seconds, which seemed hours of agony, they set off in a straight line for Beaurains, a long trail of fire and smoke issuing from the tail of the aeroplane. About half a mile away it wavered, continued on its course a little farther and then crocked up: a moment later the whole paraphernalia became a mass of flame and the smoking debris fell to earth.

The German machine was by now making its way back to the enemy lines, no doubt feeling very pleased with itself, and we watched anxiously for some fast aeroplane of ours or our anti-aeroplane guns to bring it to earth. For a time it seemed as if no one would take any notice, but our anti-aircraft gunners in Arras had seen the fight and were going to make sure of their man. Suddenly the batteries spoke out and the machine was literally surrounded with puffs of smoke. Never had we seen such good shooting: it could not fail to do some damage. Sure enough, the conqueror who had just put two of our machines out of action was himself hit and fell to earth to the accompaniment of the cheers of many hundreds – probably thousands – of onlookers.

While wandering about alone this afternoon I saw a German plane brought down. It had been hit while above the clouds, for it dived from the clouds with no wings. I do not know what happened to the wings. The engine roared as the crippled machine hurled itself at the ground. It hit the earth with a hideous impact some 200 yards from me. I ran to examine it. The engine was buried beyond view. The pilot was flung clear. He was, one could almost say, a bag of broken bones: lower limbs wrenched from hip joints, feet twisted round his neck, and had not his uniform held him contained he would have been, as to human shape, pretty well amorphous. And so it goes on. First one side, then the other. We were of course right to accept the Hun challenge (damn lot of difference it makes what I think), but the price is high and grows steadily higher.

Captain
Lawrence
Gameson,
RAMC attd. 71st
Brigade, Royal
Field Artillery

While events had proved that a precise location for a spring offensive was problematic, no one was in any doubt that one would take place. For months soldiers had been in training, learning new techniques for the attack and adapting to new machinery and weapons.

Lieutenant Alan Thomas, 6th (Queen's Own) Royal West Kent Regiment

[We] were behind the lines, training for what we all knew was going to be the 'spring offensive'. A stretch of country was chosen which more or less resembled the ground we should have to attack over. Imagination, we were told, was necessary in order to fill in gaps in the landscape and to remove one or two features that should not have been there. For the rest, our job was to 'get used to' the lie of the land ('getting to know the course', I called it in memory of golfing days) and also to accustom ourselves to the new battle formation, which involved advancing in little 'blobs' instead of in the usual line.

Arras Offensive
Canadians rehearsing the
Vimy Attack.
9 and 1917

Preparing for the Arras Offensive and the Canadian Corps' daunting task of seizing Vimy Ridge.

A healthy life it was – up early in the morning: a route march to the field of operations; a couple of hours advancing in 'blobs'; a break for lunch; a further advance in the afternoon, culminating, naturally enough, in the capture of our objective; the Colonel's pow-wow on the day's achievement; the march back with [Colonel] Dawson taking the salute as we entered the village to the tune of *A Hundred Pipers*; and so home to billets. After tea, a foot inspection or possibly a kit inspection; and the evening spent in writing or censoring letters or checking lists, while a gramophone screeched the latest tunes from the revues; or, as an occasional variation, dinner at the officers' club in Avesnes-le-Comte.

Sometimes on fine mornings Gilbert and I would get up early and go riding. Then the war was forgotten. All we cared for was the brightness of the morning, the sight of the girls, women and old men working in the fields, and the joy of living and of being in each other's company.

Not everyone recalled the extended preparation with such affection; on the contrary, Private Percy Clare remembered it as nothing but misery.

We constructed shallow trenches of 2 feet for the purposes of practice. The earth was like iron, being frozen to some depth. Then it commenced to thaw with occasional sleet and snow, followed at last by a spell of heavy rains. Our lives were rendered a misery to us then. The fields in which we were digging were simply ploughed agricultural land so that they got into a miserable state. As we tramped over them it was just one long, hard struggle to raise our feet one after the other from the suction of the gluey mud. All of France which we had not shovelled into sandbags seemed to be sticking to our boots.

So punishing was the terrible 'going' over those sodden fields that more than once I saw strong-looking men trembling and whimpering like kids. For days on end I never had a dry rag on me. Each day our cloths were soaked right through with rain and perspiration, our boots sodden, and before they could dry we were out in it again all day. No fire was allowed in or near our billet, so that after cooling down on our return each day we sat tired, cold and shivering on our soaking wet things until bedtime. Even then we had to lie in our wet things: the alternative was to lie naked under an army blanket, itself cold and damp besides stinking and dirty. All of us

Private Percy Clare, 7th The East Surrey Regiment

at this time contracted troublesome coughs which disturbed us very much at night so that we could get little sleep. A little cloud of vapour (steam) was always rising from each of us as we lay in our blankets, the warmth of our bodies drying out soaking clothes. The long drag to and fro each day, and the digging, made our feet tender and sore in the sodden state, and I suffered a good deal with rheumatism until I had worked it off each day.

The system of trenches we dug represented actually the system we were detailed to attack when the time should come. Every twist, every turn, every dugout or machine-gun emplacement was copied and correctly marked on large-scale maps; each stronghold was charted down and known to us, so that each man knew his objective. It was all very simple and beautiful in theory at any rate.

Driver Aubrey Smith, 1/5th (City of London) Battalion London Rifle Brigade

In spite of the weather, it was now practically certain that the attack was imminent. Reports from various parts of the front down south indicated that the German resistance was stiffening and the advanced elements of the Hindenburg system appeared to have been reached all along the line.

'Passing through corn fields': French farmers were well compensated for any material loss caused by soldiers.

Just south-east of our own front, a further bending back of their line had taken place, Henin and Croisilles having just been occupied. This might mean an alteration of our plans on the extreme right of the front to be attacked, but on the greater part of it everything was now in readiness. We heard reports of tanks coming up by train. I was struck by the great increase in the number of light railways being laid down behind the front, ready to cope with some of the ammunition supply.

As time passed and the day for attack drew nearer, enemy shelling increased. I then took more interest in the passages underground. The ground below the eastern suburbs was honeycombed with quarry working left by past generations of builders. These old caves were now linked by tunnelled passages and the whole system joined with the town sewers, capacious tubes of brickwork like the first 'Twopenny Tube'. ... The purpose of the vast affair was the provision of hidden safe point of assembly before the attack and of quarters for troops during the period of preparation. There was a chapel, canteens, aid posts, latrines and the rest. Many of the early caves had been hewn out of white chalky stone; in dim electric light they seemed unreal or faked, like grottoes of pantomime scenery. I never saw a plan of the system nor knew its extent, but was reasonably familiar with the part of it which directly concerned me.

One could reach the sewers by manholes dotted about the town; the main

Rue Carnot

Captain Lawrence Gameson, RAMC attd. 71st Brigade, Royal Field Artillery

The thoroughfare in Arras before the offensive, seemingly undamaged by shellfire.

entrance was I believe, was from the yard of the French barracks near the way in from the Boulevard Carnot. I could get all the way to B/71 [the battery] underground. Only twice did I go in this manner and simply to find out how the passage ran. The last part of this route was by a recently cut hideously narrow pitch-dark passage. The battery could, and did, get up its ammunition by trolley. The line ran in a different tunnel for the narrow one used for walking. It was often flooded and pretty beastly to work.

I hopelessly lost myself one day down below. Happening upon another solitary troglodyte, an Australian [New Zealand] tunneller, I asked him the way. He told me the way, and I said that I thought he was wrong. He was a good chap. Grinning, he drawled: 'Well, I guess you oughter know. I only made the bloody tunnel!'

Lieutenant Alan Thomas, 6th (Queen's Own) Royal West Kent Regiment

We moved up into Arras. But instead of occupying empty houses, this time we were billeted in cellars. Something (besides spring) was in the air and we knew that the day of 'the push' was near. For us the sooner it came the better. We had been preparing for it for two months and it was (we had been told) going to be 'a really first-class show'. To begin with a stupendous bombardment lasting ten whole days! Think of it! (they said). The old Boche will be knocked to a pulp. Ten days of the heaviest bombardment ever known in the history of this or any other war! Real heavy stuff too. Meanwhile our boys would be lying doggo-safe and away from it all – so that whatever Fritz put over in reply simply wouldn't touch us. We should be as safe as houses – or, considering the state of most of the houses in Arras, infinitely safer.

These cheering announcements we duly passed on to the men, most of whom were (like some of us) young and inexperienced enough to lap them up with glee. The war, it seemed, was going to be a walkover. But how exactly were we to be 'safe and away from it all'? What did that mean? We were soon to know.

One day, during the last week of March, we received our orders. As every movement was to be shrouded in secrecy, we did not even emerge from our cellars, lest the Germans might see us from the air. Instead we crept along them, passing from one to another, through holes knocked in the walls. Presently we came to some steps down. At the bottom we found ourselves in a large circular tunnel. A gangway of boards ran along one side of this electrically lit passage, while along the bottom flowed a stream of water. We were in fact in the main drain of Arras. The war was full of queer experiences: but we had never imagined that we should be going into battle down the drain.

For a mile or so we trudged along this drain, emerging at length, much as Aladdin emerged, into a vast cave; only here the light was reflected not by jewels but by chalk. The caves (for there was a series of them) were fitted with every modern convenience: electric light, running water, braziers for cooking, a miniature railway and even furniture, though this consisted mostly of empty crates and petrol cans. Here, in these caves, we lived for over a week. No sound reached us from the outer world. Very occasionally a small chip of chalk would drop from the roof, sign that a heavy shell had landed overhead.

From time to time we climbed to one of the exits debouching into the reserve trenches and took the air. From this part of the line we had a good view of the German positions and also of the effects of our non-stop bombardment. As far as we could see to the north and to the south, the German trenches were being pounded out of recognition. Great towers of earth were being flung up all along the eastern skyline and the air was full of whirring iron. Not much was coming from the German side.

The Germans may not have been retaliating 'much' at times, but they were biding their time, poised to strike when it became evident the offensive was under way. Those enemy guns that did return fire often targeted arterial roads that ran away from Arras, as Driver Aubrey Smith described it, 'like a bicycle hub with numerous spokes, forking out in every direction'. The Germans hammered these roads in a desultory manner in the hope of catching men and materials moving in either direction.

On the main road there was a good deal of traffic moving up, under cover of darkness, the volume growing greater as we drew near to Arras.

After several halts, short moves forward and further halts, we got to within a few hundred yards of the Achicourt-Dainville crossroads where we should turn to the right and be free of most of the congestion; but at this

Driver Aubrey Smith, 1/5th (City of London) Battalion, London Rifle Brigade

spot we stuck. The whole of the up-going traffic was apparently suspended and it was indeed tantalizing to be within a stone's throw of a quieter road and yet have to sit still on the horses, perishing with cold, waiting for an unintelligent traffic corporal to interpret impossible traffic regulations.

In spite of a lot of stationary ambulances on our right, a double-banking convoy came alongside us on the left, receiving curses from everybody. Of course, this, too, was brought to a standstill, leaving three lines of vehicles facing Arras and pretty well filling the entire road. All of a sudden we heard the report of a German howitzer on the right – that distinct pop which tells you very clearly that the muzzle is in a line with you and enables you to distinguish its sound above all the British guns firing in the other direction. The familiar 'swish' followed it and, a second or so later, the shell whizzed over our heads and burst in a field, a hundred yards or so to the left.

'Get a move on,' came in an exasperated tone from several people in the convoys. What *could* all the delay be about? Surely they were not deliberately holding up all this traffic when shells were about, just for the sake of some rule about intervals between convoys? Those who were on foot could easily find a ditch if need be, but the back of a horse seemed such an elevated and exposed position. The animals were nervous, too, standing with ears alert for a repetition of the sound.

At this juncture, downward traffic proceeded to push its way past, amidst much colliding of limber hubs, with language to suit the occasion: beyond it, forming a fifth stream, the 169th Infantry Brigade battalions were wending their way towards the firing line in single file beside the path, thus completing a good old muddle which seemed farther from a solution than ever.

Would the gun fire again? Might it not hit the road next time? What a target we presented for it – perhaps the news of the traffic block was being telephoned through to the enemy by spies in one of the cottages ahead there, as such things had been done at the Second Battle of Ypres.

'Bang! Wh-z-z-z-t!-Crump!'

The second one had landed a few yards off the road on the left: we could see the smoke drifting beyond the poplar trees which lined the path. The single lines of infantry had momentarily flopped down and were now continuing on their way again with quickened step.

'For God's sake get a move on there!'

There was absolutely no escape from the tangle. No LRB vehicle could move to right or left, owing to these idiots who had 'double-banked'. The 'down' convoy was wisely trotting past as quickly as possible; some of the infantry were doubling to put distance between them and the line of the howitzer.

'If they shorten the range again, it might land just here,' remarked Rayner. No need to dwell upon that fact! It was so patent that we simply waited our fate with pattering hearts, wishing it were permissible to seek shelter in the empty dugouts close at hand – places that had been erected for an artillery headquarters by the roadside before the German retirement had rendered them obsolete. But to leave your horses is a crime in the army: the best thing to be done was to dismount and stand by their heads in case they took fright.

Transport moving up towards Arras. Most roads were extremely congested in the lead-up to the offensive.

'They won't learn a lesson till someone gets hit,' shouted Coombs, the RAMC water cart man, making off in haste for the nearest dugout in company with the cooks. 'I'm not taking any chances.'

Still our shouts from the rear and the proximity of the shells had no effect on the blockage, whatever the cause was. For the next minute everyone was on the 'qui vive', listening intently for the dreaded 'pop'. I shall not forget the scene: Jumbo and The Grey, impatient and nervy, their noses almost touching the cooker in front in their desire to get as far forward as possible; the jammed vehicles, the convoy passing by and the LRB single files plodding along at the edge of the road: the distant firing-line rumble, the noise of passing vehicles, the curses from one and another and, near at hand, the horses' heavy breathing.

Then it came. Gun report, rush of air and shell burst came practically together. There was a cloud of smoke 10 yards ahead, shouts could be heard, and 'awky pieces' fell all around. It had landed in the middle of the road!

The downward convoy seemed to melt away, the cooker ahead of me backed into my horses, who in turn backed and then ineffectually attempted to turn round and bolt. All happened in a second.

Who was hit? It must be the next vehicle but one to mine: in the confusion I could not think whose it was. It was as much as I could do to pacify my pair and straighten out the locked wheels of the cooker.

'What's happened?' I shouted to Harbord.

'Kimbo's hit,' snapped Harbord, who was in charge of the vehicle in front. Kimbo – practically the most popular man on the section! And all through this cursed traffic block. When would we learn to control traffic as the French did?

'Get a move on,' everyone shouted again. In another minute, perhaps a second shell would fall in the road. Surely the head of our column would break through somehow, now. Ah! There was a movement in the convoy parallel to us. A few seconds later Harbord had seized an opportunity and, as I leapt into the saddle, my pair also moved forward behind him. When Harbord's emotions were aroused he cared not two pins for any man. Butting his way between two vehicles of the upward convoy, he compelled the rear driver to pull up short and let him pass through, thereby calling down all the oaths that can be imagined onto his head. I followed so close behind that there was no time for the gap to be closed and Rayner, behind me, was 'old soldier' enough to let not an inch separate him from my cooker, so that the other convoy was completely cut in two. We got right over to the side of the road and were immediately on a level with the spot where the shell had burst. In the middle of the road stood D Company's cooker with the shaft smashed and all that remained of Gog and Magog strewn about on the ground, A water cart was drawn up beside the road with the horses removed. Where was Kimbo?

The horses, who were sweating with fright, needed no persuasion to break into a trot. With a clear field before them, for the traffic seemed to have melted away, they hastened down the Achicourt road, from which we heard another shell go over and land in nearly the same spot as the last. Chrisp came alongside when we had slowed down to a walk and were drawing near to Achicourt.

'What news?' I asked him.

'Poor old Kimbo is done for.' Chrisp could hardly frame the words.

Kimbo was killed! We could not grasp it for the moment. Many a jolly evening had we spent with him; many a parcel and billet had we shared; I had known him since recruiting days at Bunhill Row. His cheery disposition when anything was going wrong and we were suffering from waves of depression had often put our hearts in the right place; and now the worst had happened. …

Our long immunity from transport casualties had given us an absurd faith in our good fortune and this had come to shatter it. … At what moment could you feel safe on any road? Demobilization seemed a futile dream, for what must inevitably happen before that were possible! How many unsafe roads were we still to traverse?

One thought was uppermost in every man's mind. Five words summed up the outlook of hundreds of thousands of men on the Western Front. What we all asked ourselves was: 'When will my turn come?'

Overleaf: A shell dump, one of hundreds in the fields around Arras – an obvious target for the Germans.

2 Opportunity Knocking

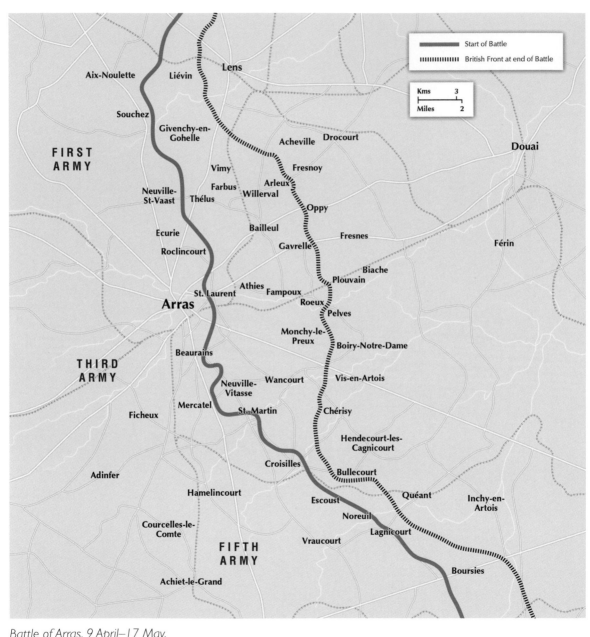

Battle of Arras, 9 April–17 May.

'We congratulated ourselves on having gone over [the top] first. It was the difference between two men with appointments at the dentist at 10 and 11, and the 11 o'clock man having to sit in the next room and hear the groans of the victim, knowing his turn must come sooner or later.'

Major Bertram Brewin, 16th The Royal Scots (Lothian Regiment)

———————

Nearly every house in the heart of Achicourt had been crammed full of ammunition, forming a reserve dump for the attack: shells were now arriving at such a rate that we had to commandeer villages to house them! And still there seemed to be no end to the convoys which passed our billet at the outskirts of the village, on their way to the batteries and various ammunition dumps further forward.

Driver Aubrey Smith, 1/5th (City of London) Battalion, London Rifle Brigade

The attack was fixed for the 9th, and on the 8th, convoys of lorries – disregarding all the regulations hitherto in force about daylight movements – passed us continually during the morning. Achicourt, in fact, presented as busy a spot as could be seen anywhere on the Western Front. RFA convoys and infantry transport limbers added to the bustle: in between all these motor and horse vehicles moved dispatch riders, groups of officers on horseback (with maps open as usual) accompanied by orderlies, and batches of infantry in reserve wandering about the village. Civilians stood at their doors watching all this unwonted bustle and excitement. Needless to say, there were delays, collisions and breakdowns; traffic regulations to be complied with; pauses while some lorry or lorries turned to right and left or performed acrobatic revolutions in the square.

The staggering number of Allied guns deployed in the attack was more than matched by the prodigious number of artillery shells. Nearly 3,500 guns, most heavy calibre, could rely on a stockpile of ammunition weighing many tens of thousands of tons. The problem was concealment of these shells from preying enemy eyes, and this proved impossible.

Driver Aubrey Smith, 1/5th (City of London) Battalion, London Rifle Brigade

About dinnertime a long line of these ammunition lorries stretched from one end of the village to the other, held up by a traffic muddle of some magnitude. We were in our billet wrestling with bully beef tins at the time and consequently did not observe either the blockage or the appearance of German aeroplanes which flew over the village, noticed the congested state of the main street and promptly signalled to their guns.

Achicourt Church and neighbouring houses already in ruins prior to the offensive. The village would be a main thoroughfare for guns, ammunition and troops.

The first we knew of it was when a loud explosion occurred – the biggest we had ever heard – which violently shook the ground and brought various bricks down from the roof into our dinner plates – or thereabouts. The speed with which we had rushed out of this same billet to watch the air fight was excelled by the rate at which we now strove to get outside to see what the present trouble was; no doubt, the loose portions of roof, etc., which were falling around spurred us on in this effort! Less than half a mile away an enormous pillar of grey smoke had

Ruins of ACHICOURT.

Achicourt Church ruins under snow.

arisen high in the air, and this was followed by another, the sound of the second explosion being even greater than the first.

We guessed the trouble: it was either bombs or shells, hitting the lorries in the main street. What an uncomfortable position for the lorry drivers and others in the village! How well we could appreciate the predicament with the memory of last night's tragedy on the Arras road fresh in our minds.

Boom! Another sudden upheaval of bricks, masonry and lorries, lost in great clouds of smoke!

'Good heavens!' said Hobson – Hobson loved to be dramatic – 'the village is simply crammed full of shells. If it catches fire, the whole place may go up.'

What was happening behind that row of houses? What of the troops in billets, the sentries at the dumps, the transport men and lorry drivers? One of the latter was earning a decoration by driving his flaming lorry into a pond. Two ASC men, dishevelled and very much out of breath, ran down the road and hardly paused to speak when we questioned them.

'For Gawd's sake, – well hop it,' said one.

'The _____ village is being blown to _____ Hell,' gasped the other.

So saying, they commenced to run again, their long coats flying behind them in the wind. In another minute they were out of sight.

Crash! The pall hanging over Achicourt from the previous explosions had hardly begun to be disseminated when another geyser of black smoke shot upwards, carrying with it doubtless many luckless individuals apart from countless thousands of pounds worth of shells. All this ammunition that was being wasted represented weeks of toil for bands of munition workers at home; fatigue parties of unfit men had spent days laboriously loading all those shells onto steamers, trains and lorries; our own folks across the Channel were stinting themselves in many ways in order to pay for them. Here they were, exploded in a flash, the only damage caused by them being to Allied life and property. . . .

All through the afternoon one big explosion followed another until it hardly seemed possible that there could be any portion of the dumps untouched. Nothing could save the ammunition now. Down in the village those who were still alive were having a terrible time of it. People would rush out to attend to wounded and the next instant a building close at hand would blow up.... One fellow whom I met afterwards told me he spent hours imprisoned in a cellar trying to pacify two women of the billet; whenever the danger seemed to have passed he started to emerge, but another holocaust would take place and he would have to retire underground again. Fellows passed us on their way down the road, with bandages on them, in such numbers that the offensive might well have begun.

Despite the inferno behind the lines and the prodigious loss of material, there was more than enough ammunition and light guns were busy, attempting to cut lanes in the enemy barbed wire, preparatory to the assault. Above, spotter planes of the Royal Flying Corps reported back the degree of success, though they were frequently assailed by German fighters, and many British pilots were brought spiralling down to earth, to the grief of comrades grimly enthralled below. Major Bertram Brewin witnessed the aerial drama with alarm, but like everyone else he was preoccupied with preparations on the ground.

Major Bertram Brewin, 16th The Royal Scots (Lothian Regiment)

Gunners were all over the place, hurriedly making last dispositions and marking down last ideas, brigade bombers with working parties swarmed down the trenches, making dumps of thousands of bombs and accessories, Royal Engineers and more parties surveying and marking down things, dumping wire, pegs, etc. and in the night-time a continuous stream of working parties bringing up trench mortar ammunition, ordinary ammunition, rations etc., till you couldn't get around and the noise was like a sheep and cow fair heard at a distance. You'd have thought things never would disentangle themselves.

Bayliss, I and runner going round meet an NCO, asked him how many in his party, 'nine' says he. 'Right ho, push along.' We flatten ourselves against the trench wall, past come seventeen swearing Tommies carrying heavy loads, barging into us, falling themselves, shouting 'Where's No. 7 Party?' 'Pass the word along there's no one behind Private Atkins', the endless stream goes on and we get fed up with being banged with every three-cornered thing under Heaven, so collar the next NCO. 'Who are you?' – '24th NF [Northumberland Fusiliers], No. 14 Party', (the word has apparently never been passed down by the party before to let us through) – 'How many men?' – 'I should have ten, Sir' – 'All right, pass the word down to halt the party after that.' We count five down and then start struggling down past the last five, find a blaspheming corporal wanting to know what _____ has stopped his _____ party. We mildly say 'We want to get through', and push along past them. After going some 10 yards, meet another blaspheming NCO who wants to know what the check is. We try to push past him and get hopelessly jammed with two men bearing a pole with ammunition slung on it. I tell Bayliss to get up on top and give me a hand, and we slither up, take a line and move off. Up starts the Boche with machine guns and we fall hurriedly back into the struggle again, and so it went on all night. It took me the whole night to get around our sector.

About 6.30 that evening there was a shout of laughter from a group of our fellows who had just had an interesting announcement. When I enquired the cause of this hilarity, I learnt that some driver had got to take a limber of hand grenades to a dump in Agny, which meant passing through a portion of Achicourt. Ha! ha! Some blighter had got to go through Achicourt. One hoped he would wear his identification disc and send a note to mamma! The sergeant was turning up his notebook to see whose turn it was for duty, and all of us were watching him anxiously. At last he looked up with a grin:

'Aubrey Smith, harness up.'

This order provoked everyone to greater mirth than ever, though as I got ready to depart, my face was no doubt as long as a fiddle. Amidst the quips and jests of all the others I eventually set on down the only possible road to my destination, praying that a further explosion might not take place and turn me into mincemeat. There had not been any disturbance for half an hour and, at the spot where I passed closest to the scene of the recent trouble, several people were going quickly to and fro. With a sigh of relief I turned off to the right, avoiding the centre of the village, and had hardly done so when there was another of these unearthly reports behind me, followed by a sound as of a cart shooting bricks into the street. Looking round, I found I was almost on the fringe of one of these smoke eruptions – another houseful of ammunition had been blown to

Driver Aubrey Smith, 1/5th (City of London) Battalion, London Rifle Brigade

smithereens a hundred yards away. People bolted and scattered in all directions and, needless to say, I broke into a canter, which lasted until I was clear of the village.

At Agny, where I stopped to unload, there was hardly a soul to be seen, though it was less than 2 miles from the line. What with the deserted appearance of this place and the quietness of our guns, it was so unlike the eve of an offensive that I had doubts as to the correctness of the rumour that the great day was fixed for tomorrow.

My return journey was serene and it appeared as though the danger were past. Our end of Achicourt had escaped intact except for odd tiles and bricks which were strewn about the road. There were few of the section about to welcome me back; it was quite dark and raining and most of the fellows had sought cover. The forsaking of the billet had meant a

Making do: soldiers improvise to create accommodation.

sudden return to sleeping on the earth in hastily rigged up bivvies, which might almost not have existed at all for all the good they did. The previous summer we had gradually accumulated bivvy material and just as the campaigning season was over the army had issued out canvas sheets: in the winter, however, the former had been discarded and the latter 'called in' for storage in a dump – where they would no doubt repose until the summer of 1917 was well advanced and the need of them had gone.

With the rain, the weather had suddenly turned cold and windy and during that night we were forcibly reminded that spring had not yet arrived. We had anticipated a sleepless night through a regular drumfire of preliminary shelling, but the guns continued to display little or no activity and our wakefulness was caused more by the anticipation of excitement, coupled with the temperature and the utter inadequacy of our 'roof', 'walls' and 'door'.

Final infantry arrangements were made on the morning of 8 April. At the battalion headquarters of the 16th Royal Scots, a meeting was held and was attended by, amongst others, Major Bertram Brewin, although he was due to be kept back in reserve during the initial fighting.

Major Stephenson and all the scrappers came to breakfast [and] we settled down to a final conference. Everything was all cut and dried, so it was only a matter of questions by company commanders on odd things and a general talk by Stephenson. Whilst we were at it the playful Boche burst a shell right in the road outside our window; luckily all glass had already gone, but it blew in all the boardings and brought endless plaster down. When we had sorted ourselves, Stephenson proposed an adjournment to a cellar in the garden and we pushed off. I was bringing up the rear as 2nd in command should, when he burst a shell in the garden and I was saved the trouble of walking down the few steps I still had to go and landed in the middle of the cellar, much to the amusement of the lads, after they had found I wasn't hurt.

Major Bertram Brewin, 16th The Royal Scots (Lothian Regiment)

As the battalion prepared to go into the trenches, Captain Stevenson [a different officer] was wounded in the shoulder by a shell splinter. He would now miss the attack and Major Brewin was invited to join A Company as it went over the top.

Major Bertram Brewin, 16th The Royal Scots (Lothian Regiment)

I was just sorting out my things preparatory to bed, when a runner came in to say that Stevenson, the captain commanding A Company, had been hit and would I go up to take over the company? I know Stephenson had wanted to take me over with him to halve the work after the Push, but Brigade wouldn't have it, Lodge wasn't very fit and Sturrock knew nothing of the line.

So I packed up and got away about 10.00 pm [and] managed to get a lorry as far as Arras; the road was like a fair with troops and transport, and we only went at a snail's pace. Gillespie [Brewin's servant], of course, came with me and carried a wonderful array of foodstuffs. It was a wretched night, trying to rain and snow and much colder; the trenches to the line were packed with working parties feverishly trying to do a week's work in one night and get safely out of the way before the flag fell. You've never seen such a mess as the communication trenches were in, just packed with struggling Tommies, hawking up heavy loads of every imaginable thing. Our HQ had already shifted down to [a] dugout which was also the jumping-off place for my company. I got in to report about 1.15 am and Stephenson made me rest and have some supper before going on. My Company HQ was in a wee dugout about 60 yards away, so Stephenson told me to come back after I had taken over.

Sergeant Rupert Whiteman, 10th Royal Fusiliers (City of London Regiment)

Easter Monday, 9 April 1917: Truly black Monday. Everyone was astir by 3.00 am; reveille was not sounded but night sentries woke officers and platoon sergeants who, in turn, got their men stirring.

A wretched awakening, pitch dark, cold, with a keen wind blowing. One can perhaps imagine the feelings of everybody that morning searching about in the darkness for equipment, chilled to the bone, half asleep, stumbling over other men's equipment and on top of all, the knowledge of a very fair prospect of 'pushing daisies up' before nightfall.

Equipment having been found, it had to be disentangled – it has a hideous habit of getting itself into endless knots if laid down for a few minutes in the darkness – then waterproof sheets to be rolled and strapped to the belt at the back, water bottles filled from the water cart and numerous other odds and ends to see to.

Breakfast was ready to be drawn from the cookers by 3.30; it having been brought 'en masse' to platoons, here was another hopeless business trying to distribute boiled bacon to every man by the light of a miserable guttering candle, with hands stiff with cold and the wretched candle being blown out by the chill wind every few minutes.

Hot tea made everyone feel twice the man he was before, and by the time breakfast was finished dawn was breaking – a very cheerless sort of dawn, however. What a strange feeling there seemed to be in the air that morning, a lull before a terrible storm, for it wanted just one hour before the opening barrage – the 4.50 'Zero'.

It was explicable this nervous tension; even the horses and birds seemed to be imbued with the knowledge that hell was to be let loose before very long. There seemed to be a strange hush hanging over every living thing, man, bird and beast.

Dawn having broken, the weather prospect looked decidedly gloomy; the sky was completely overcast with low rain clouds scudding above us. We were not to be disappointed in this at least, for it poured with rain an hour or so later.

At four o'clock the battalion moved off, each man carrying his extra ammunition, rations for the day and an extra 'iron' ration – and, perhaps, a nervous sinking feeling in his stomach. We moved out of the field, across the Arras road into the hedgeless fields beyond and down the gentle slope into the valley from which the nearest heavies had been firing.

At 4.40 we halted about 300 yards behind the first line of the heavy artillery. 'Zero' was only ten minutes off. I don't remember hearing a soul speak; that hush had still got possession of us. The eyes of each were fixed eagerly on the minute hand of his watch.

All sorts of men [were in the front line], lost, strayed and fed up. Our men were mostly sitting on the parapet, as there wasn't room for them all in shelters, or down a small sap which was handy. I got my subalterns to Company HQ and cleared the place to have a final talk (of course I knew the arrangements as well as they did), then I went round and saw each platoon, found everything quite right, and so back to Battalion HQ. The Boche was shelling us freely, and I don't wonder when I heard the noise

Major Bertram Brewin, 16th The Royal Scots (Lothian Regiment)

going on, men shouting and swearing, lost working parties shouting for directions, and sweating to get their work done and away, and altogether the place hummed like a hive of bees. The infernal Boche had already blown in one cookhouse, where we were preparing a final cup of tea for the men, and whilst I was at Battalion HQ, a message came to say he had blown in the other, so the poor lads went over without that comfort.

At 2.35, company commanders finally compared watches with the company officers, and I joined my company and passed on the time to my subalterns. At 4.00 am all sleepers were roused, and the company took up its position along the front line, ready to go over. It was a miserable morning, cold and raining, and one felt an empty sort of feeling in one's tummy. At 5.05 am the battalion was all ready, so that we only had half an hour or less to spare; one kept a pretty watchful eye on one's watch that last half hour, why I don't know, for there's no mistaking a barrage when it starts; and I suppose it is like waiting for a train, one always keeps looking at the time.

Lieutenant Alan Thomas, 6th Queen's Own (Royal West Kent Regiment)

I took a last look round, seeing that my men were in position. The formation was familiar: we had practised it a score of times and each man knew exactly where his place was and what he had to do. At first we were to advance in little 'blobs' – ten men or so to each 'blob'. After that when I blew my whistle the 'blobs' were to open out into line. Thereafter the platoon commanders were to exercise discretion, directing the men to lie down and open fire or to advance, according to the situation. The men were all in excellent spirits and anxious, so far as I could judge, to get on with the show. …

I returned to my own position in the middle of the company. My sergeant major [Harris] was waiting for me. He was standing with a little group of signallers and runners – my own particular 'blob' – and when I appeared he sprang smartly to attention, saluted and reported in peacetime parade fashion that all were 'present and correct'. The formality amused me and in a queer way gave me confidence.

A 2-inch trench mortar, also know as a 'plum pudding', just prior to being sent over to German lines.

Sergeant Rupert
Whiteman, 10th
Royal Fusiliers
(City of London
Regiment)

Only three minutes to 'Zero' – then two – one!!

Never before had I such strange sensations whilst waiting for the second of 'Zero'. Still the grey half-light of early morning. All eyes were on second hands.

Twenty seconds to go! – Ten!! – Five!!!

Zero – 4.50 am to the very second.

With a roar the heavens and earth seemed to be rent asunder; every gun along that 15 miles of front opened fire simultaneously from Vimy to Croisilles. One sheet of flame rippled along the German lines caused by the bursting of thousands of British shells being lost to sight left and right by the horizon.

None of us had ever before been eyewitnesses to such awful artillery fire. Within a few seconds after Zero, signal rockets of all colours went up from the German lines calling in vain for their own artillery to retaliate and silence our guns – but most of the Hun gunners had their own troubles to attend to in taking cover from British shells, for our gunners knew the German gun positions and shelled them accordingly. Single red rockets, rockets that burst into numbers of red balls, strings of green balls, golden rain and Very lights rose high above the inferno of flame and smoke – but to no avail, our artillery once started could not be stopped.

Major Bertram
Brewin, 16th
The Royal
Scots (Lothian
Regiment)

I shoved my men over. They went as steady as rocks, swearing at the mud and wire, but calling to one another to keep their dressing, just as they had at practice. The first wave, consisting of two lines, pushed off and then I and my little party got out.

[It is] a most desperate and naked feeling to step up over the parapet into no-man's-land – you felt as if you hadn't a stitch of clothing on, and I took the tip of a man I had met who told me he found a wonderful comfort in turning his collar up. It was such a different place to what one thought: one had only been in it in the dark, and now to be able to pick your way and avoid obstacles was quite ripping. The fireworks were gorgeous too, shells bursting by hundreds, all high explosives, with a purple orange glare, thick smoke, and up and through it all, the Boche frenzied appeals for help in green and red and yellow stars, strings of pale yellow green lights – strings of onions was the trench word for them – and the knowledge that within a very short time down would come the Boche barrage and make no-man's-land a very undesirable spot.

Every gun for 15 miles was loading and firing as fast as possible and when one remembers that each of our 18-pound field guns – and there were thousands firing in this barrage – fire off sixteen to twenty rounds of high-explosive shells per minute or 1,080 per hour, one may gain some idea of the enormous number of shells crumping into the German positions on that never-to-be-forgotten Easter Monday morning. We could not help pitying those poor chaps in the trenches yonder, for despite their nationality they were human after all – and this was a hell-let-loose.

Sergeant Rupert Whiteman, 10th Royal Fusiliers (City of London Regiment)

Nothing on earth can live in such as this. A glance to the left towards Vimy and there the scene is the same. The whole of the ridge one mass of flame and rising earth. Around us, almost deadened in the terrible din, Fritz's shells are exploding as he vainly endeavours to stay our advance. Now and then a man falls dead or wounded but we take no notice but our casualties are slight for the terrible bombardment is too much for the enemy machine gunners who are either killed or cowering down a deep dugout. We reach the first line, now almost battered out of recognition

Private George Culpitt, 10th The Royal Welsh Fusiliers

Athies, to the east of Arras, was captured on the first day of the offensive by the 9th Scottish Division.

and here we see a mopping-up party of the Jocks clearing the dugout and sending the prisoners back to our lines. Now on again to the second and third lines, which have been taken without much resistance, and here for a short space we halt. Everything has gone well so far and now we are waiting for our barrage, which is playing on the wood to lift before we do our part and take the wood. On the right edge of the wood can be seen a few of the enemy and shots are exchanged. We now move on again to the centre of the wood.

Lieutenant Alan Thomas, 6th Queen's Own (Royal West Kent Regiment)

We passed over no-man's-land, thick with broken wire, and into the enemy's lines. The trenches, as we expected, were deserted. Instead of meeting Germans, we were greeted with their gunfire. Black high-explosive shells burst overhead with that cracking, wrenching noise that blew the breath out of your body. But they did small damage. Now and then a piece of metal hurtled by with a zip and buried itself in the earth. Sometimes spent machine-gun bullets came moaning through the air. For the rest we moved forward without hindrance. The advance was beginning to look like a walkover.

Suddenly, 200 or 300 yards away to the right, a heavy shell landed among the advancing troops. For the first time in my life I saw human bodies and limbs hurled into the air. I swallowed, trying hard not to feel afraid. The Sergeant Major glanced round at me. I nodded to him as cheerily as I knew how.

'Fun's just beginning!' I shouted.

I doubt if he heard me. But he smiled. The sight of a man smiling reassured me.

We continued to move forward. The high-explosive 'crumps' were less frequent now, but the heavy shells were still falling and the machine guns were becoming more insistent. So far we had seen no sign of the enemy. As for our 'blobs', they were hardly recognizable. They had in fact opened out of their own accord. Since we were now making our way over a system of deep trenches it was impossible for the men to keep to any fixed formation. Parties of them were advancing along communication trenches. Others were running forward over the top.

Crossing a trench I glanced down and saw one of our men lying in a pool of blood. His body had been split from the shoulder, downwards, and some of his entrails were hanging out. I paused, not because I wanted to look, but because I could not turn away. I had seen a dead body before, but never one so mutilated. I did not feel physically sick. I felt frightened and shaky. My knees nearly gave way under me.

With an effort I pulled myself together and hurried on. But the image of what I had seen remained with me for hours afterwards. So long as I live I shall never be able to obliterate it altogether.

One just struggled doggedly on, pulling your feet from the mud, and cursing at the delay. The barrage lifted to the second support trench; up to then there had only been desultory machine-gun fire, it seemed like a desperate man sticking to it by sheer willpower, under very heavy shelling, yet not able to control his fire – it was wild and very sweeping, so that you really only got an odd bullet near you, as he was traversing the gun back and forward so swiftly – practically no rifle fire as I guess all the Boche were sheltering. Our old line, on looking back, seemed to be heavily barraged by the Boche, and also no-man's-land, and C and D Companies suffered a bit before they got to the Boche front line. We had very few casualties so far. We found the Boche front line badly smashed up and horrid to get into and out of, not many dead about; a few prisoners came up from dugouts; as the 'moppers up' were along with me, I had to pass on and leave them. It certainly gave one a comfy feeling, knowing that one had little chance of being shot from behind. There was no shelling round us, though the weight of metal going overhead made a continuous swishing noise. As soon as we passed over the remains of the front line, I pushed off to strike my flank party on a road which (as far as the Boche main front defence) was my right flank. The only signs of a road were the regular array of stumps of trees, and I was delighted to see a party of British on the far side of it, evidently 6th King's Own Scottish Borderers. ...

The light was very poor: one could see about 100 yards, and some smoke shells from our guns blew back and sent waves of smoke back through us, and I was the more glad when I struck the road. By this time Nos. 1 and 2 Platoons had become one line, and 3 and 4 were closing up, so I sent a runner to push them back a bit.

I was looking around, when suddenly I was pushed hurriedly from behind, and had to jump into the trench, looked up and saw my runner

Major Bertram Brewin, 16th The Royal Scots (Lothian Regiment)

hurriedly fire and then jump in: he said a Boche officer had opened on us with an automatic, so we had to stalk him down. We had no bombs, and hoped he hadn't; it was creepy work dodging round mounds and corners, and never knowing where he was, or when he might shoot. We could see our men further down now, so knew he must be quite close, when he suddenly opened up from quite close. I had a go at him with my revolver and missed, and my runner got one through his arm: he fired again and so did I and both missed, though his were very close to us, and then the faithful Gillespie said he thought he had got him: we dashed over and found him just going. The faithful one had got him through the head.

Private George
Culpitt, 10th The
Royal Welsh
Fusiliers

*A German
trench after it
was captured by
the King's Own
(Royal Lancaster
Regiment).*

Our shells are now falling with clockwork regularity on the German 4th line which runs along the far side of the wood and which is our objective. A ten-minute wait close under our own barrage and we move forward again to our objective. No resistance meets us for the Hun has long since left in an endeavour to seek safety further back. A few dead lie in the trench but no living enemy is there to meet us and we occupy the position, and commence to consolidate in anticipation of a counter-attack. We have achieved our mission without resistance and at comparatively slight cost to ourselves. We now have time to breathe fully and to take stock of our position, which is a good one: in front nearly 1,000 yards away lies the village of Tilloy on which our barrage is now concentrated, and a little

nearer in front of the village is an enemy trench, deserted as far as we can see.

The noise for a little while has quietened down and the enemy's guns no longer trouble us for he is busy trying to get them away. This for him is indeed a difficult job for our artillery is still firing steadily and accurately on all his roads of retreat and owing to a shortage of horses he cannot get them away quick enough.

It would have been reasonable to suppose, that with all that had gone before, no single Hun would have been found alive in their lines. By no means so. The majority may have been moved back but plenty had been left in the line. Their dugouts were deep and no sooner had the barrage passed than up they came, firing rifles and manning their machine-gun posts. The resistance, as these shows go, was not too heavy, but bad enough indeed to kill all too many of our comrades before their objectives were reached.

Lieutenant Arthur Worman, 6th Queen's (Royal West Surrey Regiment)

Our turn came to go over, through the preceding wave as we had been taught, to our objective – the Hun line. On the way over, my faithful orderly happened to glance my way, and saw blood oozing through the front of my tunic. I had been hit in the groin but, strangely enough, had felt nothing of it at the time, although later it proved to be quite a sizeable splinter that had got me. I have never concerned myself with telepathy or the supernatural, but it might be of interest to recall that on the night of Easter day my mother, then living in Croydon, awoke from her sleep, wakened my father and told him that she had just seen me walk into their room in uniform but with a loose white bandage wound round my middle. A strange story indeed as I had only been hit that morning and would not have been reported wounded until some days later.

My orderly covered the wound with iodine and applied my field dressing, both of which we all carried. Our barrage of the previous days had torn the Boche trench system to shreds. They had suffered heavy casualties in its wake, as witness those lying around when we got over, who would fight no more. Indeed the Hun was trained to fight. This was brought right home to me when I was moving forward with my platoon to our objective. A Hun was lying on the ground just ahead of us, apparently very dead. I had passed him and was amazed that, with such life that he had left in him, he twisted himself over and fired an automatic pistol at my batman. He was fortunately too far gone to find his mark and it was his very last effort. But what stamina and what hatred.

Sergeant Rupert Whiteman, 10th Royal Fusiliers (City of London Regiment)

It was while waiting in St Catherine Wood that we saw the first fruits of the battle, for German prisoners started to come down under escort from 'in front'; one party of about 100 passed along the road through the wood and we had to clear the road to let them pass. I had never seen such awful terror-stricken faces before; they were hardly human, they could not be after surviving our barrage. Poor chaps! One could entertain nothing but pity for them for after all, we should have looked just like that had we been through the same ordeal. Back to the prisoners' camps they staggered covered with mud, hungry, unshaven and temporarily demented by the strain of the last few days of bombardment and, on the top of that, this satanic barrage.

Prisoners gather in a makeshift cage just behind the lines, no doubt grateful to have life, if no longer liberty.

From their escort of military police – 'Red caps' – we learnt that all was going splendidly up in front – not that they had been up there to see, mark you! – and that the first division to 'go over' had taken the German front line with hardly a casualty.

On our front there has been no hitch and as far as we can gather everything has gone well all along the line. Two hours pass uneventfully and now behind us we can see the advanced line of the 8th Brigade coming to carry on from where we left off, to take Tilloy village and some ground behind. Our machine guns suddenly start on the right and we hastily turn our attention in this direction. Through a gap in the enemy trench we can see the Boche hatless, without equipment or rifle, running for his life, but not many of them get away for they run into our barrage or are caught by our machine-gun fire. By this time the advanced line of the 8th Brigade has nearly reached our trench and after a short halt to get into line they go forward across the 1,000 yards of open country to the village. We are now spectators of the battle which is taking place in front of us, and which we watch eagerly. They reach the trench without difficulty and then go forward to the ruins of the village. Here they are lost to sight to reappear at intervals among the piles of bricks and stone which were once houses.

Again our attention is drawn to the right, for here a sharp scrap is taking place. It transpires that there is a sort of brigade headquarters and here we captured an entire German Staff. A short time elapses and now the scene has changed for we see the Germans coming back, but without arms for they are prisoners, twenty or thirty in a batch in the charge of one or two British Tommies. Some mere lads, some old men, a few well set up, well-built chaps and here and there a haughty officer walking with his nose in the air. Once more the noise of battle lessens for a time, the advance is stayed according to programme. By 10.00 am the Germans have been driven back over a mile and are almost out of range of our light guns, which are now busy limbering up and moving forward to take up a position in the open. Soon on our right and left we see our batteries gallop into action, swing round, unlimber and after a few sighting shots once more proceed to harass the retreating enemy.

Private George Culpitt, 10th The Royal Welsh Fusiliers

Preparations were seen round every gun for moving up as the front line of troops advanced, so as not to get out of range of the retreating Germans. Horses were nearby in readiness and gun limbers were loaded up with the gunner's gear, including short portable bridges for running guns across trenches which, by the way, are only seen when a big attack is in progress.

Sergeant Rupert Whiteman, 10th Royal Fusiliers (City of London Regiment)

The river Scarpe near Roeux village and the infamous Chemical Works

Soon we were in the outskirts of Arras itself, where we began to see signs of our wounded. Every dressing station passed had its queue of khaki wounded waiting to be properly bandaged before being taken to hospitals still farther behind the line.

By eleven o'clock we had crossed a bridge over the Scarpe River and entered Arras proper. A few Hun shells were coming over into the historic old town, but nothing to be compared with the numbers our artillery were putting over on to them. There seemed to be plenty of troops about and plenty of wounded, and occasionally we passed batches of half-witted German prisoners. No halting was allowed as we passed through the town because Arras was not healthy!

Private George Culpitt, 10th The Royal Welsh Fusiliers

About midday the third brigade of the division goes through us and on to the attack, while the Cambrai road becomes blocked with transport, ammunition limbers, while an occasional tank is to be seen crawling up the road on its journey to the still advancing line.

4.00 pm and we are still advancing, though slowly, our guns move up again and the first batches of cavalry make their appearance. Soon large numbers of cavalry can be seen concentrating on either side but they do not go any further but stay the night at this spot. At seven o'clock we are relieved by the other two companies in our trench on the edge of the wood and return to a dugout in the German 2nd line where we are to spend the night. The first thing after we have settled down is to make a thorough examination of the dugout and to go souvenir hunting, yet in a way this is a dangerous game for the enemy is full of devilish tricks and a pull at a piece of string, a touch of a seemingly harmless knob may blow the whole lot of us sky high. But nothing happens. He was in too much of a hurry to leave to have any thoughts other than those for his own safety. Equipment, rifles, ammunition, bombs, all the implements of war, were left to us.

Black bread, coffee, tinned horse, sugar, cigars, cigarettes, fell into our hands, and were speedily made use of. The black bread did not find favour, but the coffee, was good warmed on one of his patent cookers of which there were some thousands lying about. The tinned meat (horse flesh), was not so bad and was speedily demolished. By the time we had investigated every corner of this large dugout it was well on towards midnight, so we turned in for a short rest for we did not know what the future might hold for us. It had been a good day's work, but was but the beginning of more to follow.

The day wore on and night came. The expected counter-attack did not materialize. There we were, in the middle of nowhere, everything deathly still and quiet save for the odd shell or burst of machine-gun fire and no one, so far as we could find out, on either of our flanks. As the night passed, a runner arrived from Battalion HQ telling me that I must report there immediately. Here I felt I must digress to extol the merits of these runners. Normally communication could be maintained between company, battalion and brigade by means of field telephone. In an emergency such as this, this method obviously became impossible. For this reason runners must be used. Of all the unenviable jobs, this was it. Shelling or machine-gunning was often heavy, cover was sparse and these messages just had to be got through. How often did a runner start on such a journey, in most arduous conditions, and not reach his destination? After a space of time, another runner came, yet another must be sent until one of them succeeds in getting through and back, a truly hazardous job, requiring the greatest courage.

On this occasion the runner guided me back to Battalion HQ together with my faithful orderly. On arrival I was ordered by the Adjutant to go

Lieutenant Arthur Worman, 6th Queen's (Royal West Surrey Regiment)

out and make contact with the Norfolks, who should be somewhere on our right flank, on the south side of the Arras–Monchy road. The proverbial needle in a haystack might be easy to find in comparison. However, off I went with my batman into the dark, frozen and perishing cold night with just no idea as to what lay ahead. We found, as far as we knew it, the Arras–Monchy road, stumbling over trench positions, until that morning occupied by the Germans and now shelled nearly level – the many shell holes often with their grim reminders of the battle which had recently been fought; bodies, discarded equipment and rifles, all the horror and penalty of war. We crossed the road, fortunately at that moment quiet and free from shelling, to find equal devastation on the other side. No means at all of telling where, in all this shell-torn expanse, the Norfolks might possibly be, nor, for that matter, whether we were in our own or enemy lines.

After what seemed to be an eternity of searching among the barbed wire and desolation we came across the entrance to a dugout, less shell-torn than the rest. I suggested to my batman that this must surely be where we must take a chance. It might just as well be in this hideout as in any other on this desolate front that we should find friends, or should we be unlucky, be taken over by the Huns. So, very cautiously, down we went and, on reaching the bottom step we carefully eased aside the sacking curtain and looked in. At the end of the dugout were three officers, sitting round a brazier, and by the grace of God and the greatest good luck, they were British. I moved through the curtain and called out to them 'Queen's Royal West Surreys – are you the Norfolks?' A voice which I knew well, a voice from a past life, answered 'We are indeed, are you Bank of England?' Is it believable? In all this expanse of ruin and waste we had not only found the Norfolks but I had found an old colleague from a life which seemed to be a century ago.

For once, ambitions and high expectations were not hopelessly incompatible with events. On the contrary, 9 April had been such a resounding success that British and Empire troops had almost over-achieved. The Germans were sent reeling and therein lay a problem. Such was the extent of the success it would be hard to capitalize on the results before the Germans recovered their balance and began to plug the defensive holes. In places, British troops had advanced 4 miles, 'an unheard-of distance for an infantry advance', as one soldier noted. It would also take time for the army commanders to ascertain what had been achieved, even precisely where their men were, and to formulate a coherent plan of action. In fact there would be no coherent plan for Z day plus one, and a heart-rending inertia would soon become apparent. Corps commanders knew that pressure must be maintained on the enemy, but how and where? If coherence in attack was not possible, then incoherence was better than nothing. A hastily evolved plan to use a dozen tanks supported by two divisions of men to attack the village of Bullecourt and which would be executed early morning on the 10th came to naught; the ground conditions militating against the tanks' arrival on time. The cancelled attack was rearranged for the following day.

With considerable effort, light artillery could be brought up to harry the enemy, but the ground taken was pulverized and it would take time to move up the heavy artillery. The cavalry were milling around and could be used, supported by light artillery, but immediate plans came to nothing. Weather conditions exacerbated problems, with drifting snow reducing fighting to small, incoherent and localized scraps, and in places the Germans had the temerity to counter-attack. If 9 April had been a day of action, the 10th was a day of prevarication and equivocation.

Heavy artillery hauled forward by a tractor. Most roads did not stand up to the strain of constant traffic.

Lieutenant Alan Thomas, 6th Queen's Own (Royal West Kent Regiment)

During the whole of the next day the vast activity continued. Men, guns, lorries, mules, cyclists, staff cars, and all the paraphernalia of an army on the move filled in the scene for miles and miles around us. Rumours flew from mouth to mouth. There was talk of a breakthrough, and when the cavalry came up, passing within a few hundred yards of us, on their way to Monchy, we really believed that a gap in the line had been made and that the enemy's flank was about to be turned. As the horsemen passed us we cheered them on their way.

That evening an order came to us to move forward again.... After trudging a mile or so over difficult broken ground in the dark, we halted and were told to dig ourselves in. Ahead, some sort of artillery strafe appeared to be going on. But the shells were not falling near us and we didn't worry. A staff officer gave us a line, running roughly north to south, and said that that was the position we were to defend in case of counter-attack. The word, I remember, took us by surprise. We knew that after you had made an attack, a counter-attack might be expected. But the push we had been in was more than an attack. It was an 'offensive'. To counter it the old Boche would have to stage an offensive of his own – if indeed he could stage anything at all, which we doubted. Anyway, if there had been a 'breakthrough', why worry about a counter-attack?

The troops that had taken part in the fighting that first day were now suffering great privations, hunkered down in their newly won positions. The weather was dire: relief not just urgent but vital.

Major Bertram Brewin, 16th The Royal Scots (Lothian Regiment)

Headquarters remained in the Brown Line, a small dugout, fairly crowded out; however, as the CO or myself was prowling around most of the night it didn't matter much and there was plenty of time for real sleep later. Rations came up OK about 11.00 pm, no food containers as in future days, just cold meat and bread, and some rum, which was very welcome. I slept like a top between tours and felt quite fresh at dawn [10th] when we all stood to, to see if the Boche was going to try and get his own back, but he had had enough and didn't even shell us.

Spent the morning in tidying up our line, which was complicated, as we were facing north mostly across the place where the Tynesiders should have been; however, we met with no distractions, and at 11.00 am Gavin and a patrol went out and found a battery of three 5.9s from which the Boche cleared on sight, otherwise not a sign of Boche for 600 ft east of us. What a pity, if only we had a few more divisions, and our guns could have come forward, we could have gone miles. The guns, we heard, were all bogged coming up, and of course when a few got fairly in, it stopped the whole lot. I don't wonder, for the ground was bad enough for a man on his feet and what it must have been like for gun teams and caterpillars I don't know.

Anyway, they couldn't come up, there were no reserves of troops, so we had to sit tight and watch the Boche, in full view, calmly digging himself in some 1,500 to 2,000 yards away, and not a shot could be fired at him!

It was galling.

A 7.7cm Feldkanonen abandoned by German gunners as they were overrun on the opening day of the Arras offensive.

Lieutenant Alan
Thomas, 6th
Queen's Own
(Royal West
Kent Regiment)

When night came we dug again. But the men, for all that they had spent an idle day, were tired and spiritless. The cold, I think, had got them under – and the realization that after all, the end of the war was not 'just round the corner'. Of hot food there was none. We lived on our iron rations and such extras as we could scrounge, mostly from the haversacks of the dead. For Gilbert and me one of the servants had 'found' half a bottle of whisky. Though we welcomed the find we also felt a trifle ashamed of taking it. But what could we do? There were at least 150 men with us. What was half a bottle among so many?

'We could throw it away,' suggested Gilbert, reducing the problem to an absurdity.

'Or we could give it to the Sergeant Major,' I said.

'Which would come to the same thing,' retorted Gilbert.

So we comforted ourselves not only with the whisky but also with the reflection that in taking care of ourselves we were acting in the best interests of the company. For now we were the only two officers left, Marling Apperley having been wounded and Hibbert having gone down sick the day before. We could not have been much to look at, the two of us, huddled there in our cubbyhole, with three days' growth on our chins. Nor were the conditions very grand. We were tired and cold and we knew that at any moment the Boche might start bombarding us. Yet, being together, I do not think we were unhappy.

Major Bertram
Brewin, 16th
The Royal
Scots (Lothian
Regiment)

I went round the strongpoints at midnight just to cheer the men up, for they were beginning to feel the strain and we had all been wet through and chilled to the bone since Sunday night; found two or three of the officers pretty near petered out, and so sent down for others to replace them. They had had a very heavy time for in the shortage of NCOs they were practically doing twenty-four hours' work in twenty-four hours. Most of them though were in good form, stalwarts like Martin of D, Warre of B, and others being very fit. They too were anxious for the men, who they said were getting very tired, and their feet were giving a lot of trouble; standing continuously in the slushy mud would knock most men's feet out. Mine I had rarely felt and certainly they had never been warm since Monday morning. Stephenson wrote out a stiff letter to Brigade, saying that the men were nearly at the end of their tether and that he wouldn't be responsible for them unless they could hold out a definite limit before relief was due. We got completely lost going back to HQ. The snow was blowing horizontally and the wind had swerved round and it was black as pitch; we got fairly torn to ribands with barbed wire and fell into every kind of awful place and were challenged and nearly shot by the Tynesiders in the front line.

As on the Somme, nine months before, the cavalry was held in close reserve to be used as the fastest means of exploiting a breakthrough. And at Arras, again, they were used during the fighting. On the Somme, their brief appearance had been successful, at Arras tragically less so.

During Tuesday, there had been severe localized fighting near the geographically prominent village of Monchy-le-Preux, where infantry attacks had been rebuffed. The cavalry had been available for use that day but their moment had not come.

German dead buried in the rubble of Fampoux, captured on 9 April. Sergeant Huborn Godfrey's cross identifies his half-buried body.

The attacks would continue again early the following day in a snowstorm, this time with success, for Monchy fell. That was abundantly evident from the groups of Germans seen running back in the distance while, a kilometre away, teams of horses could be seen racing up to the German guns in an effort to remove them. There was an eerie quiet in Monchy's streets, a misleading calm as senior German officers took stock and ascertained that the key position was lost. As British troops sealed the far side of the village, more men hunted round, clearing houses and cellars one by one. Between Monchy and the neighbouring village of Fampoux, which was also in British hands, the rolling countryside seemed open, undamaged, and unimpeded by barbed wire and trenches, perfect country for the cavalry to roam and wheel but the ground was also horribly exposed.

A/Captain
Douglas
Cuddeford, 12th
The Highland
Light Infantry

An excited shout was raised that our cavalry were coming up! Sure enough, away behind us, moving quickly in extended order down the slope of Orange Hill, were line upon line of mounted men covering the whole extent of the hillside as far as we could see. It was a thrilling moment for us infantrymen, who had never dreamt that we should live to see a real cavalry charge, which was evidently what was intended. In their advance, the lines of horsemen passed over us rapidly, although from our holes in the ground it was rather a 'worm's eye' view we got of the splendid spectacle of so many mounted men in action.

Private Rupert
Whiteman, 10th
Royal Fusiliers
(City of London
Regiment)

Who were those mounted men riding up the slope to Monchy from the Arras side? They were only occasionally visible but there seemed to be a lot of them, several hundreds at least. Soon the glorious truth dawned on us, they were the cavalry!

The very word sent a thrill through one. We were about to witness one of the most thrilling episodes of the war, to watch them ride through the village, down the slope on the other side, across the valley and then in amongst the advancing Germans yonder in the dip with sword and lance. Another disappointment: we saw them enter the village but they were soon lost to sight amongst the houses. Expectantly we waited for them to reappear on the other side; waited five minutes, then ten, but no, not a sign of them.

The cavalry came under fire from German artillery and machine guns, underscoring the vulnerability of the horses. They had attacked only to be driven back into the illusionary safety of the village, for the streets offered scant protection to such a large body of men and horses. The Germans, appreciating the sudden plight of the cavalry, and knowing the ranges over which to fire, slammed salvo after salvo into the packed streets.

Hideous thought! They must have halted in the village!! Of all places on the Western Front in which to halt cavalry, Monchy should have been the last. The village was developing into an inferno more and more every quarter of an hour, for the Germans were concentrating all their artillery there in the hope of being able to recapture it.

Private Rupert Whiteman, 10th Royal Fusiliers (City of London Regiment)

All their artillery, I said, but that was not strictly correct for we were getting a fair share along the sunken road. We soon began to see evidence of casualties amongst the cavalry. Those poor old horses, they commenced to come out of the village in all directions, riderless, reins flying in the wind, manes and tails stiff with terror, some limping and wounded, others galloping, down the slopes from the village to the north, the south, east and west.

It may have been a fine sight, but it was a wicked waste of men and horses, for the enemy immediately opened on them a hurricane of every kind of missile he had. If the cavalry advanced over us at the trot or canter, they came back at a gallop, including numbers of dismounted men and riderless horses, and – most fatal mistake of all – they bunched behind Monchy in a big mass, into which the Boche continued to put high-explosive shrapnel, whizz-bangs, and a hail of bullets, until the horsemen dispersed and finally melted away back over the hillside from where they came.

A/Captain Douglas Cuddeford, 12th The Highland Light Infantry

They left a number of dead and wounded men among us, but the horses seemed to have suffered most, and for a while we put bullets into poor brutes that were aimlessly limping about on three legs, or else careering about madly in their agony, like one I saw that had the whole of its muzzle blown away. With dead and wounded horses lying about in the snow, the scene resembled an old-fashioned battle picture. Why it had been thought

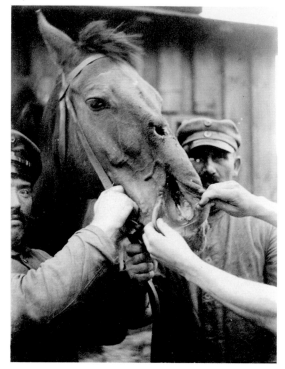

Battle-scarred German horses receiving treatment in 1917. Horses often survived quite horrific injuries.

fit to send in cavalry at that juncture, against a strongly reinforced enemy who even then were holding up our infantry advance, we never knew. Cavalry may still have their uses in some kinds of warfare, but for a large force of mounted men to attempt an attack on the enemy positions that day was sheer madness.

Lieutenant Alan Thomas, 6th Queen's Own (Royal West Kent Regiment)

As dusk was falling … we saw a runner coming towards us from the direction of Monchy. We watched him, wondering what his news was. We hoped he would tell us we were going to be relieved.

'The Colonel's compliments, Sir,' announced the messenger, 'and 'e would like to see you at seven o'clock at 'is 'eadquarters.'

'What's the news?' I asked.

'Dunno wot the news is, Sir,' replied the other, 'but I reckon as our cavalry boys 'ave copped it up at Monchy.'

'How do you mean?'

'Reckon you'll see wot I mean, Sir, when you goes up there.'

With a quarter of an hour in hand I left Gilbert in charge of the company and started off for Monchy, the runner showing me the way.

'For God's sake get us relieved,' Gilbert said, as I departed. 'The men are all in.'

I said I would do what I could.

In five minutes we were at the foot of the village. As we turned the bend of the road to go up the hill, I stopped. The sight that greeted me was so horrible that I almost lost my head. Heaped on top of one another and blocking up the roadway for as far as one could see lay the mutilated bodies of our men and their horses. These bodies, torn and gaping, had stiffened into fantastic attitudes. All the hollows of the road were filled with blood.

This was the cavalry.

When our horsemen had gathered in Monchy the Germans had put down a box barrage round the place – the four sides of the barrage gradually drawing inwards. The result of this shooting lay before me. Nothing that I had seen before in the way of horrors could be even faintly compared with what I saw around me now. Death in every imaginable shape was there for the examining.

I walked up the hill, picking my way as best I could and often slipping in the pools of blood, so that my boots and the lower parts of my puttees were dripping with blood by the time I reached the top. Nor, I discovered on my way up, were all the men and animals quite dead. Now and then a groan would strike the air – the groan of a man who was praying for release. Sometimes the twitch of a horse's leg would shift the pattern of the heaped-up bodies. A small party of stretcher-bearers, obviously unequal to their task, were doing what they could do to relieve the suffering.

I found the Colonel in the cellar. He was now in charge not only of the battalion and of the whole brigade, but also of the situation generally. He had, characteristically enough, assumed command of it on his own initiative, and when I arrived he was telling a battery commander where and when he was to fire his guns. It was a gloomy place, this cellar. It was lit by two candles and smelt of death. The only cheerful sight in it reposed on a table in a corner – an enormous ham. It was the only thing that any of us felt like attacking.

The sight of wounded horses touched the hearts of men who had otherwise become hardened to frightfulness. The suffering of these horses had been relatively short-lived, at least relatively short-lived in comparison to the men under Major Bertram Brewin's command. By Wednesday evening, his men had been in action for sixty hours without relief and in the freezing cold, the weather usurping the Germans as the primary enemy.

Major Bertram Brewin, 16th The Royal Scots (Lothian Regiment)

It rained heavily all afternoon and evening and when [Major] Stephenson went round at 11.00 pm he came back very perturbed over the state of the men. They were caving in and very exhausted: the mud and strain had fairly knocked them out. I went round about 3.00 am – luckily a communication trench ran from the gun pits where Battalion HQ had been made to the front line – I was shocked at the men, and the officers said they had the greatest difficulty to keep the men awake and feared some would die of exhaustion: they, the officers, were wonderfully cheery and as I had a water bottle of rum with me I was very popular.

Stephenson was so upset over the men that he sent me direct to Divisional HQ with a free hand to say just what I liked, and also a letter for the GSO1 – Brigade had sent us a message that Division could make no promises as to relief. It was a relief to get a real walk and be able to pick your way. I got on the Arras–Gavrelle road at the ridge top and had a very nice walk back to Arras, though the mud was appalling. Guns stuck at every point and in trying to get them out they had made a regular bog all round them. You've never seen such a sight, and so many guns hors-de-combat. Got into Arras about 10.00 am. I was a picture, torn to ribands, and mud from head to foot, not a wash since Sunday afternoon.

Saw Brain GSO1 and gave him Stephenson's letter. Oh! he said, your men have done splendidly: tell Stephenson so, and they are alright now, as there are no more operations for your brigade! I said it wasn't operations, but pure exhaustion that was knocking us out and that we couldn't go on. Brain pooh-poohed it, so I got wild and told him I hadn't seen a brigade or divisional staff officer beyond the Blue Line (the railway cutting) and that they knew nothing about it. He got quite huffy and wanted to tell me he knew all about things, so I flatly contradicted him and told him I would pilot him out to see for himself, as he wouldn't believe either Stephenson or myself.

Nicholson, the Divisional General, apparently had heard some of my trouble and came in. He was very amused at my appearance and I don't wonder: was awfully good and made me stay to an early lunch and then said Brain should go back with me; Brain didn't seem at all optimistic. Nicholson was charming and wanted to know what I was doing up there, and all about things. Then Brain and I set out on horseback, rode to the Point du Jour, and then I took him down to Stephenson. He was not so cocksure when he had got there, but Stephenson insisted on his going to the line and just as they got to the trench two poor lads died in front of them. This straightened Brain up at once, and he said: 'That's quite enough for me. You must be relieved,' and set off back.

We were relieved, what glorious news! The next thing to do was to stagger across the open snow-covered country back to Arras. There was no thought of a correct relief as per Drill Book, orders were to make it back to Arras as best as we could.

In a kind of dream we started across the countryside in scattered groups, buoyed with the knowledge that every weary step brought us nearer Arras and further from that nightmare, Monchy.

Somehow, Mantle, Swain, Haddow and Jack and a few others stumbled across each other and stuck together. It was not at all obvious in which direction Arras lay; there were no guiding stars and the surrounding acres were one unvarying vista of white. In due course a long line of trees marked the position of the main Arras–Cambrai road. When we had gained this our troubles were over for it was then only a case of plodding wearily along it.

The nearer we got to Arras the more we found that other folk also wanted to use the road, and by the time we reached the 3 kilometres peg, after numerous rests by the roadside, the road was simply packed with traffic of all kinds going up to the front line.

There were ration carts, gun carriages, gun limbers, ammunition lorries, ambulances, mules carrying shells, infantry, water carts, cavalry and wagons, all making in the opposite direction to our party. When traffic

Private Rupert Whiteman, 10th Royal Fusiliers (City of London Regiment)

Various views of the destruction in ARRAS caused by "Hun" Shell-fire.

The Station Square.

The remorseless destruction of Arras. The town's streets were eerily empty during the day, but came alive at night when shops reopened.

became too thick we took to the fields and finally reached the outskirts of Arras sometime about three o'clock Thursday morning.

Soon after joining them, the remnants of the poor broken battalion moved a few hundred yards away into cellars just off the Grande Place. Mantle, Swain, Jack, Haddow and several others occupied the same cellar and soon after getting puttees and boots off – Oh! what a relief – dinner of hot stew was ready. Someone got a brazier of glowing coke and round this on the cement floor we clustered.

The combined effect of having boots off, a fire and hot soup made everyone feel that this was the nearest approach to an earthly heaven possible. Then we slept for a few hours. About 6.00 pm we were awakened by the arrival of more 10th men. After this first party had arrived, others kept straggling in till late that night. Some men had not heard that the battalion had been relieved until sometime later so had just come in from Monchy, others had come back at the same time as Mantle and his party but had either been all this time finding the battalion or had been asleep in another quarter of the town.

Each party, as it came in, was surrounded by men making eager enquiries for news of a chum or brother. Sometimes a man believed to be dead, back there in Monchy, would come in with a party.... No one gave up hopes of seeing his particular chum until the last of the parties seemed to have come in, after that the hard fact had to be faced.

Major Bertram Brewin, 16th The Royal Scots (Lothian Regiment)

[The] next day tidied and cleaned up, shaved and generally became respectable again. Nine-tenths of the men had cut the skirts off their greatcoats – not good for the coats but quite excusable, seeing that the tails got so heavy with mud that no man could carry them. There was an awful shortage of equipment and Lewis gun ammunition drums were missing by hundreds. It was a very quiet day and after lunch I went over and did the attack on my own. They had tidied up wonderfully, heaps of salvage all over the place and all our dead from the early phases were laid outside a big crater, in which they temporarily buried the whole lot – rather a staggering lot to see, poor lads, when they were all collected, but as it was the damage of the whole brigade and nearly another, I suppose it was not excessive. They had buried those killed at the railway just short of the Bois de la Maison Blanche, from which came most of their deaths.

I saw the two tanks which were supposed to be going to do wonders: one was stuck trying to climb a Boche machine-gun post in the front line, and the other never got over our front line. The third gave up the ghost in Roclincourt valley and never appeared on the scene. There were some damned civilians looting dead Boche and odds and ends, so I scared them with a couple of shots from my revolver, and they ran like hares. It was sickening to see them, and some of the Boche were pretty well stripped.

Brewin's men had been relieved, but not everyone who had taken part in that first day's fighting was resting behind the lines. Far from it. Lieutenant Alan Thomas found his exhausted but inspirational commanding officer in a cellar, waiting for his company commanders to arrive. It was not good news.

When the other three company commanders had arrived, Dawson spoke to us. He said that things had not gone exactly according to plan. The cavalry, instead of staging a breakthrough, had been trapped – as any fool could have told they would be, except apparently our Higher Command. The result was that the whole show had come more or less to a standstill. That was the situation – and it had to be remedied at once. Every hour would make a difference, because it would give the Boche that much more time to dig in and rally his strength for a counter-attack. Our orders therefore were to press on as rapidly as possible at all costs. This meant staging an attack at dawn.

Lieutenant Alan Thomas, 6th Queen's Own (Royal West Kent Regiment)

Dawson paused. Perhaps he was waiting for one of us to say something. We knew better than to open our mouths before our opinion was invited.

'Well,' he said presently, 'have you got anything to say? You, Porteous?'

Porteous commanded A Company.

'Well, Sir, if we have to attack, we'll attack. But we shan't put up much of a show, I'm afraid. The men haven't got it in them. They're cold and they're hungry and they haven't slept for four nights. They ought to be relieved. But they'll do what they're ordered.'

Dawson grunted. Turning to me, he asked me what I thought.

'I say the same, Sir,' I replied. I told him that my men were exhausted and that if an attack was to be made fresh troops ought to be used. But I said, as Porteous had said, that we would of course do what we were ordered.

The other two company commanders said the same.

'It's all very well,' observed Dawson, 'to talk about fresh troops. But they've got to be up here in time to go over the top at half past five in the morning. It's now past seven.'

'Couldn't the show be put off,' suggested Porteous, 'for twenty-four hours?'

'If you'd listened to what I said,' retorted Dawson, 'you'd know why that's impossible.'

'Would you like to come and see my men for yourself, Sir?' Porteous enquired.

'If I had time to go round the battalion, d'you think I'd be sitting in this blasted cellar!' retorted Dawson. 'If there was anyone here at all who had the remotest idea of how to take charge or to do anything except tell me that all his men are exhausted –'

'I'm telling you the truth, Sir!' interrupted Porteous, with a temerity we all admired.

For a second I thought Dawson was going to lose his temper. But he realized in time, as we all realized, that Porteous was talking sense.

'I know you are,' said Dawson quietly. 'And you're quite right. In ordinary circumstances I'd tell the division to put the show off for twenty-four hours so as to give the men a chance – or else send new men in. But these circumstances aren't ordinary. For the last four days we've had the Boche on the run as we've never had him on the run before. I believe that even now it's not too late to keep him on the run, if we follow up at once. Remember he's checked us already. The cavalry who were supposed to go through are – well, you can see for yourselves where they are. Now that he's checked us the first thing he'll do will be to counter-attack – if we give him the time. As things are, even twenty-four hours will make a difference. That's why, if we're going to make a success of this push, we've got to go on first thing in the morning. And don't forget this. We were the leading brigade to go over on the ninth. We saw some fighting: but it wasn't so fierce and we didn't meet the resistance which some of the other brigades met – the brigades that leapfrogged us. They were up against it more than we were: and their casualties were heavier than ours. Now we've leapfrogged them and it's our turn again. I don't propose to tell the division that we can't go on.'

He paused and looked at us. He was sitting on a backless chair behind an upturned crate which was used for a table. The light from the candles cast upward shadows on his face. Behind him stood the Adjutant, whose expression showed clearly that he sympathized with us and at the same time shared the Colonel's views. His gaze was accordingly directed to the floor.

'I want you therefore,' continued Dawson presently, 'to warn your men. They'd better get all the rest they can tonight – don't put them on digging parties or anything of that sort. They must be ready to go over at 5.30 in the morning – as soon as the order comes from me.'

'We don't go over till we get your order?' one of us asked.

'You don't go over till you get the order from me,' repeated Dawson. 'But you must be ready. Do you understand?'

We all four said we understood.

After waiting about half a minute, Dawson said:

'If that's clear, there's one thing I'll add. I've been trying all the afternoon, and I'm still trying, to arrange a relief tonight –'

'A relief tonight!' one of us interrupted. 'D'you mean, Sir –?'

'Don't I make myself clear?' demanded Dawson sternly. 'I tell you that I'm trying, and have been trying all the afternoon, to arrange for the battalion to be relieved – tonight. So far, I haven't had definite word. I've told the division what I know myself of the state the men are in: and I shall tell them now what you've told me this evening. But if they can't arrange it, then we shall attack. I expect to have definite news before midnight. If the relief is coming, the code word will be 'orange'. If the relief is not coming and we have to go over, the code word will be 'green'. I'll let you have word as soon as I can. That's all.'

The Colonel rose, indicating that the conference was over.

Thomas returned to his company to relay the bad news to Sergeant Major Harris, his old school sergeant, 'stolid and unquestioning', as Thomas described him. 'You could at least depend on him to stand fast: and the tighter the corner, the faster he would stand.' After Harris had left, Thomas made a tour of his company.

Lieutenant Alan Thomas, 6th Queen's Own (Royal West Kent Regiment)

It was a dreary business. The men were huddled together in varying stages of exhaustion. A few were asleep: these were the luckier ones, unconscious of the cold and the discomfort. Here and there I was greeted with attempted cheeriness: 'Wot price a kip in the ole barn now, Sir!' 'Reckon Jerry's got to Germany by now, I don't think!' 'Wish the General could see us now, Sir!' But the majority endured in silence.

Returning to Gilbert I said that I wouldn't give much for our chances if we had to attack. Naturally we cursed the staff and wondered if they had the least idea how the show was going. We decided they hadn't. Regarding ourselves as the victims of incompetence we immediately began to feel superior. This was just as well, because whatever the truth may have been, unless we had been able to loose off our feelings on someone (and on whom better than the absent who are always wrong?), I think we might have found it difficult to carry on. As it was, we cheered up a lot and gave the ration party (who turned up about ten o'clock) a more hilarious welcome than they were expecting. The guide, it seemed, had lost his way and the Quartermaster Sergeant, a gloomy, conscientious man, had almost given up hope of reaching us at all.

In addition to the rations and the rum, he had brought up a few letters, among them one for me from my mother. Like most people, I have always enjoyed receiving letters (the joy of answering them has never been so great) and in those days the pleasure was acute – sharpened by the contrast which I invariably drew between the familiarity of the handwriting and of the Hampstead postmark and the outlandishness of my surroundings when the letter was delivered. Every letter that I got from my mother or father (and I got one pretty nearly every day) recreated for me the surroundings of my home – the desk at which the letter was written, the brass inkstand and the blotter and even the particular brown-handled pen with its 'J' nib which my mother always used. I knew the pillar box at which the letter would have been posted: it stood just down the road, opposite the station. And here in France the letter was delivered to me a few days later in conditions which neither my father nor mother could picture – sometimes in a little farmhouse, sometimes under canvas, sometimes in a quiet sector of the trenches, sometimes in the front line. The last letter had come to me when we were in the great chalk caves in front of Arras. Now here

was this one brought to me on the outskirts of Monchy, carried almost literally over the dead bodies of my comrades. There was the familiar writing. There the well-known Hampstead postmark. Hampstead of all places! I was glad my mother did not know where I was when her letter was delivered. She would have died of fright. As it was I gave the Quartermaster Sergeant a field postcard to take back. Later, when we were back in billets, I would send a description of what we had been doing. . . .

So far we had received no instructions. If we were to attack I had no idea what our objective was to be. Nor, I suspected, had anyone else, though Dawson had promised details of the plan. Even so, there couldn't be much time to study them or pass them on to the company. The only thing to tell them, Gilbert suggested, was to advance and when they met the enemy defeat him. And that, I imagine, was what it would have come to so far as instructions were concerned.

By eleven o'clock I had made up my mind that the chances of relief were nil. All I was concerned about was that we should get definite instructions as soon as possible. I knew Dawson's difficulties and the time it took to get things moving. But I knew, too, how easily mistakes were made. Even in familiar surroundings you often lost your way, as I had known to my cost. Here the surroundings were wholly unfamiliar and it

Camaraderie between this officer and his men, 1/4th Yorkshire Regiment. The battalion was badly cut up in fighting on 23 April when they lost nearly 150 men killed or died of wounds.

Two men of the 1/4th Yorkshire Regiment, 50th Division, reading letters in a trench after relieving other exhausted units from the Arras offensive, 12 April.

was dark. Easy enough for Dawson's runner to lose himself on the way from Monchy – and then where should we be? Perhaps even now he was wandering about with plans for the attack! I wondered what we ought to do if the instructions didn't come. Stand fast? Or attack? Gilbert said if he had his way a third of the company would attack, a third stand fast, and a third relieve themselves.

The minutes dragged slowly on and at half past eleven we were still without instructions. By that time a new problem had arisen. There was still a quarter of a bottle of whisky left. Should we drink it now? Should we drink it in the morning? Or should we drink none of it and take the bottle with us? If so, who should carry it? I was for taking it with us on the grounds that our plight might well become worse than it was now and then we should be glad we hadn't drunk it. Gilbert disagreed. He was for drinking it straight away on the grounds that we might as well make sure of it and that as for the morning – if we ever lived to see it – we still had our rum. The idea of taking the bottle with us was absurd, if only because we might get separated and he was certain to be the unlucky one. While we were still debating the question it began to snow. Gilbert said that was a sign from Heaven. If it was not a sign it was at least an encouragement. So between us we finished the bottle.

Just as we had finished it, I heard a challenge and a moment later Dawson's runner stood before me. Taking off his tin hat he drew a scrap of paper from the lining and handed it to me. The message contained one word – 'Orange'.

Overleaf: Tanks rolling forward prior to an attack at Arras. This image was possibly snapped on 23 April near Monchy-le-Preux.

3 Opportunity Lost

'It is really extraordinary the part played by the stomach in life. It simply rules the world, and affects all our outlook on life. We are paralyzed, absorbed, hypnotized by it. The chief topic of conversation is rations with the men, and food and wine with the officers.'

Reverend Oswin Creighton, Army Chaplain, attd. 3rd Division, Royal Field Artillery

———

The astonishing achievement of 9 April was unlikely to be repeated: too much militated against a runaway success being sustained. It was still a year before new battle tactics, learnt from experience, combined with technological innovations, to bring tanks, artillery, infantry and aircraft to function cohesively together.

In April 1917, the bombardment that could break the enemy's will to withstand an opening assault was also a key ingredient in the assault unravelling. Keeping the army moving even at a snail's pace over wet and shell-churned ground was a huge logistical operation yet momentum was critical for operational success. Crucially, the enemy was still able to bring strength and resilience to the battlefield: the Germans were not yet exhausted by war. And, of course, the Allied troops might have expected to fight an April campaign in mild, damp weather, not in a freezing blizzard more commonly found in the Russian Steppes.

The main difficulty in the constant use of large trucks or motor vehicles was that the roads could not stand the constant and heavy wear on them. Adequate maintenance of the roads for the last 2 or 3 miles was out of the question, on account of the lack of men and material necessary for their repairs, to say nothing of constant hostile shelling. During the previous winters, road control had been established, and the most direct routes to the firing trenches were often closed for weeks at a time, while all heavy traffic was routed along third-class roads, which were often double the distance of the more direct roads.

Second Lieutenant Harry Trounce, 181 Tunnelling Company, Royal Engineers

Opposite: A German 5.9-inch shell exploding: the wet, viscous mud often reduced the impact of such detonations on men even close by.

Working parties of the Scots Guards laying sleepers: the rapid construction of light railways over the battlefield was a crucial function if sufficient supplies were to be maintained to the front line.

During the first week or two of this offensive we were employed on repairing the destroyed roads or building new ones. In many places where they crossed the old trenches we were obliged to take out the timber from the German trenches and dugouts, and corduroy the roads with it. Their lumber proved very useful. In many other instances we used the only material available – brick from the ruins of the buildings nearby. These brick roads were naturally not much good, but they served our purpose for a week or two. We found considerable quantities of German high explosives in various dugouts. These we used in demolishing many of

their own concrete emplacements, being able later to utilize the concrete so obtained in our work of road repairing.

The drainage was of first importance. With the exception of the main metalled or paved roads, which invariably have ditches running along each side, the majority had no culverts of any description. It was very necessary for us to construct narrow drainage ditches along the sides and run these off into deep sumps dug in the adjoining fields from 10 to 20 feet on either side of the road. This is practically the same method that we adopted in draining most of the communication trenches. In the advance and the half-open warfare then proceeding, the infantry and gunners would carve little 'funk holes' or shelters under or into the banks of the roads, or use their waterproof sheets to cover the little huts they built with low walls of sandbags filled with dirt.

On account of the Germans having destroyed practically all of their dugouts and shelters, there was little protection for us from their constant and heavy bombardment. Our only resource was to jump into the trenches which lined almost every road. As a matter of fact, trenches are fairly good protection and we were always glad to use them. In addition to our rebuilding the highways we were engaged in making a reconnaissance of all the captured district in this area, and perfecting plans for the thorough salvaging of all enemy material left behind. The amount and value of this was very great and included rails, timber, iron, ammunition, explosives, and many other useful things. A light railway was constructed for several miles in the old no-man's-land and millions of dollars' worth of material recovered, even including the iron knife rests for supporting barbed wire. We used very large quantities of the old German dugout timber in constructing new dugouts in our recently captured positions.

Our task was to remove an [ammunition] dump from Achicourt to the captured village of Neuville-Vitasse, completing the journey under cover of darkness. Had the heads instructed us to leave at 8.00 pm, this would perhaps have been successfully accomplished, but to expect us to cover 3 miles to Neuville-Vitasse and back in four hours with traffic in its present state was, to say the least, a trifle over-optimistic.

In company with several drivers from other units, we waited for an hour while some person unknown looked for an elusive loading party, which was

Driver Aubrey Smith, 1/5th (City of London) Battalion, London Rifle Brigade

A view along the ruined street of Roclincourt, north of Arras. A picture taken by Captain Basil Peers, 7th King's Own (Royal Lancaster Regiment). Peers had been in France since May 1915.

ultimately discovered asleep in a barn. While they were being given time to don their overcoats, etc., we stamped our feet in a few inches of snow for a further half hour. Their arrival was denoted by a volume of grousing surging up from the darkness.... At about 2.00 am we eventually left the dump, loaded with small arms ammunition boxes, and set off towards Beaurains, pinching our ears occasionally to make sure they had not dropped in the road and allowing our legs to swing to and fro in an effort to regain circulation. I had been wearing a big pair of lined leather gloves, wet inside and out, but nevertheless most useful. However, one had gone the way of most gloves – having been dropped and lost in the darkness at the dump: the other lasted a few days more and was then eaten by a horse.

Between Achicourt and Beaurains, we found that the heavy guns were being moved forward, bringing the horse traffic to a complete standstill. The particular obstacle holding up the convoy ahead of us was the friendly

embrace of a lorry and a tractor, which kept us marking time for over two hours – this being the chilliest, bitterest, windiest wait that I ever had in France. We could not feel our stirrup irons when we remounted and the reins slipped several times from numbed fingers as the journey proceeded. The Boches were shelling Beaurains before and during our flight through the village, which was not conducive either to dignified bearing or good temper: but we all got past the crossroads without mishap and, proceeding up the slope on the far side of the village, emerged on territory where we had not driven limbers before.

Neuville-Vitasse, as I said previously, had been a part of the Hindenburg Line. In various parts of it the Germans had left a large 'RE' dump and considerable quantities of ammunition, which they were now endeavouring to destroy by continual heavy shellfire; consequently our own folk thought it would be a splendid idea to deposit our brigade dump in practically the same spot. It was only good fortune that prevented our new store from being blown to smithereens at its very inception: the locality was unhealthy and Fritz knew every feature of it. On the other hand, the new dump may have enjoyed long life, for all I know – I never had occasion to go there again.

It was daylight when we dropped our loads in the captured village where we could see all the signs of recent battle – dead Londoners and Germans, abandoned machine guns and equipment, a trench full of shovels and rifles. The earth about here was very much churned up by the heavy bombardment, but a thick coating of snow lay over everything, half-burying those objects that we were able to distinguish. Ahead of us the LRB and the other regiments were attacking at Wancourt and Héninel – how comparatively simple this ammunition job was to what our ration convoy would have to perform the next night, carrying their loads perhaps a mile or so ahead of this spot if the attack went well!

At seven o'clock in the morning we were back at the transport lines again, ready for a tempting breakfast of bully beef with biscuits and a cup of tea without milk. This was the fourth successive day of this iron ration diet and I felt so inclined to vomit at the thought of it that it mattered little now whether I ate or not. Fortunately a parcel arrived again at a critical moment.

The British were now in a salient of their own making and the Germans were fighting back. Key objectives set after the initial phase of fighting remained in enemy hands and would have to be taken. British attacks were, however, piecemeal and sometimes incoherent, with battalions attacking with little or no support on their flanks: the 2nd Seaforth Highlanders, in an attack on a chemical works near the village of Roeux, lost 375 men killed or wounded, 86 per cent of their attacking strength. Relief of the men in the fighting line was slow and long overdue. Arras was becoming the Somme Mark II, with progress measured in yards. There was no alternative. The agreement with General Nivelle was to attack at Arras before he launched his campaign, and, owing to a further delay because of the weather, his offensive had not even begun. Haig had no option but to continue the struggle. After all, if Nivelle's promise of stunning success were realized, then the losses at Arras would be militarily justified. The problem was that the Arras offensive was taking place within a vacuum with no clear objective other than to straighten the line. The Germans, defending, had very clear objectives: do not try to retake what is palpably lost, do not defend the indefensible but make sure that the Allied troops were made to pay, and pay heavily, for ground conceded to them.

The daily casualty rate ensured that the medical services were at full stretch. Lieutenant Colonel David Rorie's diary describes in unruffled words a plight that was, at best, ordered chaos.

Lieutenant Colonel David Rorie, OC 1/2nd (Highland) Field Ambulance

In a nook left between the end of the stretcher racks and the exit from the shelter was set a small collapsible table whereto were pinned a map of the district and a more detailed one of the trenches, both together making up the board on which you played your own special little game of chess against unforeseen circumstances. A clip took in all the 'chits' from the MOs [Medical Officers] at the various RAPs [Regimental Aid Posts], chronologically arranged as they came in, and marked with the hour of receipt, by the sergeant clerk who sat beside you.

Each message was supposed to have the hour of its dispatch written on it by the sender: 50 per cent of them never had. Many were soaked and barely decipherable – medical handwriting is somewhat peculiar at best, especially when written in indelible pencil, which had 'run'. Many demands were indefinite – 'more stretchers', 'more bearers', 'more dressings'; others asked for impossible and exaggerated quantities. Here your knowledge of the sender's mentality had to come in, and you discounted the requests of the MO who thought too imperially, and dealt with him on more parochial lines.

One MO who was a bit 'rattled' (and no wonder) might have sent off three messages one after another, all without the hour of dispatch stated; and you had to make a shot at which was the latest one (and, therefore, that to be dealt with), as messengers 2 and 1 might turn up in that order after messenger 3.

All the time, too, if you were wise (for it paid you to do it), you were jotting down a running tale of how things progressed, your literary efforts interrupted by visits here and there to lend a hand in dressing cases and loading cars; or by interviewing messengers and supervising the issue of stores in response to indents, and seeing that other indents were going back at once for fresh supplies.

A moment of relative peace if not quiet: scenes in a forward Regimental Aid Post.

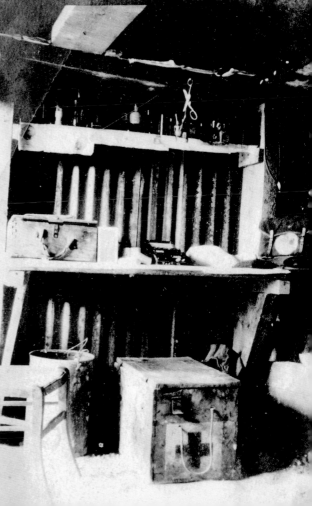

Then your map had to be kept up to date as the Regimental Aid Posts changed when the battalions advanced, and all such changes had to be duly notified to the ADMS [Assistant Director Medical Services]. Altogether you were the head of a somewhat irritable family, whose nerves, after some hours of it, were apt to get a bit jangled: knowing, too, as regards yourself, that you were the certain recipient of criticism, both from those above and those below you in rank, for all that went wrong; and at the very least expected to remedy the unexpected with the speed of Hermes and the patience of Job.

As the fighting moved forward, so did the medical services. The 1/2nd Highland Field Ambulance moved to St Nicholas, on the outskirts of Arras, where they took over a series of four parallel tunnels running into the hillside, capable of holding up to 150 casualties.

Lieutenant Colonel David Rorie, OC 1/2nd (Highland) Field Ambulance

The tunnels opened on flat ground covered with ruins, some of which had been sufficiently repaired to serve as offices, a dressing-room, stretcher and blanket stores, cookhouses, etc.; while beyond it again the ground dipped to a light railway running parallel to the river Scarpe up the valley towards Fampoux and Roeux by way of Blangy and L'Abbayette, all these places being in ruins. At the last-named was the Collecting Post; and at Fampoux Three Arches were Relay Bearer Posts; while the Walking Wounded Collecting Post was in tentage about a kilometre up the valley road. Fighting was going on at the famous Chemical Works and a steady run of casualties came in all day.

The roofs of the tunnels, unfortunately, owing to the persistently wet weather, dripped steadily; and as all ranks were underneath them this did not make for comfort, especially as the water which found its way through was not even clean. At night the unlucky possessor of an upper bunk had to tack his groundsheet onto the earth roof above him, a precarious protection at best; as in time the sheet bellied out with the accumulated water, and either tore itself from its fastenings, or at the least touch poured out onto the ill-starred sleeper from each end. The tunnels, too, could not be ventilated, smelt like a tomb, and were 'fuggy' to a degree; but there were some 40 feet of head cover, which made up for many minor deficiencies.

Till the 19th the weather continued vile, and we were busy both with cases coming in (many of them casualties from Blangy and the valley road, which the enemy shelled steadily) and with improving the accommodation – clearing fresh tracks through the ruins, forming up the incoming and outgoing roads for the motor ambulance wagons, and getting up some operation tents for 'sitting cases' when space was available. It was always a matter of duty, honour, pride and routine that those in possession should make a place of this sort better than when it had been handed over; and the outcome was that, in some of the sites where unit after unit had worked at the job for months, a wonderfully high standard was attained.

On the 22nd, in view of a new divisional push the next day, the Bearer Divisions of the Field Ambulances went up to Blangy for distribution to the Regimental Aid Posts (twelve each) and to the various Relay Bearer Posts. A 150 extra bearers (from the 5th Gordons and Trench Mortar Battery), were also in readiness, to be sent in relays, as required, by the Field Ambulance cars going up the valley for casualties.

Lieutenant Colonel Rorie was concerned to a large degree with the logistics of casualty treatment and evacuation, and the smooth, efficient running of the Field Ambulance for which he was responsible. Further down the line, at a Casualty Clearing Station, Sister Luard was dealing with the very human face of the fighting.

Monday: Just come up to lie down for an hour before the next take-in. We have filled up twice, and they are hard at it again over the road; we come next. The men say our guns are so thick they're wheel to wheel, and it is 'like playing the pianner'; the earth-shaking noise this morning did its work; the wounded Germans tell me there are a great many dead. We have a splendid 6-foot officer boy lying silently on his face with a broken back, high up. I hope he won't live long. The DMS [Director Medical Services] came this afternoon to ask me for a sister to go up to a new Abdominal Special Hospital with a Field Ambulance at a place farther up; out of shell range, but overlooking the whole battlefield.

The men, the blankets, and even their moustaches are swarming with JJs [lice], and we are getting attacked ourselves. Isn't it absolutely beastly?

Sister Kate Luard, Queen Alexandra's Imperial Military Nursing Service

I've been looking after 100 stretcher cases in the tents tonight; they are all ready now for evacuation – just heard the whistle.

Tuesday: The Senior Night Sister came up at twelve to say they were taking in again – not too bad cases, and no one need be called; so the Dressing Hut Sister and I stayed where we were and slept. Went down early this morning. They were fairly clear as there'd been two evacs., no deaths. (This new abdominal stent is making a difference there already – it ought to save many lives.) I heard a dying officer (exhilarated by morphia) gaily dictating a letter to the padre as follows: 'It is not at all serious and I am getting on all right. Don't worry about me. Love to all, your loving Son.' He is cold and pulseless and won't live many hours.

A captain of the Yorks had his leg off yesterday and makes less of it than some people with a toenail off. The glorious boy with the broken back is lying on his back now; he doesn't know about it and says he's all right, only his back is a little stiff and aching. Some of the men say they were picked up and looked after by Germans, so we are being extra kind to the Germans this time. There is in hospitals an understood arrangement that all Germans (except when their lives depend on immediate attention) should wait till the last British has been attended to, for dressings, operations, food, blankets, etc. It is only kept up in a very half-hearted way and is generally broken by the medical officers who are most emphatic about it in theory! …

The people who have been coming in all day are the left-outs in German dugouts since Monday, starved, cold, and by some miracle still alive, but not much more. … It is piercingly cold again and looks like rain.

The British liked to assert that they looked after the German wounded almost as well as their own, and once a wounded man was undergoing treatment, it hardly mattered to which side he belonged. With all the inestimable suffering, the stoic cheerfulness that Sister Luard witnessed was quite extraordinarily moving. Likewise, looking for humour in the darkest corners kept men functioning and, in many cases, sane.

The comic relief at Lille Road Post was supplied by 'James', one of our Hun auxiliary loaders. His real name, I suppose, was Heinrich Schneider or something of that sort; but as he spoke good English he was appointed interpreter for enemy wounded, and put in charge of his whole-skinned countrymen who were assisting to carry casualties down to and up from the dressing room. He had been – so he said, and there was no reason to doubt it – for ten years before the war a waiter at the Hotel Cecil, hence the temporary name bestowed on him; and his behaviour was certainly a curious mixture of the soldier and the waiter. When spoken to he came sharply to attention (military), with a gentle bend forwards from the waist (Hotel Cecil); while his prompt 'Yessir!' almost made one see the napkin over his arm. Stoutish, broadish, and – to us, his captors – affable, he magnified his office with evident relish, and treated his hoplites with true Hunnish high-handedness.

From the entrance to the dressing room I overheard my colleague, who was busy with a wounded enemy casualty at one period of the first day's work, giving James a high moral lesson, in a clear, somewhat professorial style.

'You will observe, James, that here, contrary to the custom of your countrymen in this war, we treat our wounded enemies with the same consideration extended to our own troops.'

'Yessir!'

'Before the war, James, I had travelled much in your Fatherland, and had failed to detect the degeneracy –'

'Yessir!'

'– which has since, evidently developed with such alarming rapidity.'

'Yessir!'

'Cruelty, on our part, is not made a matter of military routine.'

'Yessir!'

'You mean "No, Sir", I think, James?'

'No, Sir!'

'Ah, well! The case is dressed; summon your comrades.'

'Yessir! *Achtung*! *Zwei träger*! *Aufheben*!'

And away went James with his compatriots to load the case on a back-going car. After twelve hours of it, James came to me, saluted, and remarked:

Lieutenant Colonel David Rorie OC, 1/2nd (Highland) Field Ambulance

'Sir, I and my men are exhausted.'

'I and my men are also exhausted, James.'

'Yessir! But we had no sleep for two nights before this battle.'

'Right, James, I shall believe you and relieve you.' So, in charge of a sergeant, James and Co were sent along the trench to the divisional soup kitchen to have a good feed, and were thence taken below to an old French dugout.

Later, it was reported to me that James was missing; and although we made a perfunctory search for him, we could not find him. Two hours afterwards I was passing a small recess blanketed off from the sandbag wall of the dressing room, in which was a stretcher and some blankets, placed there for my accommodation with kindly forethought by the staff sergeant, should an opportunity for rest come along. Hearing a stertorous snort, I pulled back the blanket and discovered James sound asleep in my bed, evidently under the impression that his 'staff job' entitled him to some precedence. The humour of it tickled me so much that I left him; but his snores gave him away to others before long, and he was 'put back where he belonged'.

When the time came to hand him and his comrades over to the APMs [Assistant Provost Marshal] guard, James asked to see me, and giving his salute-cum-bow, said: 'Sir, I trust I have given satisfaction.'

'Let your mind be easy, James.'

'Sir, I hope we shall meet again.'

'When, James?'

'After the war, Sir.'

'And where, James?'

'At the Hotel Cecil, Sir!'

With which pious hope James solemnly saluted and vanished into the gloom of the trench.

The men who were relieved from the front line were almost as ravenous as they were exhausted. Living on iron rations – biscuits and tinned beef – for several days had made Aubrey Smith physically sick and he was not alone in this response. In rest, men would spend whatever money still occupied their pockets on 'grub', preferably hot, for there was little point in hanging on to cash when no one could predict what might happen the following day.

The Colonel wanted a canteen started, and that same day I found a place for one behind the guns. It was the house belonging to a doctor, an eye specialist, sumptuously built, heated with hot water, with a nice garden at the back. We soon got the canteen going there. The men patronize it all the time. It is really extraordinary the part played by the stomach in life. It simply rules the world, and affects all our outlook on life. We are paralyzed, absorbed, hypnotized by it. The chief topic of conversation is rations with the men, and food and wine with the officers. Men pour into my canteens and buy everything up. For four Sundays I have been up to Arras to hold evening service. Twice I arranged it at the canteen. The men filed out when it began, and were back again for cocoa when it was over. (I have just stopped writing this to eat a piece of cake.) I felt rather furious last time. What is the use of feeding men if they deliberately set themselves against any attempt to teach or help them see the truth? I preached at all services one Sunday on 'Man shall not live by bread alone', and said that

Reverend Oswin Creighton, Army Chaplain, attd. 3rd Division, RFA

Above: 'Grub's up!' As the Reverend Creighton noted, 'The chief topic of conversation is rations with the men, and food and wine with the officers.'

while that was the first truth laid down by Christ, it was the last that man could understand.

Wine might have been one of the two chief topics of conversation for officers, but few took their wine so seriously as to risk life and limb during a serious fire in an Arras billet.

Lieutenant Alan Thomas, 6th Queen's Own (Royal West Kent Regiment)

In the evening, just after dinner, I had gone down the road to the Casualty Clearing Station in search of news. The CCS would usually have the first news of any show in the sector. I had been away, I suppose, for about twenty minutes. When I came back I found that our house was on fire. The top storeys were well ablaze and as the only fire-extinguishing apparatus on the scene was a small French hand pump which was worked by two people taking alternate pulls at the lever and threw up a jet like a soda water syphon, it was only a matter of time before the whole building would be destroyed – as indeed it was. An incendiary shell had fallen on the house and killed a number of soldiers (Signalmen and sergeant majors' servants) who were sleeping in the attics.

I made my way through the crowd who were watching the fire and found my friend Stigand in charge of operations. This didn't surprise me, for Stigand was the sort of man who would naturally take charge in an emergency. He was an officer of long standing, wearing the South African ribbon, and should have been a colonel. As it was he was a lieutenant.

'There's one more case!' he was shouting when I reached him. I offered to go in and look for this last remaining case, whoever he might be, and fetch him out. But Stigand was already in the doorway, hailing someone else who was on the stairs.

'It's all right,' Stigand shouted back at me. 'He's got it! That's the lot!'

Whereupon the mess corporal appeared carrying 'the case' – which was not, as I had supposed, a stretcher case, but a case of sherry. After Stigand had seen to it that everyone was safe (except only the poor fellows in the attics who, I gathered, had met with an instantaneous death) he had then, in the exercise of a powerful judgment, turned to the rescue of 'the cellar'. Under his supervision, reinforced by a display of personal courage on his part that was, I believe, a source of inspiration to all who served under him, every case, every bottle, even those already in use, were saved. It was an exploit of which he was, I think, justifiably proud.

There was a pretty little incident at our cookhouse admirably illustrating the 'greenness' of the Labour Corps, that collection of dear old Johnnies – some of them on the wrong side of fifty – who toiled at road making and similar jobs, usually getting little credit for their toil. …

While going through some 'Queen Victoria Rifles' casualty kits which had been sorted out in their stores, some fellow found a bundle of restaurant bills such as you get at Lockharts, or Lyons: 'Egg on Toast, 6d', 'Tea and Scone, 4d', 'Steak and Kidney Pudding, 10d', etc. Goodness knows why they were in this man's kit, but the fact remains that they were there and one of our fellows – unknown to our cooks – stuck them up on the cookhouse door. Now there was a labour battalion stationed nearby, consisting of C2 men [weaker soldiers normally fit for home service only] who had just come out from England and were extremely 'green'. One of these poor old Johnnies came up, read the advertisements, licked his moustache, felt in his trouser pocket and then went in the cookhouse and calmly asked for steak and kidney pudding. Thinking the request was made for a joke, Waters – always ready to play up to anybody when there was fun to be poked – replied that he was sorry they would not be ready until half-past six that night. And, do you know, at half-past six that night there was a queue of some dozen of these C2 men lined up outside our cookhouse door waiting to buy their precious puddings.

New British divisions were brought in to help relieve the men in the trenches, but these 'new' men would have to acclimatize to the many vagaries of a confused battlefield and could not be expected to launch pell-mell into action. The fighting simmered for a week, with small attacks made to tidy up the line, and sometimes un-tidied by a German counter-attack. The next major offensive action was 23 April, by which time Nivelle's great scheme had already been undone. His offensive, beginning on 16 April and in pouring rain, had met with abject failure. Continued fighting over the next days – and 96,000 casualties later – brought French troops, who had shouldered so much of the fighting burden on the Western Front, to the point of mutiny. In the end, the British were compelled to continue their offensive

Driver Aubrey Smith, 1/5th (City of London) Battalion, London Rifle Brigade

Rescued just in time: a man is pulled from a collapsed dugout during the Battle of Arras.

at Arras to distract the Germans from the fact that the French Army was in a near state of disobedience and even collapse.

The renewed offensive was careful to set no over-ambitious aims and would include tanks to give extra weight to the attack. When the men went over the top, there was satisfactory success within the objectives' narrow confines, but heavy casualties and German counter-attacks drove the British back in many places. Where the 1/4th Suffolk Regiment was in action opposite Fontaine-lès-Croisilles there was another problem. At the critical moment, stocks of hand grenades were found to be useless.

Captain Charles Stormont Gibbs, Adjutant, 1/4th The Suffolk Regiment

When it was reported that our objectives had been reached there was a lull, an ominous lull. We calculated that not more than half the battalion could be left – to hold 2 miles of trench. We asked for reinforcements. None was forthcoming. Presumably the enemy would counter-attack and try to win back what he had lost.

I do not remember what time of day it started. But when the enemy was assured that the trenches in question were definitely taken by us and that none of his own men were holding out anywhere he opened his barrage on our poor remnants and put in a fresh lot of troops to drive them back.

Our men in the support trench held their ground and those in the front trench were gradually driven back. Again the wounded started pouring in. And soon came the news that we had no one left in the front trench – all were wounded or madly trying to escape with the wounded. Then came the report that our bombs which we kept hurling up to the front were duds. They were not exploding for they had not been detonated. A Mills bomb has a small detonator which is inserted at the ammunition dump under Brigade supervision before being sent up to the infantry. We had received a large number of bombs which had not received their detonators and so were useless – enough to cause a débâcle, especially when the men were exposed to heavy artillery bombardment and had been reduced by casualties to a handful.

When the enemy had driven us back for a considerable distance along our front line he was of course able to work down the communication trenches and get in behind our men who were holding their own in the support trench. When these were attacked in front and behind they tried to save themselves by bolting across the open. But they ran into barbed wire and were mopped up to a man by machine guns.

Thus by late afternoon there was literally no one left between the Battalion HQ and the enemy. Evidently the enemy were not aware of this for they worked their way back slowly along the trenches they had re-won. The Brigade must be told the exact situation. I was in the signallers' den trying again at the telephone with no effect. A runner must be sent. It would not take long and perhaps I could thus avoid what seemed certain death.

I rejoined the CO after sending back a full report to Brigade. He evidently felt the end of the war for us was approaching. He never showed fear but on an occasion of this sort he always changed and behaved in a human and cheerful manner instead of his usual rather fierce and surly way of carrying on. 'Well,' he said, 'they won't be here just yet but we had better get ready for them. We have got two men each; one of us must hold the front trench and the other the support.' We got our four men and went up. Away down towards Fontaine, bombs were exploding intermittently as the enemy worked his way along against no resistance. We decided that I should stay in the transport line with the mess cook and a runner. The CO would go down with the other two men and take the support line. I went back to have one more try on the phone. This time they had got it through; a sweating signaller was there who said he found the break nearly back as far as Brigade. So I got through to Watson who had just got my report. His cheerful matter-of-fact voice was good to hear. 'So you've got to save the 33rd Division from disaster, have you? Well, you'll have a job but good luck!'

Preparations made, we waited. There was not much danger from shellfire for the enemy gunners could not tell just how far their men had got and we were so close to the enemy that all the shelling was behind us. On the other hand, since Brigade had got our report and knew the situation they had been able to put one gun to fire heavily on the advancing enemy. This was very fortunate because the explosions of shells concealed from the enemy the fact that they were meeting with no actual resistance by bombs. They probably expected to meet someone round each corner they went, though really no one was there. So I sat as the evening drew on. Slowly but surely the enemy came on. The bombs could be seen rising and heard falling, getting always nearer until at last they reached the spot where must have been remnants of their sandbag wall and perhaps guessed they had retaken all the ground they had lost. Would they come on?

I sat with revolver aimed at the next corner round which they would have to come. How long I don't know. Certainly till after dark. And there lamely the story ends in a complete memory fade-out.

We six were, of course, relieved during the night by another battalion – 600 or so relieving six.

Reverend Oswin Creighton, Army Chaplain, attd. 3rd Division Royal Field Artillery

On Tuesday I was up at the batteries for a burial. The trench mortar working party was out and a shell fell among them, killing two men and wounding six.... The whole battery turned out, and we escorted the bodies to the grave. I talked a little about the meaning of death. But I never quite know if it helps people to realize the meaning of life and its persistence. There

are few people who definitely wish to deny it. But men generally take up such an extreme agnostic position with regard to it, largely as an escape from the sloppy sentimentalism of hymns and Christmas cards, that they stand by the grave of their friends and merely shrug their shoulders. I think it is rather a splendid attitude. As Gibbon, I believe, said, the Turks fought with the fanaticism born of an overwhelming conviction of the joys of Paradise, and the Christians fought equally courageously though they had no such certainty. I suppose the finest character springs from those who see nothing beyond the present. And yet the future seems so increasingly clear and certain to me. Death is absolutely nothing to me

Wooden crosses belonging to the 2nd Queen's Royal West Surrey Regiment in Croisilles British Cemetery, April 1917.

now, except rather a violent shock, which one's peaceful and timid nature shrinks from.

The horror of war is the light it throws on all the evil, ignorance, materialism, bigotry, and sectional interests in human nature. Surely death is not the horror of war, but the causes which contribute to war. The Cross is beautiful – the forces which lead up to it are damnable. It really does not in the least matter how many people are killed, who wins, whether we starve or anything else of a transitory nature, provided that in the process human nature is transformed in some way or another. I am not nearly so much depressed by death, or even by the thought of the success of the U-boat campaign or a revolution in Ireland, as by the absolute stone walls of ignorance, prejudice and apathy one finds oneself face to face with everywhere. . . .

Curiously enough, another incident happened immediately after the funeral. I was in the mess, taking down particulars, when we heard the sound of machine-gun fire. We rushed out and found an aeroplane battle on. Some Boche planes had come right over the town and were swooping down on our observer. No anti-aircraft guns were firing at them. The Hun planes are tremendously fast. A plane just above us caught

German pilots await burial. The man closest the camera has suffered complete immolation, a death most feared by all pilots.

fire and dropped a flaming mass to the ground just behind the convent. Instinctively we all rushed round. I thought possibly one might be able to do something. There lay a smouldering mass of wreckage. They dragged it away, and there lay two charred, black, smouldering lumps, which a few minutes before had been active, fearless men. It was not a pleasant sight to one's refined and delicate feelings. I felt rather staggered, and it loomed before me all day and night. But after all, what did it signify? – the utter futility of violence and force. Ignorance again.

When a few days later I heard I had been given the Military Cross, it struck me that there was considerable irony in these things. For I had done nothing much except to feel extremely frightened while others who deserved the Victoria Cross perhaps were dead or unnoticed. However, I could feel that on the Somme I had deserved it as much as many of the people who got it, so I did not let it trouble me.

Captain Charles Stormont Gibbs, Adjutant, 1/4th The Suffolk Regiment

It was always good to get back after a time in the line – especially after a 'show'. There was my welcoming orderly room staff, Sergeant Rowe, Corporal Herring and the two clerks – always more welcoming because they themselves remained behind in safety with their typewriters. As I sank worn out in my officer chair, or whatever substituted for one, after an all-night march from the trenches, Sergeant Rowe used to radiate sympathy and cups of tea without even speaking a word.

The trying thing for an adjutant was that after his time in the line he could not rest like the others, for he had to start at once organizing the drafts to replace casualties, writing reports, seeing people, talking on the telephone, dictating to typewriters, arranging billets, huts, tents, supplies, perhaps even attending courts martial. So he might well have several nights in the line with nearly no sleep and then come back to full days of office work, training and parades and more interrupted nights with phone calls from Brigade about the next move.

The fighting was desperate and there were many acts of valour rewarded and far too often unrewarded. Men were capable of extraordinary acts of bravery, extraordinary because often they were undertaken when the individual was also shaking in fear and fully aware of the dangers he was about to face. Four days after the Stormant Gibbs actions, an officer serving with the 1st Battalion the Honourable Artillery Company won the highest decoration, the Victoria Cross, in a not very dissimilar action when, during a German counter-attack, a desperate situation required prompt and decisive action.

Second Lieutenant Alfred Pollard had already won the Military Cross on two occasions: a man of courage but a man not devoid of fear. Pollard's battalion had been in reserve during an attack when he thought it highly unlikely he would be called upon to act. He had slept right through the barrage and the initial onslaught.

Second
Lieutenant
Alfred Pollard,
1st Battalion
Honourable
Artillery
Company

I should probably have gone on sleeping for hours had not a runner from Headquarters arrived to awake me. He bore a curt message to immediately form a defensive flank. There was no time to enquire what had happened. It was obvious that something had gone wrong. I must act at once.

I gave hurried orders to my second in command, to arrange the troops in a series of shell holes diagonal to our former position. Waiting only to see the first sections clamber out of the trench to find their positions I moved along the trench towards Oppy Wood with the idea of attempting to discover what had taken place which jeopardized our flank.

The first thing that struck me was the curious hush in the atmosphere. Neither guns nor rifles were firing. It was just like the temporary cessation in a thunderstorm when the forces of nature seem to pause before bursting out afresh with greater fury than before. The sun was shining and everything appeared ridiculously peaceful. All the same, my heart was beating wildly under an impulse for which I could not account. My instinct told me we were in deadly danger.

I was at the limit of my own trench, which was the extreme left of the divisional front, wondering what I should do next. Suddenly a bombing attack started from the direction of Oppy Wood, Bang! Bang! Zunk! Zunk! I could see the smoke from the explosions nearly a mile away. Fritz was attacking down the trench.

It went on for some five minutes without making any appreciable headway. Then, without any warning, and without any direct attack being made on them, all the troops between me and the curls of grey smoke in the distance left their trench and ran back towards the position they had started from at dawn.

Panic. Sheer unaccountable panic! As inexplicable as it was unpremeditated. The sort of thing the greatest psychologist in the world could not explain: a sudden terror which affected the whole force simultaneously. For a brief moment it had its effect on me. I felt my knees knocking together under me. I was obliged to clutch at the parapet to prevent myself from falling. Then the thought fired my brain that with all the troops having cleared out between me and the enemy, in a few minutes my own company would be assailed. And if we failed to stem the victorious torrent of the Huns the whole of the left of our division would crumple like a leaf.

How long I remained there shaking I cannot say. It seemed like some minutes; actually it could not have been more than a few seconds. Then the curious feeling came to me that I was no longer acting under my own volition. Something outside myself, greater than I, seemed to take charge of me. Acting under this mysterious influence I ran forward.

Already officers of the terrorized troops were attempting to rally them. I found a handful who were still in possession of their sense. I arranged as many as I encountered in shell holes to right and left in the trench and ordered them to fire their rifles. I did not care a damn whether or not they hit anything. There is nothing so soothing to the nerves as to be doing something. Encouraged by the example of the few I had, I rallied others to join them. Soon I had a moderate force spread out in an arc. They were steady now and I had no further fear of a fresh withdrawal. The British Tommy does not do that sort of thing twice in a morning.

Pollard set off down the trenches with two trusted bombers in the direction of the oncoming Germans. For 300 yards he encountered no one. Joined by a third man, a Royal Fusilier, Pollard ploughed forward until he met the Germans and a fierce exchange took place, during which his men, exhausting their own bombs, turned to the Germans' stick grenades, of which they found plenty.

I threw off my tin hat to give my arms better play for throwing. Next went my gas mask. Bang! Bang! Bang! Bang! The air was thick with bombs going and coming. Those that fell in the trench we flung over the parapet before they had time to explode. My two companions were magnificent. Our fusilier friend protected out front. ... The Hun attack ceased as suddenly as it had started. We were still undefeated, but we only had six bombs left.

Second Lieutenant Alfred Pollard, 1st Battalion Honourable Artillery Company

Previous page:
Two dead
infantrymen in
the remains of a
large shell hole,
photographed by
Basil Peers during
the Arras offensive.

If Fritz had only known. For that matter, if he had known we were only four he would have undoubtedly rushed us over the top. That was the tremendous luck of the affair. He did not know. He failed to take a chance. His failure cost him the position.

Pollard won the VC; his three accomplices were all awarded the Distinguished Conduct Medal. The fusilier's medal was given posthumously as he was killed the following day. The German 'failure' on this occasion had come as British troops too had 'failed'. Both sides were cancelling each other out in attritional fighting.

Driver Aubrey
Smith, 1/5th
(City of London)
Battalion, London
Rifle Brigade

The policy of hitting our heads against a brick wall was now in full swing; we were calling down all the Teutonic venom upon us because we were the only Allied army capable of maintaining an offensive for the next month. Fine fellows, we! But we did wish our heads would show their appreciation by giving us baths, clean clothes, adequate food and a reasonable amount of leave!

Most of the London Rifle Brigade's patching up was done at the Medical Officer's sick parades held amidst the shell holes. These took place every morning at seven o'clock, by which hour every participant was expected to have washed, shaved, properly dressed and duly informed the orderly corporal of his regimental number and his religion (it was of the utmost importance that a man's religion be specified on the sick list – his ailment was added as an afterthought by the doctor).

I used to wander over to the sick parade unattended, as soon as I saw the various contingents collecting together and divesting themselves of their garments ready for a good hour's dilly-dallying, half naked, in the most exposed spot that could possibly have been found for them.

Captain Riddle presently arrived looking as spick and span as though conducting a sick parade at Aldershot. He surveyed the motley throng while his acolytes, Sergeants Hammond, Koester and Humphreys of the aid post, waited at his right hand, ready to flourish iodine bottles, count out pills and dangle bandages in the breeze: then he beckoned me first. ...

While I was awaiting treatment at the hands of Koester, Riddell went round the various cases of skin trouble, boils, impetigo, toothache, internal pains, etc., accusing 50 per cent of the men of not having shaved for the occasion. His policy was a sound one. He was out to discourage malingering, and to do this he had to make sick parade as unpleasant a job as possible. Men attending it had to wake up in the dark to perform their ablutions, while their fit comrades snored on. They then had to squat in the cold wind for probably an hour, waiting for treatment, finally returning to a spoiled breakfast in the trench with 'Medicine and Duty' marked against their names. I feel convinced that nobody went on those sick parades at Tilloy unless he was absolutely obliged to do so. The regulations were, of course, a hardship to genuinely sick men.

The weather in late April and early May changed radically and the warmth of spring was a blessed relief to all and was perhaps the one bright spot in an otherwise black outlook. The fighting raged into May and was simply variations on a theme, with little to distinguish one assault from another, other than in intensity. In the spirit of attack and counter-attack, the Germans took their turn to be pummelled.

I was taking an afternoon turn at the Observation Post when the Germans commenced a series of counter-attacks on the village [of Gavrelle] and its cemetery. It is interesting to remind oneself that in the history of

Lieutenant Richard Talbot-Kelly, 52nd Brigade, Royal Field Artillery

A graveyard disturbed during the Arras offensive. Trench lines were no respecters of civilian cemeteries.

war, cemeteries have frequently been strongpoints of great resistance in a defence system, and this afternoon the heaviest German attacks were directed on the cemetery area of Gavrelle to the south of the village. Their attacks began about three o'clock in the afternoon – the day was bright, and from where I sat I could see them forming up in line out of range of our guns in the neighbourhood of two little woods. They then moved forward at a steady walk, shoulder to shoulder, their extended lines spaced at about 150 yards. It was like watching a puppet show from the gallery of a theatre. One felt quite impersonal but realized that the job in hand was to knock the puppets down.

As they moved into range, hundreds of field guns opened up on them, until the plain was so filled with the bursting puffs of shrapnel, that it was impossible without taking special steps to pick out the fire of one's own battery and to make accurate corrections for the drop in range as the German infantry struggled forwards. After one or two vain attempts I ordered the six guns in the battery to be loaded alternately with shrapnel and high explosive and to fire all guns together in battery salvos. In this way I was able to recognize my own shellfire, which appeared as a series of alternating black and white bursts all at once on the stage below me. We blew great holes in the lines, bent them and twisted them, scattered and chased them, eventually pursuing with our shellfire small groups that tried to run for cover or out of the reach of our guns.

Later that evening, in answer to an urgent call from our aeroplanes, another concentration of Germans preparing to counter-attack was dispersed and destroyed in the neighbourhood of Gavrelle windmill to the north of the village. The subaltern from my brigade, who was liaising with the infantry round the cemetery, told us that night that they had been sitting on their parapets cheering as our shells swept the German infantry away from before them. They never used their rifles and machine guns throughout the day.

The fighting around Roeux and the Chemical Works was some of the most savage of the campaign and resembled the Somme offensive when objectives, ridges, villages and woods became their own battles in microcosm. Into this inferno, Second Lieutenant Norman Collins made his way to France, returning after being

An exhausted looking Second Lieutenant Norman Collins wears a German softcap. Behind him are the ruins of Fampoux.

wounded by shrapnel five months earlier. This time he took his own camera with him, hiding it. 'Owning a camera at the front was against all regulations, so I carried it in a pocket in my khaki apron worn over my kilt. I bought the camera partly because I knew that on returning to France I would be sent to my own battalion, the 4th Battalion, and would therefore be an officer amongst the men with whom I had enlisted.' In other words, he could be confident that fellow officers would not react adversely to his flouting military law.

We received instructions to capture a certain trench last Wednesday [16 May]. The artillery put up a barrage and we went over partly through little bits of trench and partly over the top. When we got there we found that the trench was already held by our own men.

The Boche put up three lines of 'crump' barrage and I had about the worst hour going through that, that I've ever had. I was partly buried and very slightly wounded. One piece in the hand and one in the leg.

We held the line for five days and have just come out. The Germans were on our right and left flanks as it was a very advanced position. One night they assembled for a counter-attack. Our artillery smashed them up. There are hundreds of dead lying about. The trenches are blocked with them in many places and the stench is terrible. Boche lying about. We got

Second Lieutenant Norman Collins, 1/4th Seaforth Highlanders, (Ross-shire Buffs, Duke of Albany's)

some collected who had been lying out wounded for ten days. Goodness knows how they lived. Of course most of them were too far gone.

Shelling was constant as we made our way towards the front line. I was blown off my feet by a small shell. The explosion also caught my servant, Simpson, who landed on top of me.

When we entered the trench it had been extremely battered. I remember having to climb out to let the troops who had been fighting pass by while we lay on top. I remember at several places arms and bottoms of corpses were sticking out of the communication trench. A feature of Roeux was the Chemical Works and another was the cemetery. This had been blown to pieces and a lot of graves churned up, which was a terrible sight. Of the attack itself, it was something of an abortive affair, and in the end the fighting we expected didn't materialize. We didn't know that then, of course, and, as we waited to go, our chances of living, we felt, were cut down to minutes and seconds. It was dark and the shelling was merciless, although their impact was greatly reduced on the soft ground. It meant that all over the battlefield there were dud shells; the place was simply littered with them, and bits of equipment.

We went over the top and advanced quietly at first, using the dark to conceal our presence. As we went forward I remember Captain Harris waving for me to come on, and I ran forward and flopped on the ground next beside him. We were still being heavily shelled and I did a very silly thing. I took my tin helmet and I rolled it, like Charlie Chaplain used to do with his bowler hat, and put it back on again.

We dug in shortly afterwards, taking over from the Argylls. We were in the support trench, Corona Trench, and much work had to be done to try and create some semblance of order as the line has almost been obliterated. There was an overwhelming stench of death.

Among my possessions was a mud-covered map on which were marked in dots the places where I sited the Lewis guns. In charge of one of the guns was a lance corporal of mine called Meikle. At night we used to go out beyond the front line and make ourselves comfortable in a shell hole that wasn't too wet and mount his Lewis gun, as he would be there if there was a raid during the night. As a second lieutenant, I had to visit all my men for a couple of hours, wherever they were, and every night I used to go out to his forward position at the end of a sap and sit with him. He was the same age as myself, possibly slightly younger, and he worked for a Glasgow railway company as well as being a bookmaker's runner. We got very close; we used to have long, long talks and he would tell me all about his life. When the war broke out he made several attempts to enlist as a 16-year-old, but had been rejected because of his inadequate chest measurements. He finally enlisted sometime in 1915 and had gone out to France a year later just as the Somme offensive began.

He was a tiny chap – we had that in common – and he stammered and you wouldn't think he could say boo to a goose. He was such an unassuming man. His men in the Lewis gun team really worshipped him, even though he used to frighten them. When a coalbox dropped near and the fragments whistled through the air, Meikle would say to them 'You want to watch out, boys, there's death in those pieces.' It was his form of humour.

Everyone needed every ounce of humour as well as superhuman resilience to keep going. Day for day, Arras was the most costly battle fought by the British Army during the war, sustaining 4,070 casualties for each of the thirty-nine days it was prosecuted, a rate that was a third higher than that suffered on the Somme (2,950). General Nivelle was sacked in May, his failings as grand as his pre-battle boasts. With the discipline of the French Army imperilled, the British fought on to give its ally some chance of recuperation and restoration, and news of the French Army's desperate straits never reached German ears. The British line in front of Arras moved in only tiny increments after the first day of the offensive. It was brought to an end, not before time, on 24 May. To the men who took part, there was little to lift the feeling of despondency and of an opportunity missed.

Although small actions continued around Arras that summer, there was relative peace on the Western Front for a very short period, a time for British soldiers to enjoy the growing warmth as summerlike weather arrived; they took the chance to clean up and reflect.

There are moments, sometimes hours, when right at the seat of the greatest of wars, close behind the firing line, near where there have been many thousands of lives lost in the fiercest fighting of the war, one can close one's eyes and imagine all is peace again. At times when all the infernal

Second Lieutenant John Gamble, 14th The Durham Light Infantry

Men of the 1/4th Seaforth Highlanders swimming in the river Scarpe days after the Arras offensive had been officially closed down.

engines and machines at the command of the armies are subdued for a few minutes, one may realize that all the frightfulness man can invent will never kill nature. Listen, now, to the birds singing over in those trees, which are rustling gently in the mild western breeze, as they have done for hundreds of years; and that little stream which has so often run with blood since the war commenced, still makes its merry music, as it bubbles over the little stones towards the canal waiting to receive it.

Close your eyes with me here, and listen to nature gently protesting that she still does, and always will, hold sway; that war will not continue for ever, and soon she will reassert herself in the stricken land, and with the aid of time, gradually cover up and remove all the appalling signs of the forces which have endeavoured to upheave her.

28 May: The weather is still very hot here. I am surprised that it is not in England. The battalion is going into the front line for a few days tonight, but I am not going in this time.

The night we were relieved last week my headquarters (just an old door with 2 inches of soil over the trench) got a direct hit by a shell and finished three officers and a sergeant major of the regiment that relieved us. Lucky for me, wasn't it?

The Boche aeroplanes are very busy at present. I see in today's paper that you have had them in England.

Some of the Boche prisoners are very pessimistic while others are still confident that they will win. There are a lot of local 'scraps' in this sector but the main battle here is finished.

I had a swim in the river [Scarpe] yesterday. It was lovely.

Second Lieutenant Norman Collins 1/4th Seaforth Highlanders, (Ross-shire Buffs, Duke of Albany's)

Sunday, 3 June 1917

My dear old Rachel [niece]

You can't think how I loved getting your letter telling me of your animals and the carrier pigeon. It is such a different world that you are in to what I am with war going on, but some day I shall come back and see all your things, and keep some perhaps myself like I used to do. I am writing this in the middle of cultivated fields where we are practising. In the hedges here are lots of caterpillars; some in bunches in thick webs which they

Lieutenant Andrew Buxton, 3rd The Rifle Brigade (The Prince Consort's Own)

*Training after
their exertions in
the trenches.*

have made, and some lovely coloured ones with yellow lines, and red and black lines down their sides.

I am wearing 'shorts', so my knees are getting sunburnt and quite sore. At present I am in a farm with lots of white pigs about, which the farm people try to sort out and put in different sties, etc., calling out all sorts of funny noises to make them come. The same way they shut up ducks at night and calves. They had a great hunt after two calves yesterday, which got out into the corn. My men helped get them in. The war is going very well, and the Germans must be feeling very uncomfortable, I think.

Private Henry
Russell, 10th The
Worcestershire
Regiment

The craze for button cleaning and pack and equipment scrubbing had developed to be dreaded by the man who had omitted any detail affecting his personal appearance. 'CB', in large and frequent doses was the order of the day, and the mournful notes of the prisoners' bugle call, *Defaulters, at the double*, was answered with the currying of many feet.

The provost sergeant, a one-time prize-fighter, was doing a roaring business and enjoying it, and on his none too innocent head was poured the silent curses of a multitude of delinquents.

On parade, the battalion sparkled with brightness and polish, and if victory had rested on 'Soldiers Friend' and 'Blanco', it would have been ours without more ado. The badge of the Worcestershire Regiment was emblazoned on our helmets and, therefore, in future the enemy would have no difficulty in identifying his opponents, should they be lying out after a stunt.

Under the category of cleanliness shirts took second place. True, we had shower-baths and changes of underclothing at varying periods, but even the sterilizing process did not rid the washing of all the parasites which clung to it, and a few days after a clean change men would be seen half-stripped carrying on the never-ending war of extermination. ...

I was becoming accustomed to the habit of war. Ordinarily a clean-minded and peaceably disposed citizen, I hardly noticed that a marked change was taking place in my attitude towards life. I was, perhaps unconsciously, becoming akin to the beasts of the field. I could sit by the side of a corpse long since dead and scrape out a tin of pork and beans

Spotless army lorries in an unknown French town, mid-1917.

with evident relish. The instinct of self-preservation was developed to the full. Life was sometimes horrible, but life was sweet, and I wanted to love. The sight of the bloody wounds of other men was revolting, but while I escaped and continued to escape I was more than satisfied.

Driver Aubrey Smith, 1/5th (City of London) Battalion, London Rifle Brigade

In view of the perfect weather, the inevitable inspection was no hardship to us; there was plenty of time in which to go mad, everything looked smart and glittering, and so the General was delighted. For days the stables resembled a Brasso shop and the number of shirts and nosebags torn up for harness-rag beat all records. The Brasso was purchased on this occasion by the Transport Officer instead of the men, but there was little diminution in the amount of grousing, in return for the gift. Harness cleaning had become an infernal monotony, and one or two of the old drivers were giving up the

Sergeant Huborn Godfrey's foot. The caption states he was taking the photo 'under difficulties'. Was he trying to take the picture surreptitiously in the knowledge that cameras were banned?

job in disgust, contenting themselves with a single horse job (officers' horses and pack ponies) which were gradually developing from the most despised to the most coveted positions on the section.

The next item on the programme was a battalion concert held on an impromptu stage rigged up in an open field by the pioneers. At this the Quarter Master was to supply free white wine and whisky for the artistes, which caused such a number of performers to offer their services that the arrangement of the concert became a different matter. At length a programme was drawn up which was estimated to last three hours without encores; needless to say, the transport had secured a very full share of the places. There is no space to describe fully the farce that followed. The London Rifle Brigade now consisted of a great variety of individuals from all walks of life, so that Figg's baritone solo was followed by a 'comic' song given by someone who sang without music or even intelligible sounds – a song that made even the CO blush with shame, yet called forth lusty applause from a little knot of the performer's sympathizers who had probably arrived in his draft. Meanwhile the consumption of liquor proceeded apace behind the scenes and, when I came away from the outskirts of the audience (where I had taken my stand after assisting with sundry accompaniments), I found on looking into the artistes' quarters that not only the performers but many intruders were sharing in the refreshments.

Parades usually ended at half-past three, and after tea had been issued a general exodus would be made to the village. It was an enterprising little place, whose inhabitants catered for the troops, and enriched themselves immensely by doing so. Estaminets would be filled to overflowing, and the choruses of popular songs would re-echo through the streets.

Private Henry Russell, 10th The Worcestershire Regiment

Tommy out of the trenches was no sentimentalist. He drank his beer or his coffee with gusto, and called for more. He chatted with Madame and flirted with Mademoiselle. He bought silk postcards and sent them home to Maud and Anna, and he contrived to cram into an evening the pleasures of the week. A man could sit from six o'clock until eight and be quite happy and comfortable on less than half a franc. Not that everyone went to the estaminets. Some preferred the wholesale atmosphere of the villagers' houses and enjoyed the inevitable eggs and chips.

The band of the 1/4th Seaforth Highlanders strikes up to entertain the battle-worn men.

Occasionally, in the camp, the divisional band would give a concert, and men would heartily sing *You'd be far better off in a home*, and the band conductor, a stoutish jovial man, would dance about and wave his stick, and they would sing louder and laugh merrier and feel the better for it.

At seven o'clock each evening the buglers sounded 'Tattoo', and immediately afterwards the drums and fifes would commence a series of tunes and marches, which seemed to hold an irresistible fascination for those who had preferred to stay in camp.

It impressed me greatly. Even in after years it would produce that curious feeling, that reaching back of the mind to scenes that were forever sacred. It produced that insatiable desire to revisit the battlefields, to commune, as it were, with the spirits of the dead. The call of the Somme and of Flanders must for ever be in the blood of those who suffered there.

Captain Harold Bidder, 1st South Staffordsire Regiment, attd. Corps HQ

I had a curious experience a day or two ago in revisiting my early haunts of December 1914. I took the Ford car which is allotted to me (and a very good one too) and started off early. I went through Armentières (which I had never seen before except in the distance) towards our village of 1914. I stopped the car at a place a mile or so short of it and walked on. You may remember my describing the billet my company used to go back to between the village and the trenches – an old farmhouse, with the old farmer and his wife and Marie, a pretty girl of seventeen. Even then a shell had blown away a bit of one of the outhouses, and I didn't much expect to find them now two and a half years later. The village itself, I knew, had been blown to bits in the meantime. However, I walked in that direction. It was a jolly day. The country looked much more cheerful in its spring green than when I knew it, sodden and bare. I got to the road where the billet was and came upon a field absolutely torn up with shell holes, with the ruins of a farm near.

Apparently the Boche had been strafing some horse lines there, and not long ago either. At first I thought the ruins were my farm, but there were no remains of the large shrine I remembered at the crossroads. I walked on; and 300 yards further on the shrine and billet hove in sight. After what I had just seen I felt more certain than ever there would be no one there.

I passed my old room looking out on the road (how well I remembered it – I could almost feel the snow and rain) and walked into the house. Curtains in the windows had rather surprised me. The place seemed occupied. I turned into the kitchen. The sensation of a jump back in time grew stronger and stronger. The kitchen was just as it used to be – a large pot on the fire, the long settle under the window with the table before it. A woman I did not know was sitting working at another window – a nice-looking woman of about thirty. She rose as I came in, and I concluded another set of people had taken the house. Then I began to spot a likeness to the girl of 1914. '*Êtes vous Marie?*' I asked. She looked puzzled.

'*Mariée?*' she said. '*Non,*' I said, '*Marie-vous.*' 'Oh,' said she, '*le capitaine des Ouest-lands.*' It was Marie, grave, good-looking, about ten years older.

They had stayed in the farm all this time, in spite of the shelling all round, and worked the land and kept their cows. Only a week before, the Boche had strafed some battery positions in the paddock, 100 yards from the house. There were no guns there, but the positions were knocked to bits. The farm had never been hit again, by wonderful luck. I asked where they went when the shelling was on, and Marie said 'Oh, into the cellar or the kitchen', as one might talk of coming in out of the rain.

She was very ready to talk and remembered people in a wry friendly way. I sat in the kitchen and had a glass of beer, and we had a long talk. Her

A farmer's wife and child: only old men or young boys remained to help with the onerous work.

father came in halfway through; at first he didn't recognize me, and then said, 'Ah yes – your brother was at Bailleul and came to see you.'

The mother was away in Armentières with the son, returned on leave from Salonika, home for the first time for nearly three years. I was very much touched by their cordiality. We were the first people to be billeted on them, and since then they had mostly had Artillery. We sat and chatted about the people of those early days. Marie Louise, a friend whom you may remember, was now in Paris. Her brother had been killed. The curé of the village had gone, as he had no church: it meant a long trudge now to Mass. I was glad to hear that no one else had succeeded in making the fireplace in the next room draw, which we had had to give up so ignominiously. A girl came in while we were talking, from the billet down the road where C Company and its commander used to be. Yes, she remembered him perfectly, the officer with the eyeglass.

I cannot tell you how strange it was, sitting there as if two and a half years had been wiped out, and one was back as a beginner in France. So much, so very much has happened in that time; and yet, in the curious way memories revive, it seemed only a week or two since I left the place. And with one was of course very strongly the thought of all those companions and friends of those days who have gone across. A. of the eyeglass, sweet-tempered and friendly; B., who came out with me, capable and energetic; C., my subaltern; D., even in those days already wounded in Ypres; E., the cheery, the last to go; my company sergeant major, very young (all the old NCOs had already been knocked out at Ypres) but willing.

Of the officers whom I knew well only two are left. There may be one or two of the other officers.

I left the billet and walked through the village. The last time I went along that road, full of trench fever (for which I may be truly grateful) seemed as yesterday. But the village was untouched then: now it is a ruin, and the church a mere shell.

I walked round other well-known spots, and found them full of company; not that there was anyone to be seen. I went past the house in the Rue Delpierre, where C and D Companies used to share a mess when we were further back. We used to come there, caked in mud, direct from the trenches.

And so back to the car and home.

Overleaf: *One of the nineteen mines blown on the Messines Ridge, 7 June 1917. A picture taken and annotated by Sergeant Huborn Godfrey.*

TAKEN. 24 hrs AFTER EXPLOSION.

4 Summer Success

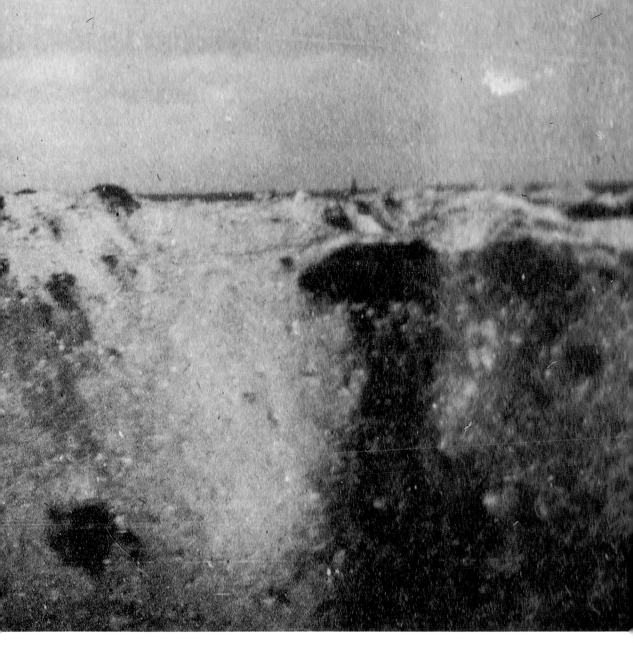

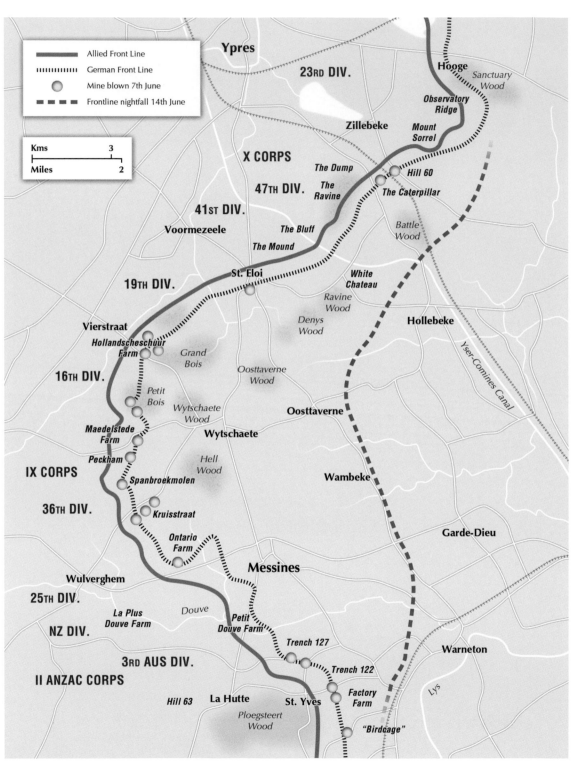

Legend:
- —— Allied Front Line
- ||||||| German Front Line
- ● Mine blown 7th June
- – – – Frontline nightfall 14th June

Kms 3
Miles 2

Ypres

23RD DIV.

Hooge
Sanctuary Wood

Observatory Ridge

Zillebeke

Mount Sorrel

X CORPS

The Dump

Hill 60

47TH DIV.

The Ravine

The Caterpillar

41ST DIV.

Battle Wood

Voormezeele

The Bluff

The Mound

White Chateau

St. Eloi

Ravine Wood

19TH DIV.

Denys Wood

Hollebeke

Vierstraat

Hollandscheschüür Farm

Grand Bois

Oosttaverne Wood

Yser-Comines Canal

16TH DIV.

Petit Bois

Wytschaete Wood

Oosttaverne

Maedelstede Farm

Wytschaete

Peckham

Hell Wood

Wambeke

IX CORPS

Spanbroekmolen

36TH DIV.

Kruisstraat

Garde-Dieu

Ontario Farm

Messines

Wulverghem

25TH DIV.

Douve

Petit Douve Farm

NZ DIV.

La Plus Douve Farm

Trench 127

Warneton

3RD AUS DIV.

Trench 122

II ANZAC CORPS

Factory Farm

Hill 63

La Hutte

St. Yves

Lys

Ploegsteert Wood

"Birdcage"

Battle of Messines, 7–14 June.

'I don't know if we are going to make history tomorrow,
but at any rate we'll change the geography.'

Major General Sir Charles Harington, General Staff

––––––––––

South of Ypres lay the strategically important Messines Ridge. This had been firmly in German hands since autumn of 1914 and gave commanding views across Allied trench lines and supply routes. The Germans had fortified the entire ridge with concrete pillboxes in the sure and certain knowledge that the British would make detailed proposals to take it. British preparations for such a strike were begun in late 1915 but it was the audacious nature of the final plan to seize control of the ridge that was not anticipated by the German High Command, though they were warned by their own Commander of Mining of just such an eventuality.

Taking the Messines Ridge was crucial to the campaign of 1917 as a whole. The French Army, still in disarray after the Arras debacle, would appreciate a distracting offensive far from their beleaguered positions on the Aisne. At the same time, if the British Army was to launch a summer offensive at Ypres, as the Commander-in-Chief dearly and explicitly wanted, then it would be imperative that this commanding position was cleared so as to make enemy observation of British preparations far more difficult.

Over the course of two years, a series of tunnels was dug underneath key enemy positions. It was an extraordinary technical achievement through different geology including sand and clay, each material posing further challenges for the tunnellers, some of whom worked on the venture for eighteen months. At the head of these tunnels were placed twenty-five charges containing, in all, nearly 450 tons of high explosive. On a signal, these mines would be detonated in quick succession with the result that the enemy would be literally blown off the ridge. The devastating explosive percussion would enfeeble enemy resistance, killing almost simultaneously thousands of enemy soldiers in dugouts and trenches, as roofs collapsed and earthen walls concertinaed.

The mines would be the stupefying prelude to a limited offensive at Messines – a 'bite and hold' operation as it was known, one that had a good chance of success because of the meticulous preparation coupled with a clearly defined, tangible objective, similar in certain ways to the Canadian Corps' storming of Vimy Ridge. General Sir Hubert Plumer, given charge of the operation, had proposed merely to take the crest of the ridge, but his commander-in-chief wanted to go further and so the plans were adapted. Once under way, the men would advance up to 3,000 yards, up, over and down the far side of the ridge, taking the German first and second lines and the heavily defended village of Wytschaete. It was a sensible suggestion for it reduced the likelihood of a German counter-attack regaining the ridge. Despite the more ambitious approach, the offensive would be short, a matter of days, but nevertheless it was intrinsically linked to the ambitious plans for the salient. If successful, the artillery used to support the Messines offensive would be speedily moved north to help with the opening bombardment at Ypres.

The bombardment of the German positions began on 21 May and was gradually ramped up over the following days as nearly 2,300 guns and 300 mortars targetted enemy batteries and strongpoints. The troops would advance under a creeping barrage supported by seventy-two tanks, artillery fire, gas, and a barrage from massed machine guns.

Major William Watson, D Battalion, Heavy Branch, Machine Gun Corps

In June the back area of the salient was like a disturbed ant heap. We were making every possible preparation for an attack, and apparently we did not mind in the very least whether or not the enemy knew all about it. The countryside was 'stiff' with light railways, enormous dumps, fresh sidings, innumerable gun pits, new roads, enlarged camps. No advertisement of the impending attack was neglected. The enemy, of course, realized what was happening, and acted accordingly. He had brought up a large number of long-range guns, and his aeroplanes flew over on every fine day. He had, too, the advantage of direct observation over all the forward area. The results were unpleasant enough, even in June. Dumps would 'go up' with a pleasing regularity. Camps and railheads were always being shelled. Bombing continued by day and by night. In front we destroyed the German trenches, breastworks and fortifications, and shelled their batteries. They retaliated in kind, and the unprejudiced observer would have found it difficult to award the prize.

We drove first to Ouderdom, a vast and enticing railhead, which the enemy shelled methodically each night, much to the annoyance of B Tank Battalion, who lived, for reasons of state, at the edge of the railhead. Their tanks were housed with disarming frankness in a series of canvas stalls surrounded by a high canvas screen. The whole erection was perhaps three-quarters of a mile in circumference. The tanks were so obviously concealed that the enemy never suspected their existence. The shells that dropped each night into the camp were the ordinary courtesies of warfare, although they did at last produce a move.

Men of the 3rd Worcestershire Regiment rest while on the march along the Bailleul– Armentières road.

For several months we had been in the line opposite Wytschaete and we knew every trench, dugout, snipers' and trench mortar posts, where it was safe to walk above ground and so forth on our side. Also we knew every dump, machine-gun post and trench railway of the Boche as we had been firing at them continually. In fact, we thought we knew all there was to be known about that part of the line. As for a chance to get into Wytschaete –

Lieutenant Alan May, 49th Machine Gun Company, Machine Gun Corps

the place we had been looking and firing at for months – well that sounded like the best of news.

Innumerable new roads, miles of them, were made over the surrounding countryside. Tram and rail lines were laid down according to schedule, so many miles a day. These were used the following day to bring up supplies for the further continuance of them. Old roads were widened and repaired and those without drainage were ditched. Special tracks across country were laid out for troops marching up and for empty wagons returning, thus saving congestion on the forward line of supplies. Signposts designated all roads and tracks showing where they led to and where they came from. Had the main roads been heavily shelled, the cross-country tracks were to have been used instead. A full gauge railway using ordinary engines was installed to just behind Kemmel 2 miles from the front line. Overland tracks were from York Road (a road running parallel to the front line about 900 yards behind it) to the front line bridging all our trenches and gaps cut in the wire. The foremost signs pointed to Wytschaete church, to Oostaverne and so on. Parties were detailed for continuing the overland tracks as soon as some of the ground had been taken.

During these preparations we were for a while at Klondyke Farm on the main Locre–Kemmel road about halfway between the two places. The traffic along this road was unbelievable, guns of all calibres going up to Kemmel. Ammunition columns were on the road day and night and tons and tons of RE material also went up every day. I don't think we ever saw the road other than chock full, though with much traffic the movement was slow. Never could understand why the Boche did not shell that road day and night for they could have created real havoc. Even when ammunition dumps and RE dumps were established at the sides of the road, the Boche did not bother them.

One evening a jolly old 15-inch howitzer ambled along and settled down just in front of Klondyke Farm. In due course it was camouflaged, shelters were built for the ammunition and dugouts for the men. When the gun commenced firing we were of course interested and would go and watch. A 15-inch shell is after all very different from our machine-gun bullets. When standing behind the gun we could see the shell leave the

muzzle of the gun going up and up and at the same time looking smaller and smaller in the distance until it vanished from sight. The concussion from these howitzers is great; it took all the tiles off a farmhouse close by and some off our place too.

Heavy artillery parked briefly by the side of the road on its way to a new location, mid-1917.

Signaller Sidney Banyard, 215 Siege Battery, Royal Garrison Artillery, putting out telephone cable days before the Messines Offensive.

Lieutenant
Martin Evans,
9th The Welch
Regiment

29 May: The area here is lousy (forgive or overlook the expression): let me alter it to thick with guns. By night, they come up into position behind hedges and ensconce themselves in hidden emplacements; it is a bigger concentration than on the Somme, our factories must have put on a spurt. This time there will be no mistake. It will be a gunner's battle and we shall walk over. Every night we are toiling on working parties; we trudge up to the forward lines, keeping close to hedges covered in May blossom, past ruminating cows with a better chance of longevity than ourselves, past cunningly concealed guns unleashed as yet, our track is a carpet of green covered with buttercups.

Too obviously, the Divisional Follies [concert party] have moved nearer; there is a sameness in their repertoire, the same white-faced clown with his parting shot which never fails, 'too late, too late, the canteen's closed'; the same dark-haired, mournful tenor; he sings to us of Wine and Monks; not tactfully just now, he renders prophecies about Gabriel and the Last Trumpet; it sends us away with dew-laden eyes.

3 June: I took the NCOs to see a model of the landscape we propose soon to project Jerry from; it is real artistry, ruins are shown with bricks, trenches by concrete, roads of wood, woods by twigs; most ingenious, contours are indicated, more than that, they are clearly defined. There should be no mistake. I talked to my platoon about it. I could not rise to the heights of Henry Vth's eloquence, but we came a good second. The setting for my *en avant, mes enfants* harangue was in keeping with the increased tempo, the tapestried background, the ceaseless rumble of traffic, the mutter and roar of guns working to a frenzy, in a crescendo of open diapason....

Opposite: *Before
the stress of
battle, men of
the 2nd Queen's
Royal West
Surrey Regiment
enjoy their free
time.*

In a few intervals left to call time our own, many of us take the chance of a swim in a nearby pool or muddy pond. It is better than nothing. No one sees the notice board 'No Bathing allowed'. Why it should not be allowed, no one knows, as there are no disgruntled and peeping Mrs Grundies and no ladies to come and watch us as they did on the lower reaches of the Somme....

I take off my hat to our Divisional Field Guns, everywhere we go, they follow like ministering angels; when called upon to cut the Hun wire or to put down a barrage or answer an SOS they ran down a hail of iron,

spreading like a curtain over our heads. The guns are sleek, businesslike and kept spotless, green wheels and shining brass hubs, the crew as usual have a totally inadequate protection. No praise can be too high for these gunners. Somehow, except for occasionally meeting the Forward Observation Officers, we do not get the chance to make their acquaintance.

These gunners would deliver their 'hail of iron' in a creeping barrage. Behind this curtain, the troops would advance on a series of objectives coloured with red, blue, green and black lines and the final trench map objective, if all went well, known as the Oostaverne Line. It was vital that the infantry was protected from the severe percussion of the mine explosions and the subsequent fall of spoil. Detailed instructions were issued ordering trench and dugout evacuation where necessary, troops being required to remain a minimum of 200 yards from the blown charge and for at least twenty seconds after detonation.

Lieutenant Martin Evans, 9th The Welch Regiment

6 June: It is the eve of a great day, perhaps the most momentous in our lives; from hints you will have gathered where we are. It has been a strenuous time getting all in order. One night the routes up had to be reconnoitred for an overland track, nothing is left to chance.... Everything is ready, flares for plane contact, rifle grenades, wire cutters, bombs, fans for plane signals and I shall carry a Very light pistol. Bazentin [on the Somme] licked us into shape to face this. Must confess it gives that feeling of waiting for the pistol to unleash us for the Half Mile.

Lieutenant Alan May, 49th Machine Gun Company, Machine Gun Corps

On 6 June I tried to get all my men to sleep till noon but only a few of the old timers were able to do this. After lunch I called a confab with the men who were going over with me. All were in fine spirits and anxious to get started. The previous day I had taken these men to see a scale model of the ground we were to advance over, all the trenches, strongpoints, mortar and machine-gun positions, overland tracks and so forth being shown and marked. A fine bit of work done by the Engineers. While here I cross-examined the men to see if they knew what to do, where to go and how to carry on should I happen to get knocked out.

The men who were going with me I had chosen from the section, all good, sturdy, reliable hardened soldiers, not windy, although possibly the intellectual capacity of some of them was not all that could be desired. After all, they needed physical stamina and guts rather than brains for this job. No orders had been received as to prisoners but we would be too busy anyway to bother with them. However, it was sort of understood that any prisoner had to help us, carrying back our wounded, carrying rations, ammunition and so on. The Boche had his choice in this. I suggested to all my men that it would be a good idea to collar the first Boche he could lay his hands on and make him carry the load.

At seven o'clock I had my men fall in. A certain proportion of every unit is always held back so as to form the nucleus of a new unit; these men are called B echelon. As soon as my men fell in, the B echelon lads turned up to wish 'good luck' and 'see you later'. Bellamy and Fairlie had fallen their men in at the same time and we each gave a short talk as there might not be much chance after we got up the line. I remember spouting something about the honour of the company and so forth though there was no need for this.

At 9.00 pm, Lieutenant May set off, stopping to see his commanding officer so as to synchronize watches and to drink a quick cup of tea before meeting his men in the communication trenches. The weather was still sweltering hot, despite the advance of evening. There was to be no smoking or talking on the move-up, while underfoot empty sandbags had been laid on the duckboards to muffle the sound of footsteps.

Throughout this whole day I realized I had not been particularly excited but anxious and keen that things would prove out as I anticipated. It seemed the most natural thing in the world to be taking shelter in a puny trench waiting to do my wee part in the biggest battle of the war. The men too did not show any excitement, they were calm and seemingly indifferent. I even had to wake one man up just a few moments before we went over. He rubbed his eyes and said 'Oh, hell' to himself, not because he was about to take in the push but because he had had his sleep broken up. Of course I had expected to be extremely high strung, possibly nervous or windy but I felt none of that. It is true that we had been informed just *where we* would be buried if we went west but no one paid any attention to that. As a

Lieutenant Alan May, 49th Machine Gun Company, Machine Gun Corps

matter of fact it was in an addition to the Canadian Cemetery just off York Road. Quite a nice place and easily accessible.

Lieutenant Martin Evans, 9th The Welch Regiment

The night was calm, so were we in this atmosphere of suppressed excitement and expectancy. There was a slight heat haze. The guns were keeping up a desultory fire, nothing out of the ordinary and no shells came back to us. A plane flew over us a few times as though searching; we imagined it must be an enemy, suspicious. Later we learnt that they [Germans] were not certain when the attack would commence. From their vantage points they must have known something was afoot. Colonel Godfrey rode along with us and tried to make conversation. I must have seemed unresponsive, there was so much to think about and so little time left.

We got to the jumping-off trench at midnight, saw all the men settled into their allotted places with scaling ladders for the jump to come. Saunders, Morris and I rested in a shelter, the time went quickly. At 2.15 I gave rum to half the company. Nearly every man was asleep, which was most sensible, if there had been time we could have also slept.

Our watches on wrist had been synchronized; there was nothing we had forgotten. In my hand I carried a card showing the exact minute at which we should reach certain coloured lines, the time and place where the barrage would lift and fall, we were to keep close to it. I carried too, a Very light pistol with coloured flares in case needed.

Captain Harold Bidder, 1st The South Staffordshire Regiment, attd. Corps Headquarters

I was up at half-past two. Nothing would come in [to Corps Headquarters] for a bit, so I walked up the road. A little way out of the village it tops a rise, and from here I could see the horizon behind which lay our front of attack.

It was very strange and very tense. I had never seen a battle from so far off before: it was like looking through the wrong end of a telescope. And then one thought of all those crowded trenches, full of men and boys silently waiting for the signal, longing by that time for it to come. As I said, even back there it was very tense.

It was the end of an exquisite summer night. There was an almost full moon behind one, a little cloudy. The stars were paling, and to the left of our front the sky was growing light. It was a very peaceful half-lit scene

– grey stretches of field, black masses of wood. There was the wonderful fresh smell of a summer dawn on a gentle breeze. There was some sound of firing, but not much. The impression was stillness. A cock crowed somewhere. Frogs croaked in a pond near. On the horizon, the white stars of the German Very lights lobbed lazily up as usual and flickered down again. That was all good – he had not spotted our concentration during the night. Five minutes yet. A whirring behind, and a great black shape sailed by under the moon. It was the first contact aeroplane going out to battle. Then another and another, like great bats against the pale stars. The Very lights still shot up and floated down, occasional and unsuspecting; the first bird sounded a note or two.

Towards dawn the fire on both sides slackened and just before 3.00 am we were ordered to leave the trench and lie out in the open. It was an impressive time – the gunfire ceased altogether with the exception of an occasional shell here and there – a thick mist was over the land and we had to lie full length, partly because of the shock that would result from the explosion of the mines and partly to prevent Fritz seeing us in the growing dawn. There was a strange groaning and rumbling from behind us and presently, looming out of the mist came a tank, moving straight towards us. We began to scramble out of its way, but it turned off to the left and was soon buried again in the mist. Out of the silence came the sound of blackbirds from a clump of battered trees.

Sapper Albert Martin, 122nd Signal Company, Royal Engineers

With a muffled rumbling crash the guns opened in unheard-of numbers – not absolutely simultaneously, but growing quickly into one tremendous throbbing roar. The whole horizon became a mass of darting red rockets as the Boche called frantically for help. And, half-right, a stupendous thing happened. A vast shape of lurid fire grew from the horizon and unfolded itself till it seemed to stand for a second, a solid bowl-shaped expanding thing of flame. The earth shook – it was one of the big mines. Then the flame died down; and after that the flashes of the guns revealed, towering higher and higher, the great mountain of smoke it had caused. The flashes were incessant, and played backwards and forwards across the horizon like some giant's fingers doing a tour de force on a great keyboard.

Captain Harold Bidder, 1st The South Staffordshire Regiment, attd. Corps Headquarters

Messines Crater. blown up
June 7th 1917

111975

Hundreds of dead laying about, died
with th stock.

A crater at Messines and the devastated ground beyond, with Sergeant Huborn Godfrey's original note on the reverse of the picture.

I stood watching the opening of this terrific drama with bared head. Then I turned back to the office. The daylight was rapidly broadening and the bird-chorus growing. The office looked out into a pleasant garden: the potato bed and the walk between fruit trees was soon bright in the sunlight. The village woke up. The hundred or so cheerful little girls who, with the nuns who teach and manage them, share these headquarters, began to be in evidence as one passed through the court. There were only the wires that came through to remind one that, a few miles on, our men were sweating, stabbing, falling, pressing on, facing, daring, holding, winning – for us.

Lieutenant Alan May, 49th Machine Gun Company, Machine Gun Corps

When I heard the first deep rumble I turned to the men and shouted 'Come on, let's go.' A fraction of a second later, a terrific roar and the whole earth seemed to rock and sway. The concussion was terrible, several of the men and myself being blown down violently. It seemed to be several minutes before the earth stood still again though it may not really have been more than a few seconds. As I looked at the uproar it appeared that the whole earth was shorn apart as far as one could see. Flames rose to a great height, according to the papers some 1,400 feet though they did not last long. Silhouetted against the flame I saw huge blocks of earth that seemed to be as big as houses falling back to the ground. Small chunks and dirt fell all around. I saw a man flung out from behind a huge block of debris, silhouetted against the sheet of flame. Presumably some poor devil of a Boche. It was awful, a sort of inferno.

Going on slowly with the men it was hard to see because of the dust and debris. Suddenly I noticed that some of the infantry were running back, presumably terror-stricken by the mines. Naturally I did my best to stop them, shouting at them, brandishing my revolver, and succeeded in stopping a few. Must say they appeared a bit ashamed. One of them told me he thought he would be crushed by the debris.

Shouting of course was futile for no one could possibly hear, though those close enough to see in the near dark could understand gesticulations. There was confusion on all sides, many men were lost to sight. While

A tank advances up Messines Ridge. This remarkable picture was taken by Captain Robert Perry, 3rd Worcestershire Regiment.

looking for my men to get them together again I came across Sergeant Riddle and Private Davidson, but where were the rest of them?

Continuing to look around and futilely shouting, I eventually found enough of my men to get together a gun team and sent them off. After waiting a few more minutes hoping some of the others would show up – none did – I decided that Riddle, Davidson and I would try to make up a gun team. Riddle carried the gun and one box of ammo. Davidson, a small chap, carried three boxes of ammo and I carried five. We had no tripod but anyway, ammo was more important.

The darkness cleared gradually and I saw that there were no infantry waves at all, everyone seemed to be going ahead on his own and all the units seemed to be mixed up.

Lieutenant
Martin Evans,
9th The Welch
Regiment

The whole earth gulped, heaved, shuddered and vomited a vast spume from its bowels. The debris shot up, towered up hundreds of feet and hurtled down. By then the first wave was over and racing ahead. ... At this stage a few shells came over, for which and for once I salute the German gunners for their bravery in being able to stand up to the pulverizing avalanche falling around their batteries. They must have been swamped; we had located every battery.

At first faint gleam of dawn, we took the great plunge towards the unknown. The smoke from the mines and fog created an artificial darkness into which we leapt. In the vast crater that had been the Nag's Nose, a blue flame was flickering; we had to traverse this and had to tread lightly over the damp, spongy subsoil.

Our guns had cut all the wire and a new invention. Thermite, which burns anything or anybody and gets hotter on exposure to air, had cleared the way. ...

Our first objective, the Blue Line, existed only in name, no trench was left, everything except a few pillboxes was beaten out of recognition. At this stage Saunders and I pulled out our maps and had a lucky escape, we were within an ace of being blown up by one of our own shells falling short, it fell at our feet; it was a miracle – no other word for it – how we survived that day. That was not the only near shave. But, I say this without bragging, nothing seemed to matter, one could have walked into hell, as indeed we were, without a tremor. I cannot understand it myself.

It was an experience which I shall remember very vividly for the rest of my life – all the phases of the preliminary bombardment, the calm silence that succeeded it suddenly broken by a most terrific uproar, the weird sights of moving men and things in the semi-darkness, the rolling clouds

Sapper Albert Martin, 122nd Signal Company, Royal Engineers

A brief pause during the Messines Offensive, 9 June. Sitting nearest the camera is the Adjutant, 3rd Worcestershire Regiment, Second Lieutenant Lawrence Piper, aged 37. He was killed the following day.

of smoke picked out every now and then with shooting tongues of flame, all formed a tremendously wonderful sight. It was stupendous beyond the imagination.

As daylight increased I looked directly onto the line that was being battered and the sight was so awfully impressive that the real horror of it all was temporarily quite obliterated. On our left, Fritz was sending over cloud gas – he also had an observation balloon up but this was soon put out of action by our aeroplanes. The prisoners came over in dozens and scores and passed behind us into safety. About five o'clock 'Hookey' Walker took us out of the trench and we advanced to the Dammstrasse. Ordinarily he has a languid sort of bearing that would give one the impression that he was rather dull and unobservant but he led us across that open, shell-holed country that only two hours before had been held by the Germans since 1914 as if he knew every inch of the ground. He didn't hesitate for a moment and took us straight to the dugout in which the 124th Brigade Advance Signals had established themselves. The Dammstrasse is 1,200 yards in front of, and overlooking, our old front line. It is a sunken roadway about 6 to 8 feet lower than the surrounding country and therefore of considerable military advantage. At times we have imagined that Fritz has given us a tidy battering, but judging from the frightfully mutilated state of the ground, we have given him ten times as much as he has given us. His front line has been completely wiped out and is only traceable by the remains of his barbed wire, and it was only possible to find little bits of any trench.

Private Henry Russell, 10th The Worcestershire Regiment

It was bewildering. The volume of sound made men sweat in an agony of fear. Looking over the parapet we could see nothing but smoke and the flames of exploding shells.

Our turn was not yet. For half an hour the barrage played on the German first system of trenches and then lifted to the second line. Presently, wounded men began to appear, followed by a few Germans, white, haggard, and half-crazy with fright. One big German, naked to the waist, and with horrible wounds to his face, chest, and back, staggered in our direction.

Shorty bawled to him to cross the trench by the bridge which had been placed near us overnight. The wounded man misunderstood, and thinking that some fresh horror was overtaking him, suddenly gathered strength and took a flying leap into the midst of us. This was rather starling, but with the help of a certain amount of dumb show, we directed him to the nearest dressing station, and after we had assisted him out of the trench he went his way.

Not far in advance of our front parapet I saw a couple of our lads who had gone completely goofy, perhaps from the concussion. It was pitiful; one of them welcomed me like a long lost friend and asked me to give him his baby. I picked up a tin hat from the ground and gave it to him. He cradled the hat as if it were a child, smiling and laughing without a care in the world despite the fact that shells were exploding all around. I have no idea what happened to the poor chap but if he stayed there very long he must have been killed. Crossing no-man's-land I had a narrow squeak. I was carrying two boxes of ammo in one hand and three in the other when a bit of shell went through one box and stopped in the next. Can't understand why the ammo did not go off but it did not. Would have lost my leg but for the boxes. Telling the others to wait I went back and got two more boxes. Surprisingly enough there in the middle of no man's-land there was some green grass and I also saw one or two yellow iris, though how these plants and grasses escaped destruction I cannot imagine. ...

From here on, the ground was completely torn up, not a square inch left unturned by shells. The Boche wire was completely destroyed, only a few strands lying about. Their front line was utterly napoo, blown to bits and more or less filled with dirt from the mines. A bit further on and we had to rest for we were carrying heavy loads and dripping with sweat. It was just breaking dawn and the dust was still falling. Where we rested there were two dead Germans and believe it or not, Davidson used one for a seat to rest on. They had been killed by machine-gun fire, ours I hoped. All this time I realized that I had not been a bit windy though maybe I should have been. Probably too anxious to do a good job and too interested in all I saw. Some gas shells had been coming over and both Riddle and I were feeling the effects of them badly. We tried a cigarette to see if it would help. It did not.

Lieutenant Alan May, 49th Machine Gun Company, Machine Gun Corps

A German concrete pillbox reduced to rubble by a direct hit.

I saw that the infantry were not advancing in waves as planned but rather in groups varying from about thirty to five or six. Not good. Some men appeared to be bored, others were picking up souvenirs while some seemed keen to get on with the job. There was no excitement anywhere, everything seemed so routine it was unbelievable.

It was slow and heavy going for all the ground had been chewed up by shells and mortars. There were many large deep holes from the shelling and these we had to go around or down them and then up again – one as bad as the other. We knew there was a stream called the Whytschaetebek but this almost non-existent. If I had not sunk in mud up to my knees I would never have known it was there.

We jumped out of the trench, relieved that the long wait was over, and after getting into some sort of order, we marched in formation across the open ground. I felt curiously helpless. The din of the guns behind and the shells in front prevented us from hearing whether the enemy artillery was in action, but no shells appeared to be bursting anywhere near. I fully expected to hear the sudden roar of high explosives, or the crash of shrapnel, but it was singularly absent and we gained confidence with every step. The platoon officer, as fussy as ever, quickly became annoyed because we failed to keep together.

'You'll all get lost,' he shrieked. He was like a sheepdog rounding up the strays but his efforts were to no avail, for the ground was intersected with shell holes, which necessitated much breaking apart. We crossed the enemy front line, which was but the wreckage of a trench system, and when nearing the second line we opened into extended order just as we had done in the rehearsals of a few days before. Still not a hostile shell was noticed, and it became fairly obvious that the German batteries had either been disabled or withdrawn.

We were now on top of the ridge, and glancing back I could see the earthwork of the old British trenches plainly visible. It seemed strange that we had been allowed to live in those obvious targets. Stranger still that those operations had actually commenced without even an attempt to flatten them out. Quite slowly we advanced. Here was a man ablaze with the fire of a dozen Very lights which had become ignited by some unknown means. He was beyond all human aid and his body was left to the mercy of others with more time to investigate.

The second line was garrisoned with khaki-clad soldiers, who were busily engaged deepening and strengthening the trench, and slightly in advance of this position we were required to wait while the barrage reduced our objective, the Black Line. We crouched in the shell holes watching the vivid scene, and some tried to converse, but their voices were lost in such a terrible clatter. I heard Shorty shout in my ear:

'Where the deuce is Jerry's barrage?' but I shook my head. I wanted to look around.

In a nearby shell hole sat the commanding officer looking cool and unperturbed, and close to him were various details from the headquarters

Private Henry Russell, 10th The Worcestershire Regiment

Collecting the wounded on Messines Ridge, as other men dig in.

unit. To the right, to the left, and to the immediate front, the barrage, lifting columns of earth, which was falling in a nerve-broken cascade. I wondered what the enemy was doing in that hell but a few yards away. Lying low, I thought, waiting grimly to meet bayonet with bayonet. I was wrong. We had no fight for the possession of the third line. Even before the barrage had lifted some Germans began to run the gauntlet of the shells, and directly it passed over them they swarmed out of the trench without weapons and with hands extended upwards.

Sapper Albert Martin, 122nd Signal Company, Royal Engineers

When we reached the Dammstrasse we were fairly in amongst the shells for this was now our front line and Fritz was concentrating all his efforts in the attempt to prevent us from getting any further. Also many of our own guns were firing short, and spiteful 18 pdr shrapnel was bursting all round us. The western bank of the Dammstrasse was lined with dugouts, now in various stages of demolition. The one chosen for our Signal Office was fairly sound, being constructed of reinforced concrete about 3 foot thick. Lieutenant Walker and Corporal Aitken went in to take over, leaving us outside in the remains of a trench which was labelled 'Engel Weg'. Colonel Carey-Barnard (known as Carey-Whizzbang by reason of his rather explosive nature) came along leading the 15th Hants [Hampshires]. Of course he wanted to know who we were, what we were, and all about us. The trench was rather cramped so we moved across to the east bank of the Dammstrasse. Looking over the top, no Germans were visible but we knew they were lurking in shell holes and hiding in Ravine Wood and Pheasant Wood, both of which were only a few yards away.

We sat down on the bank waiting for orders and wishing to goodness that our 18 pdrs would lengthen their range. On my right was Dagnell and next to him was Coltherd. One of our 18 pdr shrapnels burst about 6 yards above our heads and the bits came hissing down viciously. I wasn't touched but Dagnell got it in both knees and Coltherd in the left knee. We ripped their breeches open and bandaged them up. I used my own field service dressing on Dagnell and subsequently got into trouble for being in action without one in my possession. We carried them across the road to the dugout, where they remained till 8.00 pm before we got hold of any stretcher-bearers. It was about 5.30 am when they were wounded. The Dammstrasse is a slough – mud, water and shell holes. A shell burst right on top of the Signal Office and we went over expecting to find the place blown in but it was quite unharmed inside – evidence that Fritz knows how to build dugouts.

A tank arrives to assist a comrade bogged down on the Messines Ridge. A captured German pillbox is to the right.

Opposite:
*Battle-worn
men of the 3rd
Worcestershire
Regiment resting
after their
exertions on
Messines Ridge.*

Presently the tanks came along. They had to drop down the bank about 6 or 8 feet, wallow through the mud and climb the opposite bank. One came over the top of the Signal Office and again we feared for the safety of those inside but there was no need to worry. Another got stuck in the mud and refused to budge. At 6.30 am the advance was continued for another 1,000 yds to the final objective of the division, the attacking battalions of our brigade being the 15th Hants and the 11th Royal West Kents. There was not much opposition except from a machine-gun nest in Pheasant Wood. The bullets came 'zipping' over our heads until the Kents stormed it at the point of the bayonet.

The Signal Office was small, and with two wounded men in it and one end under water, there was only room for one operator at a time; yet at certain periods it was necessary to have two instruments working, so I took a buzzer outside and rigged it up on a mound where the trench had been blown in. The dirt gradually wore away and disclosed the bare buttocks of a dead man so I moved into the Dammstrasse where the only comparatively dry spot was alongside a dead German, but he was not badly mutilated. An infantryman close by me was hit in the face by a quantity of shrapnel dust and his tears trickled down his cheeks. He cried out 'Oh my eyes, my eyes! My God, I am blind!' The sudden realization of his blindness seemed a greater agony than the pain of his wounds. I shall never forget that terrible cry of anguish. A big German prisoner passed me with his left arm badly shattered. He begged a drink of water but I shook my head because I had only a little drop left and had no idea when I should get any more. Two other prisoners came over, one unhurt, the other wounded in the arm and side. The former scrambled up the bank leaving his wounded comrade to struggle alone. There was a yell of execration from all the Tommies round about and it put the wind up him. He threw his hands up above his head and yelled '*Kamerade*', and we made him go and help his companion along.

Lieutenant Alan
May, 49th Machine
Gun Company,
Machine Gun
Corps

A group of twenty Boche prisoners came by with their hands on their heads in charge of one small Tommy. This chap walked nonchalantly behind them, rifle slung, smoking a cigarette, apparently the most unconcerned individual. The prisoners were indeed poor specimens, either very young

or old. They appeared to be half starved and green with fright – as well they might be. Some of them carried bits of dry bread in their hands, perhaps they thought we had been starved out by their U-boats. The big concrete strongpoints and dugouts we saw had been blown to bits. From the remains of one of these I saw a miserable little Boche run out. Here was my chance to shoot a Boche personally but he raised his hands when he saw me so of course I could not. I judged him to be about fifteen years old, weak and about half my size. He looked at me like a dog that knows he has done something wrong and croaked 'Kamerade'. By shouting and gesticulating I made him understand that if he wished to live he was to carry some of my load. The agility with which he picked up two boxes of ammunition was astounding considering his physical condition.

Sapper Albert
Martin, 122nd
Signal Company,
Royal Engineers

Time passed very slowly – I looked at my watch, thinking it was afternoon and found it was only twenty past eight. I took off a message from the Kents saying that the Huns (500 of them) were massing for a counter-attack. Walker seized his revolver and went forth to meet them but soon came back as he had left his ammunition behind. This attack was repulsed by the Kents, who killed twenty-five of the enemy and took twenty unwounded prisoners. We were due for relief at noon, but the relieving division was delayed somewhere or other so we had to hang on, feeling very tired and hungry. Also we sent back several demands for cavalry as our advance had been so successful, but apparently the state of the country was such that rendered it impossible for cavalry to get up. The 47th Division on our left met a fiercer opposition and failed to take their final objective. Of course our 'lines' (telephone wires) were continually being broken – our stock of pigeons was soon exhausted – and our runners were on the go perpetually. In the afternoon I took a message forward to Lieutenant Taylor. By this time things had quietened down considerably. I climbed up the bank and looked forward. With the exception of a solitary tank that had come to anchor just in front of me there was no sign of humanity except that displayed by the general devastation, and the explosion of an occasional shell. My only guide was the 'line' which led me to a large shell hole in which Lieutenant Taylor and his party had settled themselves. Fritz had ceased making any attempts at counter-attack and seemed to be content to settle down in his new position.

The Germans had been routed, their erstwhile deep and complex defences completely shattered in a matter of hours. By 9.00 am, virtually the entire ridge was in British hands. Almost all the mines had detonated and only where charges had failed was there any concerted enemy resistance. Small counter-attacks melted away almost before they had begun. The Oostaverne Line was captured in the early evening, permitting men on the ridge to consolidate their positions, a job that continued for a week until the offensive ended.

The Black Line had been entirely evacuated, but it was not now the practice to hold enemy trenches, and we pushed on to some distance in front and there commenced digging. Presently, another regiment came along and leapfrogged through us and dug in a few hundred yards ahead so that we were again in supports. This one-sided battle was now developing in an unexpected manner. Considerably more than the original objective had been taken and apparently the German front on this sector was broken.

Half a dozen tanks came wobbling along and disappeared through a wood which lay half-right from where we were entrenched. A British aeroplane, which had been flying backwards and forwards dangerously near the ground, was hit by a shell and burst into flames, and it was with intense pity that we watched it go to its doom, for the pilot had been a source of inspiration from the commencement.

Private Henry Russell, 10th The Worcestershire Regiment

We reached our final objective, the Green line bordering the road from Wytschaete to St Eloi. Here we started to dig in. Most of our men hale from the Rhondda Valley and they dug then as though back in the mines. … Then the men called for me. At such times they must turn to someone. I went along and looked down. On the floor of the new trench poor little Waggett of my platoon was dying from loss of blood, an enemy shell had hit him and there was nothing we could do. His white face and slender body was piteous, he looked sacrificial. So young, so innocent, so at rest after the storm. I must have seen hundreds killed, but this memory will never be effaced. One noticed as so often, how kindly death comes, it draws aside the mask we wear leaving a poise, a serenity. …

They must have thought me heartless when I turned away. I had no words. They buried the poor fragile body in a shell hole nearby.

Lieutenant Martin Evans, 9th The Welch Regiment

Lieutenant
Colonel
Rowland
Feilding, 6th
The Connaught
Rangers

Within six hours of the first assault, parties were already at work, making roads across the mutilated zone and even laying water pipes! All objectives had been reached punctually to scheduled time. At 10.00 am our guns were still pounding, though at reduced pressure, and the enemy had ceased to reply at all.

There was nothing to keep me any longer at the telephone, and I went forward to study results. German prisoners were carrying back wounded. Already our Field Artillery was on the move forward – a stirring sight which always fascinates me. As I watch them, though I have nothing to do with them, I feel a kind of pride in them. I, as everybody else was doing, walked freely over the surface; past and over the old front line, where we have spent so many bitter months. Then over no-man's-land. As we stepped out there my orderly, O'Rourke, remarked: 'This is the first time for two years that anyone has had the privilege of walking over this ground in daylight, Sir.' We visited some of the huge mine craters made at Zero hour, and huge indeed they are.

Our tanks were now advancing – a dozen or more of them – going forward to take part in the capture of the fifth and sixth objectives. Their

Digging a communication trench on top of the ridge.

duty is to reduce local opposition, when it is encountered, and there they were, lumbering along, picking their way through the honeycomb of shell holes and craters, getting into difficulties, getting out again, sometimes defeated, but generally in the end winning their way through the area of devastation, where nothing has been left alive, not even a blade of grass.

Mark suggested that we should do a little exploring, and as the ground was safely hidden from direct observation, we agreed. Within easy reach lay several dugouts, which we duly inspected. Every indication of a hurried retreat was to be seen. Rifles, with bayonets fixed stood outside. Equipment was strewn about, and in the dugouts we discovered partially eaten meals. One dugout, which we judged to be that of a general, or some highly placed person, was luxuriously furnished with armchairs and couches, and boasted a splendid carpet, which, had it been possible, we should surely have bought back with us. An abundance of bread was found, but we knew better than to sample it for it was extremely probable that poison traps had been laid to catch the unwary.

Private Henry Russell, 10th The Worcestershire Regiment

The spirit of 'souveniring' seized us and we commandeered bayonets, rifle bolts, and many odds and ends, which not long afterwards we were glad to get rid of because of the trouble of carrying them about. Enemy bayonets and other curiosities might look nice at some future happy date, hanging on the wall at home, but to the infantryman who carries his belongings on his back, every pound of additional weight becomes so much extra burden. I led off with a collection of six bolts, two bayonets and a detonated egg bomb, and when finally I landed in England only the egg bomb remained.

Lieutenant Raphael, the Surrey cricketer, was up here this morning for no earthly reason as far as I can make out, other than that of souvenir hunting. He brought his batman with him and both were killed by a shell in a dugout which he was exploring. By the evening we had given up hopes of getting relieved today. Aitken and I settled down in the trench and tried to get a little sleep but Fritz started sending shells just over our heads to a spot about 200 or 300 yards away, and the shriek as they whizzed past was more than sufficient to keep us awake. He also treated us to some

Sapper Albert Martin, 122nd Signal Company, Royal Engineers

shrapnel – one burst just above us and a small piece hit me on the arm. It was long and thin and by a stroke of luck it struck me lengthways just where my sleeve happened to be rucked in several folds. If it had come end-on it would have gone through. I picked it up and put it in my pocket. It is the only souvenir I brought back although I could have had hundreds of belts, buckles, buttons, bayonets and such things as some men pride themselves in collecting. Outside the Signal Office was a great pile of arms and clothing together with black bread and sausages but although we were hungry we knew better than to touch any of it. ...

We were all dead-beat and about 10.00 pm we crowded into the dugout to try and get some sleep. Yet one man had to be on duty so I proffered to carry on till 3.00 am, when MacDougall would take over till 8.00 am. I was kept busy all the time for although things were quite quiet, we were the only front line Signal Office. Once I had to go out and find a runner and managed to slip into a shell hole of slimy mud and water. The poor wretch was, if possible, more worn out than I was but war is no respecter of weariness and I had to make him go on his journey. From the length of time he was away he must either have gone to sleep or have been too tired to find his way.

Private Davidson for some reason hardly seemed to be affected by the gas, but Sergeant Riddle and I were having a bad time. I was leaning over vomiting when an officer came up and asked 'Are you hit?' I straightened up and said, 'No, just gas.' Then I was bowled over like a rabbit. I felt as if a whole shell had hit me in the back. Maybe I was out for a few minutes but certainly not very long. It was painful to breathe and one of my legs was jerking and kicking and I had no control over it. Riddle held my leg and I remember the officer saying something to Riddle before he went on. Riddle cut off my equipment and stuck on some bandages and left to find a first aid man. I wondered if I could carry on but with the leg unmanageable and the trouble I had breathing decided I had done all I could. It was a terrible disappointment to realize I would never get to my objective. Then I thought about how upset Mother and Father would be when they heard I was a casualty – nothing I could do about that at the moment. Stretcher-bearers came and dressed the wounds,

Opposite: *Captain Robert Perry supports a notice on the edge of Messines village.*

Lieutenant Alan May, 49th Machine Gun Company, Machine Gun Corps

actually very little blood and as far as I could see no apparent damage to the leg. The bearers rolled me on a stretcher, a painful process but my breathing was easier. I told Riddle and Davidson to carry on and said Goodbye.

Sapper Albert Martin, 122nd Signal Company, Royal Engineers

At 3.00 am I roused MacDougall and lay down with my feet in water and with my steel helmet for a pillow. I slept for a few minutes only, when I opened my eyes and found MacDougall shaking me vigorously. 'Come on,' he said, 'get up. Fritz is coming.' 'I don't care,' I said, 'I'm tired,' and turned over – but he pulled me up and shouted that it was our relief that had turned up. So I staggered to my feet and got my equipment on. By this time Walker and all the other fellows except Aitken and myself were out of the dugout. I seized my lump of mouldy bread, picked up a tin of jam that belonged to somebody else, poured some of it onto the bread and shared it with Aitken. We were the last two in the file and I was feeling very fatigued when stepping on a soft patch I slipped and went over my knees into watery mud. Aitken helped me out but I was too exhausted to stand so sat down for about ten minutes to get my breath and a little strength. When we resumed, the remainder of the party were out of sight. We only had a vague idea of the direction in which we had to go, and after passing an immense mine crater (an old one) in the forward side of which Fritz had built some strong concrete dugouts, we eventually come to Stragglers Post. We had seen numerous dead bodies in all the ghastly horrors and mutilations of violent death, men with half their heads blown off and their brains falling over their faces – some with their abdomens torn open and their entrails hanging out – others stretched out with livid faces and bloodstained mouths, and unblinking eyes staring straight to heaven.

At Stragglers Post the guard could not direct us to our Brigade HQ so we wandered here and there making scores of fruitless enquiries until suddenly we met Bill Rogers and his runners coming from the Relay Post. Of course they knew the way and took us only a short distance past Stragglers Post to the dugouts at ET10 (Voormezeele). This is the first deep dugout that I have been in since the Somme last October. It is about 30 feet deep and has two or three galleries. When we reported in at the

Signal Office Buchanan gave me a mug half full of rum but my hand was so shaky that I spilt most of it down my clothes. It was now 8.30 am and for forty hours we had been on the go without food or sleep. Early in that period, too, my nerves had been badly shaken, so it is no wonder that I felt absolutely laid out. The cooks got us some breakfast and I almost fell asleep over it, and then lay down outside the entrance to the sap but was warned that it was not a safe place to go to sleep in as a man had been killed there yesterday. So I washed and shaved as well as my shaky hand would let me and went down the stairs. Sergeant Oxley lent me his bed and an overcoat and I was soon fast asleep.

10.6.17: My hand still shakes too much to permit of letter writing without causing people to wonder what is the matter with me. This afternoon Davidson and I went up as far as the old no-man's-land and had a look at two of the new mine craters. One solid concrete dugout had been blown up and rolled over bodily. The dead body of a German was still inside. All our own dead have been buried but there are still a few German bodies scattered about. The RE Field Companies are working

After battle: men of the 3rd Worcestershire Regiment rest. The battalion lost forty-six men killed or died of wounds on Messines Ridge. The divisional sign, a horseshoe, can be seen stitched to their tunics.

hard on pit-prop roads and trench tramways. They have carried them as far as the old front line and are now working across no-man's-land. Their hardest work is now commencing. It is an extraordinary scene of animation. Wagons and lorries full of materials are arriving in constant succession and hundreds of men are unloading and carrying and putting in place, all within easy reach of Fritz's artillery but he is not being very bothersome; probably he is tired after the big counter-attack he made the night before last along the whole of the new front. He was repulsed everywhere although the attack lasted from 7.00 pm till midnight. The official reports issued to the English press state that all the objectives were captured early in the morning of the 7th, but we know that the 47th Div. is still held up some distance from its final objective and it is quite likely that some of the divisions on our right have failed to get as far as they were supposed to.

Lieutenant Martin Evans, 9th The Welch Regiment

10 June: An artilleryman has promised to post this [letter] with others. I wrote to you yesterday from near the Grand Boise, which for years we have been looking at and now it is ours. It was thought we were to go further up, after much discussion, reorganizing and redistributing of material we had orders to come back to our old front line. Got in at 11.00 pm and slept the sleep of the just and today we had intervals of 'dosses'.

We go forward tonight only to hold on until relief arrives. Will write when we get out. The chief need is water. Most of the morning has been spent in writing recommendations as some medals will be on their way; I put forward Saunders and Morris, but for the others I had largely to rely on what the sergeants could tell me, as in the hurly-burly I could not see everywhere. The next need is a wash, it is a risk which I take, using water from any shell hole, at the moment they are dry. The other Morris had lent me a razor. Three days without. Different from when I first came out, the Colonel had me on the mat for not growing a moustache. It just could not be done then. The papers say Haig has pushed, they ought to say Plumer, it was entirely his affair; we gained every objective, it has been a model attack; the most complete within defined limits, in history.

I suppose I have to tell you some time, I can hardly bring myself to do so. Words fail me when I say that my most loyal, devoted companion and friend, my Platoon Sergeant Owen was killed. It goes without saying that my batman Davies was wounded, how badly is not known. Among the ten killed are Corporal Manning and little Waggett from my platoon. God bless you. I trust we shall all get home someday.

The attack was a complete and overwhelming success. The whole of the ridge, which for so many weary months had dominated our lines, was captured at a low cost. A and B battalions of tanks were useful but not indispensable. The ground was difficult and in places impossible. Many tanks became ditched. Certain tanks retrieved a local situation finely by the stout repulse of a strong counter-attack. We received the impression that, if the weather had been wet, tanks could not have been used. ...

The taking of the Messines Ridge was encouraging, and for a time we cast covetous eyes on Lille; but, thinking it over, we began to rate Messines at its true value – a very notable but local success.

Major William Watson, D Battalion, Heavy Branch Machine Gun Corps

Overleaf: *A group of Royal Engineers taking a break from their vital work.*

5 Fresh Air and Exercise

Dear Brother
    I can't tell you where I am, but I am at the place which I left to go to the place where I've come from. I think that should baffle the Censor, don't you?

Anonymous

───────────

Opposite:
Second Lieutenant Norman Collins carries Denise, the daughter of a farming family on whom the officers of the 1/4th Seaforth Highlanders were billeted before the Third Battle of Ypres.

Everything had worked in the Allies' favour at Messines. The weather had been perfect, not just during the offensive but before it, allowing General Plumer to prepare his forces devoid of distractions, and to observe the enemy without impediment. Clear skies permitted the pilots of the Royal Flying Corps to fly sortie after sortie over the ridge, directing artillery fire and signalling back the extent of advance. Unfettered observation of the enemy had been a key determiner of success and although the artillery had churned up the ground, the fine weather ensured the earth was dry for tanks. The net result of capturing the Messines Ridge was that it enabled Field Marshal Haig to press ahead with his plans for an offensive in the Ypres Salient.

Marked peaks and troughs in military activity characterized trench life on the Western Front and, in the summer of 1917, there was an obvious trough as Haig prepared for Flanders. So far, 1917 had been an undeniably violent year, and soldiers took every opportunity to enjoy the relative lull, to appreciate the weather and, if they could find them, comforts amongst the civilian population far back from the front lines.

17 June: I wish this war was over. It is absolute murder now. There is too much machinery about it. I hope it finishes about next spring then I can have a nice six-month holiday during the fine weather. I am afraid this is a dream though as we will not be demobilized for at least twelve months I should think.

Why did I join the infantry? And an assaulting division at that. I think the Royal Garrison Artillery would have suited my 'gentle disposition' better.

Lieutenant Norman Collins, 1/4th Seaforth Highlanders, (Ross-shire Buffs, The Duke of Albany's)

Opposite: *After resting, battle training resumed. Men of the 1/4th Seaforth Highlanders advancing across open ground.*

You can see I am in a fed up mood today. Probably the heat is the cause, the weather is very hot.

Well, tea is ready so *au Revoir*.

Norman

23 June: Many thanks for the nice parcel you sent. I nearly finished it in one night. A wee French kiddie about five years of age assisted me. You will see her photo soon.

When we left our last billet (yesterday) the people belonging to the farm shed about a bucketful of tears.

They were very good to us giving us honey, milk etc. for nothing.

For a week or so I was sleeping in white sheets. My French is improving greatly.

Norman

An impish grin: Denise charms the officers of the Seaforth Highlanders.

Private Alexander Simpson, 1/4th Seaforth Highlanders, aged 18 standing in a farm doorway. Simpson served as Norman Collins's servant and was killed at Ypres in September. His body was never identified.

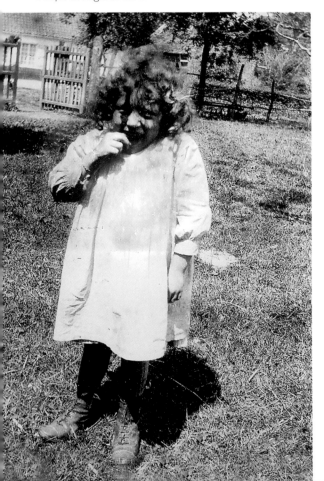

Officers and men watch a battalion boxing bout, July 1917.

We were billeted at a farm and it was a delightful place to be while we trained. It was lovely sunny weather and, when we got time, we used to ride on the farm horses. There were no young men there, but it was full of their children. I have snapshots of the little girl, Denise, and she is riding on my shoulder. I also have pictures of my servant, Simpson. He was aged eighteen, but had been at the front fully a year and a half. He had been a farm boy and for recreation used to hoe the farm vegetables: I often wondered what he was thinking about. When he'd finished, the farmer gave him a bottle or two of cider or wine.

It was a very agreeable interlude. I remember the scent of the broad beans, a lovely sweet smell. I took pictures of fellow officers, Lieutenant Pitcairn and Captain Harris, also the pipe band and boxing matches between the troops, as well as pictures of the men advancing in open order and practising their musketry.

New drafts were sent out to join the battalion. After the mauling we had had at Arras, we were now once again more or less up to strength, fit and ready for the next offensive. And that was how it was. If you survived one assault, you went back; you trained again for another show, when once again you had to accept that your chances of living could be cut to minutes and seconds.

One of the many diversions which occurred during our period of rest was when arrangements were made to take the battalion in motor lorries to Boulogne, some 40 miles distant. Whether the idea was to give us a day's outing, or whether it was considered we could do with a thorough scouring with sea water, I cannot say, but we welcomed the trip with open arms. We were due to meet the lorries at a point about 4 miles from where we were staying, and clad in walking-out dress, and carrying groundsheets, we set out gaily on this unexpected adventure. Arrived at the starting point, it was decided that we might need our water bottles, and so we were marched the 4 miles to billets and back to the lorries again. This was an unhappy augury and was the cause of much swearing, for we were already dog-tired and the day was well advanced. Some of the men wanted to forgo the pleasure, but it was not one of those kinds of trips where you could change your mind at the last moment, and I rather think that if it had been decided that we must fetch the remainder of our kit in instalments we should still have been compelled to go.

Apparently everything was now satisfactory, for we were allowed to climb into the lorries, and the excursion began. Such a little matter as a 12 miles' enforced march was not wont to disturb the tranquillity of a whole battalion, and for three solid hours we rode through village after village cheering like children on a Sunday school outing.

To those who had expected a joyful afternoon in a big French seaport came a blow, big and sure. With extra strong field glasses we might have seen the colour of the brick buildings that showed faintly in the distance. Here we were by the side of the sea, with a portion of the beach reserved for our exclusive use, splashing about to our heart's content, and men were grousing because military police kept guard on either side. They wanted to roam to their heart's content. Maybe they would have liked to imagine just for a few hours that the war was over, and that they were again at Blackpool, or Weston, or Brighton, or wherever they used to spend their

Private Henry Russell, 10th The Worcestershire Regiment

summer vacations; but those military police! Even a battalion naked to a man, with nothing but tattoo marks to awaken suspicions of militarism, could not look on them and pretend there was not a war on.

We enjoyed ourselves thoroughly, and after a few hours of inhaling ozone, and vainly trying to obtain a glimpse of those white cliffs that are forever England, we re-entered the lorries and sang away the 40 miles to billets.

Lieutenant Colonel Rowland Feilding, 6th The Connaught Rangers

I am getting rather bitten with agriculture. No wonder these peasants get rich; – or, if they do not (and I really do not know), I should say there must be something radically wrong with the whole system of land tenure in this country.

They are the most industrious and the thriftiest people I have ever seen, and though during this time of war the work is done by women, children, old men, wounded men, and men hopelessly unfit for active soldiering – with a few soldiers (very few) released temporarily for the purpose, I am sure it must be impossible for those who have not seen it to realize what cultivation means in France and Belgium, or to picture the seas of corn and potatoes and roots, extending as far as the eye can reach and further; the forests of hops, weedless; without a barren patch or a neglected spot anywhere.

In the farm where I am billeted there is a farm-hand – a girl of about eighteen. She sleeps on the straw, on the floor of a stable. She is up, bursting with life and spirits each morning at five o'clock; and she works, at top pressure, without ceasing, till dark. Then she returns to her straw. She is slim, but has the strength of an average man. She handles the farm horses with a single rein (attached to one ring of the bit only), and by word of mouth. Apparently, she neither eats nor drinks.

It is the 'manure' season. That is to say, it is the time of year when they carry out the loathsome liquid accumulation of the past twelve months and spread it over the fields, and so wrapped up is this girl in the work, that you would think she revelled in it.

She moves always at the double – whether through the chicken run, whence every bird flies scared and panic-stricken at her wild approach, or *through* the manure heap (for she never goes round it). Each time I pass her she looks up with full face and a cheery grin. I don't suppose she ever washes, and she must reek of manure, but she fascinates me because of her extraordinary vitality.

Soon after this interlude we were given another ride in motor lorries; a rather long ride which finally landed us within measureable distance of the line. It was on the outskirts of Meteren, and Meteren was a place beloved by troops because of its capacity for supplying the needs of the moment. Here D Company was quartered in sheds attached to an estaminet. The proprietor also owned hop fields and a farm. It was hop-picking time when we arrived, and men strolling through the hop fields noticed that the owner had a pleasant habit of visiting his workers with great jugs of beer. D Company started hop-picking after parades.

Private Henry Russell, 10th The Worcestershire Regiment

Norman Collins: 'When we left our last billet (yesterday) the people belonging to the farm shed about a bucketful of tears.' A close relationship was often forged between officer and men and the families on whom they were billeted.

Butter churning was another pastime for anyone who was hard up and possessed a thirst, but it was a monotonous task, and after the first hour of swinging the flat tub which served the purpose, and after sundry peeps inside to see how much butter had formed and finding only a few yellow floating spots, the amateur churner usually remembered he had his buttons to clean.

Conscripted men now made up the majority of drafts leaving for France. By mid-1917 there were almost 2 million men with the BEF on the Western Front, with tens of thousands of men arriving each week to replace losses. In July, Lieutenant George Brown arrived for the first time, naturally curious to see what life overseas was like.

Returning officers standing on the sea front in Boulogne.

Officers of the 1/4th Seaforth Highlanders take a train back to the battalion: some were returning to France after recovering from wounds.

Well, here I am at the base; you'd hardly believe it, but it took seven hours to get here, about 25 miles. There's not much news, but I thought you'd like a letter. This is not a wildly exciting place. The thing that strikes one most in France is the quantity of black. I know that it is worn much more than in England, but it is a depressing sight. Why do people, especially widows, parade their grief and depress others in this way? – to grieve, I suppose, is human, but not this show. And the little children, too – it's too bad.

I have been posted to the [9th Suffolk] Battalion, so look out in the Gazette. I shall stay here probably till the end of next week.

The life here is distinctly good, in its own strange way, enough work to fill your day, 7.30 am to 5.00 pm, though sometimes, such as tonight for example, one is at it from 5.45 pm to 12 noon; but in those cases the rest of the afternoons both before and after is one's own. This afternoon I am going into ___ about 4 miles away, where I dined last night. There's a splendid spirit of comradeship and optimism. The general feeling here puts the end of hostilities much earlier than I do, but then one never knows, one can only pray for the best. I have a strange feeling that I shall see you much sooner than any of us think.

With all its privations and little hardships, which, after all, are nothing to speak of, I like this life. I am getting fitter and browner day by day. What are the privations? To live in the open? Surely not in the semi-tropical sunshine – just to march about under a broiling sun, carrying more weight than is comfortable and to wear always a tin hat! That, and the chafe of having rules and regulations. Here one takes life at its true value; wealth loses its significance and health becomes one's primary asset. Behind is the wealth of civilization, in front the nameless quality of war. Surely we who come back will do so with new standards and new ideals, and so the countless sacrifice will not have been in vain. And to those who don't return, what after all are ten, twenty, thirty, even forty years off a man's life viewed in the light of all eternity?

How strange it is to think that after all one is fighting for the freedom of one's enemies. All night long the guns boom out up the line not many miles away, and all night long train after train takes its load to the railheads. Death and destruction for the freedom of those to whom we are dealing it out!

Lieutenant George Brown, 9th The Suffolk Regiment

'Today's needs', as they say in St James' Street, 'a portable drinking cup, a tin of Eno's oil to keep flies off, and a fly strafer'.

The work here is naturally hard, but one gets whole afternoons and even days off, and then to the coast to bathe, and imagine that one is just here for a summer holiday. The other afternoon I spent on the dockside; it was a revelation and an education. Men from Fiji, China, Japan, Soudan, India, Burmah, New Zealand, Australia, Canada, Belgium,

England, Scotland, Ireland, Wales, USA, Portugal, and prisoners from Germany and Austria, French Colonials from Algiers – all working away as units in the mighty mechanism that can take a heavy gun from a ship and have it pouring shells into the German lines just a few hours after. Truly the British Nation is one of the wonders of the world. Another thing, fancy cakes and tarts for tea; excuse the bathos, but these letters are just impressions to serve me as reminders when Peace comes. One learns instinctively to use the capital P. It seems so distant and so sacred, the idea of Peace again.

Have you ever reflected on the fact that, despite the horrors of the war, it is at least a big thing? I mean to say – that in it one is brought face to face with realities. The follies, selfishness, luxury and general pettiness of the vile commercial sort of existence led by nine-tenths of the people of the world in peacetime are replaced in war by a savagery that is at least more honest and outspoken. Look at it this way: in peacetime one just lives one's own little life, engaged in trivialities, worrying about one's own comfort, about money matters, and all that sort of thing – just living for one's own self. What a sordid life it is! In war, on the other hand, even if you do get killed you only anticipate the inevitable by a few years in any case, and you have the satisfaction of knowing that you have 'pegged out' in the attempt to help your country. You have, in fact, realized an ideal, which, as far as I can see, you very rarely do in ordinary life. The reason is that ordinary life runs on a commercial and selfish basis; if you want to 'get on', as the saying is, you can't keep your hands clean.

Lieutenant Henry Jones, Machine Gun Corps (infantry)

Personally, I often rejoice that the war has come my way. It has made me realize what a petty thing life is. I think that the war has given to everyone a chance to 'get out of himself', as I might say. Of course, the other side of the picture is bound to occur to the imagination. But there! I have never been one to take the more melancholy point of view when there's a silver lining in the cloud.

Certainly, speaking for myself, I can say that I have never in all my life experienced such a wild exhilaration as on the commencement of a big stunt, like the last April one for example. The excitement for the last half hour or so before it is like nothing on earth. The only thing that compares with it is the few minutes before the start of a big school match. Well, cheer-oh!

A picture taken inside a dugout in reduced light: an officer having a meal.

There were men who undoubtedly enjoyed soldiering and, by extension, enjoyed war as a supreme test of their character; then there were those who simply enjoyed the thrill of extreme danger and of fighting. Lieutenant Jones, while seeking to reassure his family that he would accept death in the pursuance of a higher cause, also appeared to enjoy service at the front. Like others of his generation, he exulted in war as an act of self-purification. He was keen to pursue life stripped of its meanness and selfishness, stripped to its bare essentials of survival and comradeship, where ownership and property – base civilian pre-occupations – were immaterial. He was not the only officer facing the strong possibility of death to write in such a manner.

As Lieutenants George Brown and Henry Jones shared their feelings with loved ones, Lieutenant Harry Lawson, a 40-year-old headmaster of Buxton College in Derbyshire, was in teaching mode. He wished to disclose to his former pupils important lessons learnt past and present and, in this case, fusing the two in a letter, this time on the subject of duty, honesty, and 'playing the game', as Lawson himself was now doing. He had only been in France a matter of weeks and school was still very much in the forefront of his thoughts.

Lieutenant Harry
Lawson, 325th
Siege Battery,
Royal Garrison
Artillery

3 July, 1917

My Dear Boys

I wish I could be with you in person to say goodbye to you all, and to hand over my headmastership to my successor. Instead, I'm writing from a dugout, to the sound of guns, the sort of message I want you to have before term ends. But although I am in a dugout at the front, I am picturing myself as sitting in my study at the college in the midst of surroundings of busy boyhood. I see the war-potato field and the cricket pitch – the wickets casting a dark shadow in glaring contrast with the thin, white line of the block. Momentarily I think of the need of camouflage for concealing the position from the observation of hostile aircraft. Only for the moment, I'm back again in the study, and a bell, rather jaded and weary, has sounded the end of a period.

I've got one thing in particular to say to you all – just the main thing we've talked about together in its different bearings in the past – just the one important thing which keeps life sweet and clean and gives us peace of mind. It's a Christian thing, and it's a British thing. It's what the Bible teaches – it's what the Christian martyrs suffered in persecution for. It soon found root in England and began not only to fill the land, but also to spread abroad and become the heritage of the Empire. It's the story of the Crusaders, of the Reformation, of the downfall of the power of Spain, of our colonization, of the destruction of Napoleon's might, of the abolition of slavery, and of the coming awakening of Germany. The thing is this: Playing the game for the game's sake.

Now I've had many opportunities in years gone by of having a talk with you about this, and I've always found that we've got a clear starting-off point. For whether I have been talking to a boy alone, or to a class in its classroom, or to the school met together in the New Hall, I have found opinion quite clear and quite decided as to what the game is and what the game is not. We've had a sure foundation. And the difficulty for us all consists, not in knowing what the game is, but in trying to live up to the standard of life which our knowledge of the game puts before us. Don't think that I am referring to the breaking of school rules. I am not. School rules don't live forever, and, further, school rules suffer change. I am referring to deeper things than these, to rules which do live forever and which do not suffer change. I am thinking of high honesty of purpose and of the word duty.

I'm going to tell you a story of something that happened at the college in days, I think, not within the memory of any of you. I pick this story because it illustrates well what I have said about school rule and deeper rule.

On a certain school day afternoon in the Lent term some years ago, the Vth Form made a raid upon the IVth Form. The IVth barricaded themselves very securely in their own classroom by piling up desks and furniture against both doors. The raid was still in progress when I came along at half-past three to take the IVth in English.

I passed through the IIIrd, where there were evident symptoms of excitement, and came to the door of the IVth. The door wouldn't open. But my voice acting as a kind of 'Sesame', the barricade was quickly removed and I entered. The classroom was pandemonium, desks littering the place in wild confusion, and in particular concentrated against the door opposite to that through which I had entered. I held a court of enquiry – pronounced judgment – went to the study for my cane and dealt with the IVth Form ringleaders on the spot. This, mind you, for a breach of school rule. Desks are not designed to be used for splinter-proof dugouts. Now the enquiry showed clearly that though the IVth were guilty, they were not nearly so guilty as the Vth. So peace once more reigning in the IVth, I went along to the new hall to have a talk with the Vth. I told them what had happened – what punishment had been meted out to the IVth, and I said, 'You've got the IVth into a row and you are the guiltier party of the two. I have caned the principal culprits in the IVth, and I shall be in the study at five o'clock and shall be glad to cane there those of you who feel you ought to turn up.'

At five o'clock seven of them arrived and received their caning. Before they left I said to them, 'I'm very proud of you chaps, and I've got to thank you for the first caning I've ever enjoyed giving.'

They felt they ought to turn up. They did turn up. I need say no more. . . .

Lieutenant George Brown was yet to experience the rigours of trench life, but he was already anticipating his own emotional response to the trials ahead by watching and speculating about those who had already fought. How would they adjust to life back home in the fullness of time? It was hard to imagine that it would be a swift and easy transition.

One sees these English Tommies who probably never left their native village and to whom life was bounded by the village pastures, and thought by the chatter of the village pub; one can see these same men swaggering about perfectly at home in Continental towns; talking of London and Paris; sitting in cafés or estaminets hearing stories of the world from those who have been pioneers in strange lands, citizens of strange cities, and one wonders what will be the end, the great result! When Peace comes, how will these men, steeled by the horror of war, tempered by the close familiarity of death in its most gruesome form, whose minds have been broadened to an extent unrealized before, how will these men treat life in the village pub again? How many of those who have tasted the joys of free life and fresh air, who have dabbled in the great passions of the world, in love and lust, in hunger, thirst and war, 'where life means strife and strife means knife', how will they take it all again? Must not the very foundations of our social life be uprooted – our ideas shattered and rebuilt – I wonder.

Lieutenant George Brown, 9th The Suffolk Regiment

The answer was speculative. Nevertheless, there was enough evidence on the ground to suggest that when the war finally ground to a halt, reintegration would require more than a return to homes, a jobs market and the grateful words of a nation.

This man acts orderly corporal for our platoon and distributes letters, rations, papers, etc.; has been in the firing line during the spring advances and experienced their horror.

He told me of a horrible experience he had in the trenches. After a costly advance on the Thursday of 23 May (I think), near Fampoux, I expect a kind of brain fever had seized on him, a final overflow of bile from the dreadful sights he had encountered, mere fragments of men, limbs, heads, bodies, sundered and dead, lying in heaps, especially in a quarry near the village – a whole communication trench choked with his own comrades killed by shrapnel.

Speak to him of the trenches and he will burst out into bitter expressions of despair, as one with whom nightmare has been a living thing and a constant bedfellow. That is the great impression one gets of the man, that he has passed through a time of horror. It gleams in his

Private Hugh Quigley, 12th The Royal Scots (Lothian Regiment)

eyes, in his nervous manner of speech, the queer fits of pawky cynicism will come over him and inspire sharp utterances of uncomfortable truths about life. … He has been in the pit, breathed an atmosphere of decaying mortality until even the quiet delight of a holiday under the trees has not complete power to banish memory or bitter recollection. A soul arrested in its passage through darkness to light, dimly aware of past happiness and suffering still from the haunting miseries of death seen face to face. In quiet civilian life he won't be able to forget, and even when war is over and become a thing the mind willingly forgets and shrinks to remember, when everything of life will be concentrated on the arts of peace, he will remain a twofold being, not entirely at rest nor entirely reminiscent of war – something of both, not all of one.

Lieutenant George Brown, 9th The Suffolk Regiment

It would seem as though most of those who come over here have a dual personality, a dream-life and a real one. To some, the life of England is the dim and half-remembered dream; now lost, now flashing with startling vividness on the 'inner eye'; to them the war is the real life, and on the whole they are the happier, I think. To others, the life that lies behind is the real, while that of today is a dream, often a nightmare, but a dream from which we shall awake some day.

Many a time here I have found myself wondering if this or that is really happening, and if I were real. I feel as though my real self were sleeping in that England I love so much. …

What a pathetic picture a war cemetery is – just its rows of little crosses, some of stone, some of wood – most just bearing a name, and some that best epitaph of all, 'Here lies an English Soldier'. One wonders what motives moved the minds of those who lie so peacefully in this 'Norman countryside' to come here. To some perhaps death came as the great release, to others as the greatest sacrifice. Many came seeking glory and found it. And surely these must have found atonement, whatever their lives may have been.

The success at Messines did not obliterate the bitter feelings of failure at Arras, nor the bitter disappointment of the Somme, where expectations of decisive victory had once run high. Almost everyone longed for peace, but what would peace mean to those who came home? No one could be sure. Moreover, how would they be received by civilians who would be shocked at the coarseness of these men, men emotionally retarded and aggressive? Those who had fought debated about peace and how it might not work for the erstwhile soldier. Sixteen-year-old Private Thomas Hope, illegally serving under age, arrived in France in July and naturally he hung on every word of his war-gnarled comrades.

Two graves of officers belonging to the 1/4th Yorkshire Regiment, killed while holding the line after the Arras offensive ended in May.

Night, with the full moon shedding a soft light through the barn, the hooting of an owl outside, the rustling of leaves and the sound of restless cattle – these are the things we can appreciate while we puff contentedly at

Private Thomas Hope, 1/5th The King's (Liverpool Regiment)

our pipes and cigarettes as we argue far into the night. When will the war end? What will happen to us? Questions we can never agree on.

The first we can find no definite answer for; it is something only to be dreamed about, something that, deep down in our hearts, we doubt if we'll ever live to see. Nevertheless that does not prevent us from speculating and surmising on just what will happen to us when the miracle takes place. ...

'I'll tell you what will happen to you duration soldiers. You'll have the time of your lives, you'll be hugged and kissed, treated and petted, they'll have banners strung across the streets: "Welcome Home, Our Heroic Tommies", you'll be received with open arms, they'll let you mess on their doorstep and thank you for doing it, you'll be the heaven and earth and all that therein is for just one month, then some morning they'll wake up and realize the war is over, and that's when you fellows will have to start using your own toilet paper. You'll get the cold shoulder, as they'll have no more use for a penniless, out-of-work, fighting man who stinks of trench manners and speech. Hell, the very people who have fattened and prospered on your blood and sweat will be the first to denounce you; you'll be shunned like a lot of sewer rats.

'Ah, you can laugh, boys; you're little tin gods just now, but when it's all over you'll find you've not only had to fight the war but you'll have to fight the peace as well, and a damned sight harder too, if you're going to win through, so get it out of your thick heads that you're in for a cushy time, and put all that in your pipe and smoke it.'

As Webster proceeds to light his pipe, he waits with an amused twinkle in his eye for the storm of abuse he knows will follow his shattering of our dream, and he hasn't long to wait:

'Let's ram this sock in his mouth'; 'Smother him, somebody, he's too cheerful', 'Kick him, he's still breathing'. ...

When the noise subsides, Taffy attempts to carry on the argument. With his head to one side and his pointing index finger wagging away in tune with his ideas, it is evident he has given the subject some thought. ...

'It's useless trying to prophesy what will really happen when the war is over, boys. All I know is that there will be a couple of million men suddenly thrust back into civil life, many of who, war has stripped of their thin veneer of civilization, men accustomed to look on life cheaply, all of them coarsened in different degrees by the exacting life they have been forced to live. As in war, so it will be in peace, and anything might happen.

'Some of you, of course, have jobs to return to. For you, the war will merely have been an episode, but there are others like Mac, Duggan, Barham and a few more who had just started an apprenticeship. To them the war will have been more than an interruption; the most valuable years

Men of 215 Siege Battery, Royal Garrison Artillery, relaxing and chatting in a wood.

of their lives have been wasted here; they'll have to start all over again, handicapped by age. Then there are the babes, like Jock there.'

'Hold on, Taffy,' I interrupt.

'It's quite true, Jock, there are dozens like you out here, straight from school into this, men before you were youths, the only trade you know – that of killing. Yes, unless the old country can dig up a Solomon, peace is going to bring one glorious mess, an unequal fight against a public who will soon forget our sacrifices, and new generations who will know nothing of the war and what it meant to those who served.

That is what peace is going to mean for us, boys. It makes me wonder if those who return are going to be so fortunate as they think they will be.'

Driver Aubrey Smith was to find out at first-hand how hard the transition would be when, in July, he was given leave. It was only his second leave in two and a half years and it began with a tortuous three-day journey to England and the coast, arriving as German aircraft flew over the coast to deliver a severe daylight raid on London. 'From a blissful seaside holiday I had been transferred into the midst of war's alarms and, paradoxical though it seemed, the farther I got from the firing line the nearer came the sound of [anti-aircraft] guns.' Smith returned to his home in Kent and a new and different reality.

Driver Aubrey Smith, 1/5th (City of London) Battalion, London Rifle Brigade

A few days' leave from the front acted on one's spirits like a dose of Alpine air. Everyone at home seemed to possess such confidence in an early victory, such optimism in regard to even the most discouraging events, that after a few hours of their inspiring talk one was apt to become as cheerful and unreasoning as they.

The folk on the home front may have had doubters in their midst, but they were not much in evidence in London or Kent, at any rate. It seemed as if the majority had been served out with rose-coloured spectacles through which every cloud appeared a blue sky, every reverse as victory. To the cynic just returned from the Western Front that was at first rather riling (and nearly everyone was a cynic by now, at least if he had been in France a good time). The cynic knew that a fruitless attack by several divisions, relieved only by a small gain of ground at X, would be described as a 'successful attack at X', with scant reference to the remainder of the front. The optimist at home merely read in the communiqué that that had been a 'successful attack at X', put down his paper and beamed with delight.

Or the optimist might read: 'Our planes destroyed five enemy aeroplanes and forced ten to descent. Two of our machines are missing.' At which he would make a single calculation and joyfully exclaim that we were thirteen machines to the good on the day. The cynic had perhaps himself seen three of our machines brought down on the British side of the line, but he knew that as these were not 'missing' they were not included in the reckoning: in other words, he drew no conclusions from the official announcement, which was misleading. ...

A great deal of the ever-cheerful attitude was due in the manipulation of the war news by the ingenious press correspondents, who dwelt eternally on the slight losses incurred by our side and the appalling slaughter of the enemy: on the adroit success of every British trench raid and the complete failure of every German attempt; on the utter demoralization of the enemy when it existed in their own perverted imaginations.

But after I had been home a few days I came to the conclusion that it was better so. It was preferable to have a hopeful, cheerful populace than a world of weeping Jeremiahs: it enabled them to endure their privations with less grumbling and goodness knows they had enough to harass them, with their air raids, food queues and lighting restrictions. It was a good thing that the jaded warrior should return to find the folk at home still smiling: he preferred his friends to be happy than to see them depressed and glum.

Except for the occasional firing of anti-aircraft guns and the cruising of aeroplanes, the countryside surroundings were much the same as they had been in pre-war days. No army lorries passed the little Kentish lane where we lived; but for a few cyclists, billeted in the cottages around and enjoying years of training at home, you might have forgotten the existence of an army. Labourers worked in the fields, the baker came round with his bread as of yore, little children played with their tops and their skipping ropes. Was I not back in the summer of 1914, the victim of a hideous nightmare?

No! Several things told me I wasn't. In the first place, I could hardly frame a dozen sentences without wishing to introduce some word that would have offended the civilian ear. Conversation had not been such a

Leave: men on board a ship. The extent of their smiles indicates in which direction they are going.

strain in 1914! Then, again, it was rather a trial to attend a dinner party. The natural inclination was to reach out for whatever you wanted, take your plate onto your lap, peel potatoes with your hands and call out 'Chuck us the bread' to your hostess. In 1914 I fancy I behaved rather better than that. As a civilian I had been a law-abiding citizen, but now I noticed a tendency to cross railway lines contrary to regulations, to jump on the back of a milk cart without permission if it meant getting to my destination quicker, and to regard all the neighbouring fields and woods as public property if they looked tempting for a stroll. There was also an inclination to feast one's eyes on every pretty girl one saw, almost to the extent of being impolite.

I called at the office as usual, to find them getting on splendidly without me: profits were better with their staff of girls and overage men than they had been in pre-war days. This, as the manager said to me with a smile, was scarcely an incentive to the company to be impatient for the demobilization of its young men.

Aubrey Smith returned to France ten days after he had left, landing back at the port of his disembarkation in 1915. The reception had radically altered from first time around.

In the blazing heat I climbed up the steep hill to the leave camp at Boulogne with thousands of others as silent as myself. It was very different to the time when we had sung popular songs amidst a throng of onlookers at Rouen in January 1915. Even as far back as that, the cavalrymen had laughed when we had shouted, 'Are we downhearted?' 'But you ___ well soon will be,' they had replied. Now, nobody raised a cry, nobody sang, no crowd gathered to watch us; processions like ours passed to and fro every day and we were not particularly beautiful.

Driver Aubrey Smith, 1/5th (City of London) Battalion, London Rifle Brigade

When a grateful government is paying for a holiday abroad, it seems a pity not to see all that there is to be seen, and so I set out, and I was glad I did, for the humour of seeing English Tommies at home was worth it. Here and there one saw a woman, a child or an old, old man – but all the rest were English Tommies, gathering harvest, mending roads and doing the hundred and one jobs of everyday life in a country village – and enjoying it, too. At 4.00 pm we got the train (we, being my servant and I, for here they seem to consider that an officer is incapable of looking after himself if let loose alone – and where you go your servant goes too – I must say they are very useful). As we were not travelling by troop train, the train was only about five minutes late. Apparently, there is no shortage of paper in France, for my railway ticket is 1 foot wide and 2 feet long. At 4.30 we reached our first changing place, and having learned what to expect in the way of connections, I was not surprised to find that there was no train on to the next stop till noon tomorrow. I packed my servant off to the nearest camp, and had tea – a tea such as you can't get in England – as much bread as you want and hot fresh cakes. Thence to a concert, for here one is on the fringe of civilization. A meal, and here I am writing by candlelight in a commandeered French house.

I have, as I mentioned before, a servant, quite young and with a sense of humour – how great I have yet to find out, and until then must remain on my guard, lest worse befall. Yesterday he informed me that he had found

Lieutenant George Brown, 9th The Suffolk Regiment

a place for officers to have hot showers in (subtle words these), and so I ordered one. I was duly informed that one would be ready at 6.00 pm, and at six I arrived. My suspicions were aroused when I saw various men carrying pans of hot water into a green tank. I was shown into a room labelled 'Officers Only', where I undressed. I was then conducted to another similar room – did I say room? – a misnomer, a tin partition 8 feet by 4; across the top of this a ¾-inch pipe ran in the form of a Z. At one angle-piece I saw a disc exactly the size of a penny containing eight small holes. Considerable clattering not unlike a 'noise off' proceeded from the upper regions and a strange voice asked if I were ready. On my replying in the affirmative, very slowly and majestically five of the eight holes in the aforesaid penny emitted a slow trickle of water which scattered into drops about 6 inches below the point of discharge, a sixth hole dribbled at intervals, while the other two remained barren of watery offspring. This was my bath; with the greatest ease I stopped it with my thumb. But more was to come.

Finding the water too hot, I asked for cold to be turned on. Two more buckets were carted onto the roof, and a distinct fall in the temperature was obtained. Having stood there for twelve minutes, during which quite two pints fell, I dressed, first removing a large family of black insects which had spent the day trying to share my underclothes with me. On looking at these they turned their tails over their heads in a haughty manner.

Last night was one of heavy drifting rainclouds, and before going to bed I stood and watched that arc of fire that lies to the eastward, marking the scene of the conflicting forces of mankind. Impressive and awful, and yet without the terror that gunfire and shell bring, for here the noise was muffled to a low murmur, punctuated every now and then by the dull thud of a bursting shell that fell behind the lines. Arcs of vivid white crept slowly through the air – sudden flashes now green, now gold, and now an angry crimson, from star shell, Very light and gun, from bursting shell and burning farm. An awful yet a wonderful sight – war viewed from peace!

Haig's long-held desire to fight in the salient was now achievable and he gave operational control to his trusted commander, General Sir Hubert Gough, commanding Fifth Army. Detailed planning for the offensive in Flanders began just three days after Messines Ridge had been secured and while that offensive was still under way. For three years, the British had been held in an unforgiving stranglehold in the Ypres Salient. One hand had been removed by taking the high ground to the south; now the grip of the other could be loosened, vastly improving the tactical position for British and Empire troops. By pushing the Germans back over the series of low ridges that overlooked British-held ground, the offensive would help secure the Belgian coast while also threatening the enemy's key railhead of Roulers, a vital supply line to the region. Haig also hoped to continue the wearing-out process of the Germany Army, an objective that was encouraged by Intelligence reports suggesting low German morale.

German soldiers pause for the camera. In the Ypres Salient many farm buildings were turned into small concrete fortresses.

The offensive in the Ypres Salient was of an entirely different order and scale to Messines: no mines here with which to stupefy the enemy. The British could rely on overwhelming firepower. Some 3,000 heavy and light guns would be available to Gough and, crucially, shells manufactured to finer tolerances and therefore less likely to fail. Of course, the Germans could be expected to learn from their mistakes at Messines and lightly hold their front line trenches. Gone were the days of German profligacy when it came to expending soldiers' lives; saving manpower was critically important to the High Command.

The British had a transparent superiority in manpower, airpower and firepower. The Germans, anticipating the need for defence, constructed a remarkable fortress of concrete pillboxes, built with the best possible fields of fire but sited also to ensure that each position helped in the protection of the next. To help counteract the threat from these pillboxes, the British could use their aerial superiority to help direct artillery fire onto them. This accuracy would depend on detailed mapping of the ground through photographic reconnaissance and this was immediately undertaken. Supporting the infantry would be tanks. These fearsome machines had performed well at Messines in dry ground. However, with a high water table in the salient, dry ground would be crucial if they were to be used as successfully again, as the crews well knew.

Major William Watson, D Battalion, Heavy Branch Machine Gun Corps

The thought of tanks in the salient made those of us shiver a little who knew the country. The salient had swallowed up so many reputations and made so few. With water everywhere just below the surface, and a heavy preliminary bombardment, the ground would be almost impassable for tanks, and if it rained.... Surely, we felt, there could never have been a more hopeless enterprise! It was an ugly business. Yet I must confess that in the eager hustle and stir of our preparations we became almost confident; those who had never seen the salient made light of our fears; they would never send the tanks to the salient if they had not made sure. We allowed ourselves to be encouraged....

Over 200 tanks would be required for the offensive and these were brought up towards the line and then hidden from view. The crews too went under cover, although hiding was not as easy as it might have seemed at first.

In a laudable attempt at hiding our camp, though the whole salient was an open secret, we had pitched our tents among thick undergrowth and some saplings. Orders had been given that the undergrowth was not to be cleared, and life in consequence had its little difficulties. At first to walk about the camp at night was simply foolish, for, if you had the courage to leave your tent, you either plunged into a bush, collided with a tree, or tripped over tent ropes decently hidden in the vegetation. But man cannot live in a forest without itching to make some clearance – it is the instinct of the pioneer – and before we had been long in the copse I am afraid that one or two of the more tempting bushes had 'disappeared', paths had been trodden, and the inevitable 'temporary structures' raised on what to all outward appearance had recently been young trees. ...

Soon afterwards the crews and tanks were relocated. The first softening-up bombardment of the German lines was soon to begin.

At dusk we drove down to the ramp at Oosthoek Wood. The train backed in after dark. We brought off our tanks in great style, under the eye of the Brigade Commander, who was always present at these ceremonies. The enemy was not unkind. He threw over a few shells, but one only disturbed our operations by bursting on the farther side of the ramp and so frightening our company dog that we never saw her again.

There was no moon, and we found it difficult to drive our tanks into the wood without knocking down trees that made valuable cover. It was none too easy without lights, which we did not wish to use, to fasten the camouflage nets above the tanks onto the branches. The track of the tanks from the ramp to the wood was strewn with branches and straw.

That was on 11 July: the next twenty days were crammed full of preparations. Every morning the men marched down to the wood, wondering a little if the shelling during the night had done any damage – and Oosthoek Wood was shelled every night. Gradually the tanks were 'tuned' to the last note of perfection, the new Lewis guns were fired, and finally the tanks were taken out on a cloudy day to a field close by and the compasses adjusted. ... Names and numbers were painted. Experiments were made with the new and not very satisfactory form of 'unditching

Major William Watson, D Battalion, Heavy Branch Machine Gun Corps

Major William Watson, D Battalion, Heavy Branch Machine Gun Corps gear'. Supplies of water, petrol, and ammunition were taken on board. Everything that the crews could do was done. We were told soon after we had arrived in the salient that during the first stages of the great battle, D Battalion would remain in reserve. There was, in consequence, no need for us to make any elaborate reconnaissances of our own trench system, because by the time that we were likely to come into action it was probable that we should be beyond trenches and operating in the open country.

If a tank company is ordered to attack with the infantry on the first day of a battle, no reconnaissance can be too detailed and patient, for on the night before the attack a tank can do untold mischief. There are wires, light railways, emplacements, communication trenches, dugouts to be avoided, and a specific spot to be reached at a given time. Tanks unfortunately are

Members of a tank crew rest up in woodland. The cover of trees helped hide the presence of tanks from the enemy.

not allowed to roam wildly over the battlefield either before or during a battle. The route that a tank will take from the moment it starts to move up on the night before the battle to the moment it rallies after the battle is only a few yards wide. It is chosen after the most painstaking examination of aeroplane photographs and the daily reconnaissance of the enemy country. To our own front line the route is taped, and forward it should be taped – in the mind's eye of the tank commander.

We had only to reconnoitre the routes to the canal, and make a general study of the sector in which we might be engaged. Nothing, I suppose, sounds more elementary than to take a marked map and follow a tank route from a large wood to a canal which cannot be avoided. In practice there are not a few little difficulties. First, it is necessary to extricate the tanks from the wood without knocking down the trees, which may later be required to shelter others from aeroplanes. This requires care and skill. Then the tanks proceed along a cart track until the route crosses a main road by a camp, where it is necessary to swing sharply to avoid important wires and some huts. Beyond the main road we trek across a field or two until the track divides, and it is easy enough in the dark to bear to the right instead of to the left. Then there is a ditch to cross, with marshy banks – a good crossing in dry weather, but doubtful after rain – and we mark an alternative. We come to a light railway, and this under no circumstances must be damaged. We arrange for it to be 'ramped' carefully with sleepers, but it is just as well to carry a few spare sleepers in the tanks, because some heavy gunners live nearby. The track, which by this time is 2 feet deep in mud, again divides, and bearing to the right we find that an ammunition column has camped across it. So we suggest that tanks through horse lines at night may produce dire results, and a narrow passage is cleared. Another main road crossing and a bridge – we are doubtful about that bridge, and walk down the stream until we come to something more suitable to our weight. Along the route we look for woods, copses, or ruins, so that, if a tank breaks down, we may know the best cover for the night: you cannot afford to leave a tank lying about in the open, however skilfully you may camouflage it.

I shall never forget those hot arduous days when we tramped in the moist heat over all the possible routes, plunging, after it had rained, through sticky mud often up to our knees, setting up little signposts wherever it was possible to make a mistake.

In those days the German gunners gave us no peace. It was a magnificent duel between the two artilleries. The enemy knew, of course, that we were about to attack, and they determined that, if shells could spoil our preparations, our preparations should be spoiled.

Just as the tanks would drive in a straight controlled line towards the enemy, so the rate of advance would be even and controlled too. Messines had succeeded because everyone worked broadly at the same speed and the advance into the enemy trenches was as uniform as it was possible to achieve. It would be sensible to try to repeat the success with the infantry advancing behind a creeping barrage. The Germans would once again be demoralized by artillery and the troops would advance at a steady pace – 25 metres per minute – crossing the Germans' first and second lines with the artillery moving up in a matter of hours to resume the shelling. The advance would begin again as soon as possible towards the Passchendaele Ridge. It was ambitious but achievable, if the weather was good, impossible if it turned bad.

Lieutenant Edward Allfree, 111th Siege Battery, Royal Garrison Artillery

17 July: There was one continuous and unceasing whistle of our shells passing over the whole day. I counted 150 large shells pass almost immediately over the OP in five minutes; that is 1,800 in an hour. The same thing was going on all along this front, all day and every day for a fortnight before the attack! The expenditure of shells in connection with this operation must have been colossal. A certain number of Boche shells were bursting behind me. But the number coming our way was not to be compared with the number we were sending over.

My telephone wire got cut with shellfire, and I had to send the linesman out to repair it. It was some time before I could get through to the battery again. I then learnt that the battery was again being heavily shelled. The road on my way back was being shelled, so we had to make a bit of a detour to avoid it. I got back at 7.30 pm and found the shelling had ceased. But it began again just as we were sitting down to dinner, and we had to clear, and were kept from our dinner for two hours. We then returned to the mess and had dinner. I was hungry after my day at OP, with only light lunch and no tea. The shelling shortly started again, but we stayed in the mess, as we came to the conclusion that we were not the actual target. The shells were falling very near our sleeping huts, however, – too near to make our beds very enticing, so we all stayed in the mess till about 1.00 am. The gas alarm came through on the phone, and soon the gas got pretty thick, necessitating the wearing of gas masks. Cripps sent and warned the men, and gave orders that they were to wear their gas masks. This gas was rather mysterious, as we could not hear the familiar sound of gas shells bursting, and there was not a breath of wind to bring the 'cloud' of gas over from the Hun lines. We came to the conclusion that the Hun now puts gas into some of his high explosive shells, such as were bursting in the vicinity of our sleeping quarters. If so, this was new.

A member of 121 Siege Battery, RGA, stands in a larger than average shell hole.

19 July: We had been having rather a wearing time. The work had been hard – always firing the whole day and after a hard day's work on the guns, the men had to spend part of the night getting in ammunition, which always came up by night, and had to be unloaded. It was no light work humping 100 lb shells about; and the rest of the night they were probably prevented from sleeping owing to gas or shelling. ...

21 July: OP for me again today. I started at 6.30 am and arrived there at 7.10 am. The Major came down later in the day. We ranged the guns on one or two points, as the Major wanted to see how the guns were shooting. He was a remarkably good observation officer. In the battery he had come out with, he had been battery observation officer, and did all the observing for his battery. It was not usual now for one to do all the observing, but all junior officers of a battery took their turn. He was able to point out to me many features in the landscape I had not seen before. He could always see

what the map told him ought to be there! He looks at the map now and says:-

'Can you see General's Farm?'

I reply, 'No.' I had often looked for it, but could see no sign of it.

'Well, let's have a look now. It should be eleven degrees from the left-hand corner of Wood X.'

He looks through the periscope, and to my annoyance says:-

'Oh, yes, you can see it all right.'

I then look to where he directs me.

'No, I can't see any bally farm.'

'You can't be looking in the right place – do you see the wood?'

'Yes.'

'Well, count off eleven degrees to the left from the left-hand corner.'

'Yes, I've got exactly 11 degrees from the left-hand corner.'

'Well, you must see it there just this side of that slight mound.'

'I can see what looks like a couple of bricks on the ground.'

'Well of course, my dear fellow, that is the farm. You don't expect to see anything else but a few bricks on the ground after all this shelling, do you?'

'No, perhaps not, but I still should not like to be sure that is the farm; someone might just have kicked that brick there.'

'Well, we'll get Cripps to put a couple of rounds on that farm, and we will see where they fall. He can get the exact range from the map, and No. 1 gun, which we have just ranged, is shooting very accurately.'

So the battery is buzzed up, and No. 1 gun is got into action.

'No. 1 ready, Sir.'

'Fire No. 1'

An artillery battery near Langemarck with camouflage netting above.

'No. 1 fired, Sir' – from the telephonist.

'Look in.'

'There you are, dead line and just minus.'

'No. 1 repeat.'

'No. 1 fired, Sir.'

'Line and short plus. Is that good enough for you Allfree?'

Yes, I had to admit that was the farm.

22 July: It had been arranged that our battery was to take up a position in Boesinghe after the push, which was shortly to come off. And this afternoon I went with Cripps to put up boards to indicate the position, which had been allotted to us. This meant going down near our front line. On arriving at the spot, we had to climb out of the trench to plant the board. It was not a matter to linger over, as one was in full view of the Boche here. It was a broiling hot day, and we had to hurry, as this afternoon we were putting over a test barrage. We expected that the Boche would retaliate on our front and support lines, as soon as this started, and we were anxious to get our job finished and take cover in our OP, before the barrage began. We had just planted our board, and were hastening through Boesinghe, when a shell burst just short of us, followed immediately by another just

over us. So we had to make a dash along Boesinghe street to our OP. As a result of this hurrying and dashing I arrived very hot and very thirsty. Marshall was at the OP, and he gave me a drink from his water bottle.

We viewed the test barrage. It was, indeed, a wonderful sight – an absolute torrent of bursting shells along the whole line, with shrapnel bursting above. Then suddenly silence, and then down it came again a few

An unknown officer photographed by Colonel Perceval-Maxwell at 'C21 Hammond Corner'.

Opposite: Camp routine behind the lines: pay parade, drumhead service, fixing bayonets and the much anticipated arrival of mail.

hundred yards further on. It would have been absolutely impossible for any living being to exist in it.

We waited for a bit, but the Boche did not retaliate, and we then returned to the battery.

The dry weather that was urgently required came and then went, thunderstorms and very wet weather alternating with fine, hot weather. The infantry preparation was coming to a close and men prepared for battle, still uncertain as to when the day would be.

Private Sydney
Fuller, 8th
The Suffolk
Regiment

24 July: The Archbishop of York gave the 53rd Brigade an address or sermon, his 'text' being a part of the 20th verse of the 6th Chapter, 1st Epistle to Timothy, 'Keep that which is committed to your trust.' He said, 'You must all do your best in the coming operations, which may, if successful, bring about the end of the war in a short time.' His address was given from an old wagon, the brigade forming three sides of a hollow square in front of him. During the day, we tested the new message-carrying rockets. They were about 3 feet long, were made of steel, having a hollow 'stick' in which the message was carried. They had a 'Very' light or flare on the tail end, which ignited automatically when the rocket was fired, and a 'siren' whistle on the nose end which sounded when the rocket was in flight. They were fired from a grooved trough at an angle of 50 degrees for maximum range, which was about 1,800 yards. They were for us in action, for sending messages through heavy barrages, or in any cases where telephones or runners were useless. They had to be left for five minutes after being fired, before they were cool enough to be touched by hand. The first one we fired dropped short, very near a farmhouse which had a thatched roof. (Wind up!)

Second
Lieutenant
Thomas Floyd,
2/5th The
Lancashire
Fusiliers

25 July: Very wet. All preparations made for moving. Drummers, Pioneers, and all men who were not going into the line, moved to a Corps Reinforcement Camp, leaving the battalion at 3.00 pm. Our blankets were rolled and handed in. About 5.00 pm we received fresh orders – the move was cancelled. We therefore got back to billets again.

Just a line to let you know that I have received all your letters up to 20 July, and the parcel, for which I thank you very much. I have been simply awfully busy – chiefly with maps and operation orders re coming offensive – and have not been able to write home during the last few days as a result. We are supposed to be resting, but I have hardly a moment to spare. General Stockwell lectured all officers and NCOs of this battalion here in the field on Monday afternoon. He said that he was going to tell us everything that he knew himself about the coming battle, but did not tell us anything we did not already know! I do not think he told us all: if he did tell us all then I don't think much of the idea. The General had a cigarette in his mouth and his hands in his pockets the whole time he was speaking; he was quite jovial, cracking jokes all the time. He impressed upon us the importance of sending messages back when we reach our objectives; he said that if we do not do so, it will mean his coming up to the front line himself for information, 'and I don't want to have to do that,' he laughed, 'but it will come to that if necessary,' he went on in a more serious tone, 'and it will be woe betide the platoon commander whose negligence has brought his brigadier general's life into danger!' At the conclusion of his speech the General asked whether any of us had any questions to ask. I could have asked one, but I know he would not have answered it; so I remained silent!

27 July: The weather just now is glorious – too hot to move. Just by our tent is a military railway constantly carrying things and men up to the front line. The engines and trucks are quaint little things. They have a bell which sounds like the trams running from Blackpool to Bispham and beyond. One expects to see the sea when one hears the tinkle, but one merely sees … well! One sees life at the front; one hears the roar of the guns; and if one cares to lift one's eyes to the sky one sees copious observation balloons and aeroplanes. The day is very near now. This will probably be my last letter before going into action, so do not worry if you do not hear again for a week.

Cheer up. … All's well that end's well!

I took my turn at OP, and on other days acted as section commander on the guns, occasionally working out the targets for the guns, and finding 'the error of the day'. The error of the day always had to be ascertained several times during the day. This consisted of taking the calculations necessary to correct the effect of the weather, and climatic conditions on shooting. The temperature of the air, the temperature of the charge or cartridge, the state of the barometer and the strength and direction of the wind, all had an effect on the distance the shell would carry, or rather on the elevation to be given to the gun, to get a particular range; and the wind would also necessitate a correction for line. Every battery received what was known as a 'meteor message' six times in every twenty-four hours, which gave this information, including the strength and direction of the wind and the temperature of the air at varying heights. It, of course, depended on the range you were firing at, how high the shell would have to go, and you therefore wanted to know what the wind and temperature were like up there.

We were getting rid of an enormous number of rounds every day. Our targets were, for the most part, enemy trenches and wire entanglements. Sometimes an aeroplane would observe for us, reporting the fall of each round in its relation to the target, in code by wireless.

My dear old friend Marshall left us at this time, much to my regret. He was sent back with a nervous breakdown and neurasthenia, and got to Blighty with it. He had been clearly getting worse for some time, and I think the experience he had one evening 'put the lid on it'. I forget exactly where he had been, but the Major had sent him somewhere, and on his way back he had to meet a lorry load of our men to take them to some back billets, the way to which they did not know. On coming through Woesten by himself, the place was being heavily shelled, as it frequently was, and there, near the crossroads, he found a lorry which had just had a direct hit on it. It was in charge of only the two drivers, both of whom had been wounded, and one of them severely, and would undoubtedly bleed to death unless he received immediate attention, which the other appeared quite helpless to give.

Now, Marshall was one of those highly strung, sensitive, imaginative people, with a horror of blood and a dread of shelling (most of us had the

Lieutenant Edward Allfree, 111th Siege Battery, Royal Garrison Artillery

Overleaf: Scots Guards being issued with shovels before going up the line.

latter to a greater or lesser degree), and, as I have said, with his nerves already in a very bad state. He possessed, however, a stronger characteristic, and that was a keen sense of what he considered his duty and of what was right and wrong, and he never let his sense of fear prevent him from doing what he felt he ought to do. It only made his anguish keener and his task more difficult than it would have been for a fearless, unimaginative man. Marshall was therefore, to my mind, a truly brave man. A brave man is surely not one who knows not fear, but rather one who, though fearful, and with a lively sense of danger, yet acts nobly.

So with the shells still bursting near on the crossroads, with that horrid shattering roar, he gave directions to the other man, and together they bandaged the wounded, and got him on a passing lorry. He then took him to a Belgian dressing station, which, though some way off, was the nearest one, and after some persuasion, succeeded in getting them to take them in. He could speak French well, and was therefore able to make strong representations to those in charge. But they were very reluctant to accept the man, as he was English and not Belgian.

He then went back to the battery, arriving in a badly shaken condition, and almost in a state of nervous collapse, and reported to the Major what had happened, and that he was quite unable to take the men in the lorry to the billets. So Hartley was sent.

I am afraid his evening's performance was not properly appreciated by the Major, who was inclined to adopt rather the attitude that would cause him to give expression to such words as, 'What the Devil does he go tinkering about with wounded lorry drivers for, instead of doing the job I sent him to do?' Marshall himself said he felt a worm for allowing someone else to do his job. I thought he had acted quite rightly, and I tried to console him by telling him so.

That night it was Marshall's turn for duty in the map room, so I stayed with him. He was not at all in a fit state to be left on duty all night alone. We did in fact have a target come through on the phone that night; which I worked out, and got the guns in action.

The next day, Marshall was sent off to the CCS, feeling, as he said, that he was a rotter, and 'swinging the lead'. But there is no doubt that he really was in a very bad state.

Our packs arrived at 1.00 am, and we turned in until 8.30 am. The day was spent in preparing for the 'stint', which, we had been told, was to be 'the biggest of the war'. Not feeling very optimistic, I made my will on a small leaf provided for that purpose in the paybook. Saw several air scraps over the lines, towards evening. Orders were issued for us to move at 9.45 pm. Started off at 10.00 pm across country.... The track for our division was marked by small direction posts at intervals, and at short intervals were small iron rods, on top of which were small iron discs, painted white, with the divisional sign painted in black. The Battalion's Scouts had been posted at intervals along the track (they had been shown over the ground during the time we were back at rest) as a further precaution against our going astray in the darkness. Our guns, especially the 'heavies', were very active. So were the enemy's, and shells were flying all over the place, many being gas shells.

Private Sydney Fuller, 8th The Suffolk Regiment

The tanks had been fine tuned and prepared for action. On 27 July, they were renamed too. Gone was the opaque moniker, Heavy Branch Machine Gun Corps, and in came the Tank Corps.

After mess on the 30th, I strolled out with Cooper to the corner of the main road. It was dusk, and the coolness was sweet. We waited, and then battalion after battalion came swinging round the corner, where guides stood with lanterns. Some of the men were whistling, a few were singing, and some, thinking of the battle or their homes, had set faces. Soon it became too dark to distinguish one man from another, and I thought it as well. What did it matter if one man was singing and another brooding over the battle to come? They were shadowy figures, dark masses, just so many thousand infantrymen marching to the battle, just so many units to kill or be killed. One grave is the same as any other, and one infantryman should be the same as any other; for it is difficult to endure war, and at the same time to think of the fear, the love, the songs, the hope, the courage, the devices of the individual men who fight. There is nothing noble, glorious, or romantic in war, unless you forget the souls of the men....

The squealing mules with their clattering limbers plunged round the corner, and we returned to our tents. It was hard to sleep. In a few hours there was a momentary silence. Then right along the line an uneasy drone

Major William Watson, D Battalion, Tank Corps

broke the stillness – the weary tank crews had started their engines, and the barrage fell with a crash on the German trenches.

Lieutenant Edward Allfree, 111th Siege Battery, Royal Garrison Artillery

The infantry attack, for which we had been preparing for the last fortnight, comes off tomorrow. We have been given our programme for the part the battery is to play. 'Zero hour' (that is the time the infantry are to kick off, and which is kept secret till as late as possible) has been disclosed. The barrage opens at 3.30 am. All watches have been synchronized to the second. The Major and Hartley are working out the lines and elevations for our barrage targets, which will keep them employed till well into the night. I have to be up early, so go to bed early.

Private Sydney Fuller, 8th The Suffolk Regiment

Reached the ruins of Zillebeke about 12.30 am. A good deal of gas was in the air, smelling like mustard, but it did not appear to do much harm. We had some difficulty in finding our signalling apparatus, which had been brought up to the village by limber. Saw one of our tanks burning fiercely near the village, and behind some bushes, lighting up the ground for some distance around. Two other tanks could be seen nearby. We were led wrongly in the trenches, and were wandering around like lost sheep, amongst the mud and shells, until just before the barrage started, when we stumbled, more by luck than judgement, on a trench called 'Wellington Crescent', which was our proper position.

Everything was set and the troops were poised to advance. Last instructions were given and then everyone waited for the final furious bombardment before going over the top. It was raining again, a steady drizzle, enough to make the men waiting feel annoyingly damp. Waiting, too, were the men of 419 Field Company, Royal Engineers. That tense night of 30/31 July they were surprised to receive an instruction from the War Office. It was printed on three closely typewritten foolscap pages and it dealt with discipline in the army, emphasizing in particular the necessity for the men to properly salute their officers. This proper but untimely message, arriving just as the offensive was about to begin, had come hot on the heels of another much more incongruous note, which stated that owing to the shortage of fat, 'men were allowed to dip their bread on the bacon fat on one side only'. They had been warned.

Opposite:
Massed artillery opening up a final, furious bombardment of the German trenches.

52. 3RD BATTLE OF YPRES.
3.45 AM 31st JULY -17.
THE BOMBARDMENT AT ITS
ZENITH JUST BEFORE DAWN
PHOTO TAKEN SHOWING SKY LIT UP
BY FLASHES FROM THOUSANDS OF GUNS

It was still practically dark, and exactly at the appointed time all the batteries opened fire, hundreds of them – batteries of all sorts and sizes from 12-inch to 18-pounders. The darkness was at once dispelled by the flash of guns, and the stillness of early dawn was rent by the sudden roar. Anyone who has not seen a gun fired by night, I believe, has no idea of the brightness of the flash. It does not give one the idea of fire, but rather of an electric flash. The flash from one gun fired at night will light up the sky like a flash of lightning, and will be visible from miles away.

Lieutenant Edward Allfree, 111th Siege Battery, Royal Garrison Artillery

Overleaf page: *German soldiers looking pensive. The prolonged British bombardment drove many of the enemy to the verge of madness.*

6 Armageddon Calling

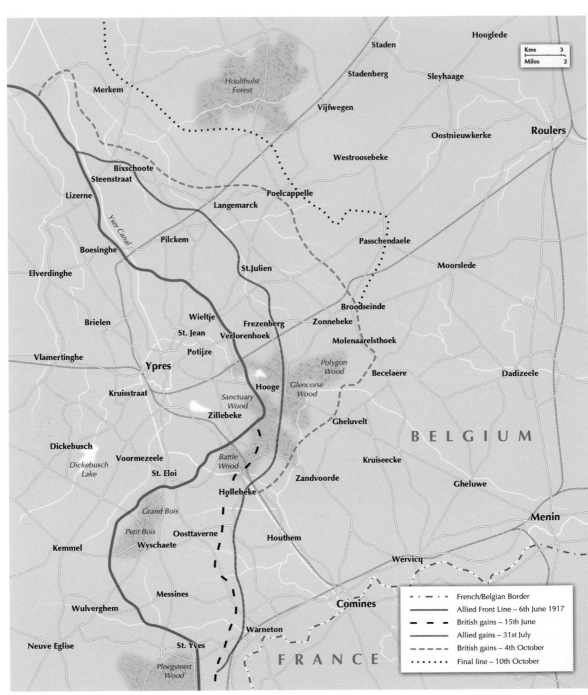

Battle of Third Ypres, 31 July–10 November.

'We could expect no help from the rear. The artillery wouldn't put down a barrage to save us – everything had been destroyed by the bombardment. The second line, the third line? Probably a few men still remained alive in them – a miserable handful who could give us no support, no covering fire from their machine guns.'

Leutnant Georg Bucher, Platoon Commander, German Infantry

————

Ever since the ferocious battle for Verdun, the German Army had been on the defensive in the West. Indeed, in trenches opposite the British, that state of affairs had existed since the Germans had tried and nearly succeeded in breaking through at Ypres in April and May 1915. The German strategy was to deal with their enemies on the Eastern Front, knock Russia out of the war first and **then** focus on the Western Front. Their defensive plan had been defined by this policy, and the desire to preserve their strength. With this at the forefront of their minds, they had created their fortifications: the deep and sophisticated trenches and dugouts on the Somme and, in the Ypres Salient and the Hindenburg Line, the inter-connecting and multitudinous concrete pillboxes. These defences gave the Germans a certain assurance: the Allied troops would require extraordinary pluck and guile to break through.

But prolonged 'back-foot' fighting required a very special form of defensive valour too. Morale could be undermined if soldiers stood in their trenches only waiting for the enemy to attack. It took self-possession and discipline to stand one's ground when under siege, for these men soaked up artillery bombardments that had the percussive power to drive them insensible as they were simultaneously suffocated by cordite fumes and gas. There they would wait to confront the inevitable assault delivered by soldiers whose aversion to killing was suppressed by severe combat stress and the desire for life. The following accounts from the German side, one by an infantryman, one by a gunner, give an impression of the frantic nature of defence just prior to the Third Battle of Ypres and on its opening day. These recollections are illustrated by images taken in the Ypres Salient by an unknown German infantry officer. They are believed to have been taken just prior to the offensive.

German troops cleaning their equipment prior to a move into the line.

Leutnant Georg Bucher, Platoon Commander, German Infantry

There were increasingly frequent indications that the enemy was preparing for an offensive. The days had become blazingly hot; and evil-smelling vapour rose from the mud as it dried and crumbled – the foul stench of decomposing bodies for the whereabouts of which we searched at night. We found them; but there was nothing we could do, for the dead in no-man's-land were buried beneath barely a foot of soil and the shells were continually uncovering them. Some of them were in rotting field grey, many in khaki.

During those sweltering July nights we sat together and exchanged opinions about the state of affairs in our immediate neighbourhood. Such scraps of news about the horrors of the Wytschaete sector as had filtered through to us were discussed ad nauseam. Burnau's hoarse voice was unforgettable: 'Thousands annihilated by mines in a single blow! Whole divisions! That isn't war – it's butchery! Butchery in the interests of the war-makers!'

From a hundred signs, a hundred noises that reached us through the night, we knew what the enemy meant to do in that Flanders sector. We became more alert and sent warnings to the rear – that was all we could do. In the meantime the Tommies remained suspiciously quiet.

One morning several long-range batteries became active, firing deliberately at the ground behind us. They felt their way with light-calibre stuff first of all, and then the heavies joined in. The result was that the cooks got the wind up and our ration parties had to tramp a mile and a half further. Nobody was very pleased about it.

Next day the English put up sausage balloons and kept our airmen well at a distance. There were always four or five of their planes at a time flying around, and our machines were chased back whenever they tried to attack the fat sausages.

We who were in the trenches felt very restless and chattered excitedly far into the night. Sonderbeck recalled, for no apparent reason, the Joffre patrol in 1914. How long ago that seemed! The years that had passed since then reminded us that we were getting older.

Riedel came in from duty; he had been in a sap where there was a listening post. He nodded as we looked up at him. 'There must be a few hundred lorries moving about yonder – you can hear them distinctly,' he said.

Many of us could hear much more than that – we knew what fate was preparing for us during those sweltering July nights. Before I turned in I stood with a sensation of bewilderment, looking over the parapet near the dugout. The Company Commander came by, nodded to me and passed on. The hair was snow-white on his temples – it didn't seem to go with Kranz's very soldierly bearing. I saw an undersized form approach him and stand to attention.

'NCO on duty – everything in order, Sir.'

It was little Sonderbeck, reporting that everything was in order. But was it? My eyes glanced up at the starlit sky. How beautiful it looked!

I listened intently to the confused rumble that came from the English lines. How disturbing it sounded, how threatening! And how sultry the night was!

I went into my shelter and lay down fully dressed on my waterproof sheet. That rumble yonder! It wouldn't let me sleep. . . .

I couldn't have slept very long. The ground shook and resounded – a fierce bombardment was raging over Flanders, over the sector where we lay. My runner had already lit the candle when Sonderbeck burst into the dugout – he was the NCO on duty. 'The big offensive has started!' he panted, his eyes rolling. I had never seen him in such a state of excitement. 'Already three men have been blown to bits,' he gasped, and hastily swallowed a mouthful of rum.

In a moment I was ready and hurried up the steps with him. There was an absolute downpour of earth and shell splinters – on every side the night was lit up by the explosions. Three of Sonderbeck's men were plastered on the walls of the trench or lying in fragments on the ground – the mess couldn't be cleared away while the bombardment lasted. I glanced at my wristwatch: it was time for Gaaten's spell of duty. I ran to his shelter. Armed figures were standing in the flickering candlelight, which gave their faces a strangely wild and threatening expression.

'Time to go on duty!'

Five men followed Gaaten and me out of the dugout, which, as things were, was the only place of safety. I wondered whether their hearts were beating as wildly as mine. Shells were exploding all about us. The five silently took up their positions – they could only trust to luck.

There was a terrific explosion somewhere in the direction from which we had just come – a hissing column of flame and earth rose up from the trench. Gaaten's dugout and the four men in it had ceased to exist – a 15-inch shell had landed directly over it.

'Missed it by half a minute, Georg!' Gaaten shouted, his face ashen. I shook his hand and hurried away to the Company Commander's dugout, where I arrived just in time to help carry Lieutenant Kranz down the steps. He was already dead – a big splinter stuck out from the rent in the crown of his head.

'I'm taking over the command of the company,' young Von Mall said in a choking voice. Kranz's servant was blubbering in the corner.

That 20-year-old subaltern was responsible for 160 men. I saw his calm, steady hand grasp the telephone – his body stiffened sharply as he heard the reply from the other end of the line. His boyish voice rang out as he reported: 'C.1 sector, fifth company …'

There was nothing for him to report to the battalion except our helplessness – the situation was beyond our control.

We spent the whole of 30 July moving up to the wagon lines, and that night, at 2.30 am, we went straight on to the gun line – in pouring rain and under continuous shellfire; along stony roads, over fallen trees, shell holes, dead horses; through the heavy clay of the sodden fields, over torn-up hills, through valleys furrowed with trenches and craters. Sometimes it was as light as day, sometimes pitch-dark. Thus we arrived in the line.

Our battery is the farthest forward, close behind the infantry, so that we can see the English position on the left. Our position is a perfectly level spot in the orchard of a peasant's ruined farm. In the square of trees, on each side of the road which runs through the middle, stand two houses. One is a mere blackened heap of bricks; the other has three shattered red walls still standing. The whole place is in the middle of arable fields reduced to a sea of mud, churned up to a depth of 15 feet or more by the daily barrage of the English 6, 8 and 11-inch shells, one crater touching another! Nothing can be seen far and wide but water and mud. From this position, the hill gradually rises to the front line.

In order to have some cover our two guns stand under a tree to which extra green boughs have been added. We can't have a proper dugout because the ground is so soft and wet, only a sort of rather superior wooden hut, covered with tarred felt, sand and leafy branches, so that when it rains, as it generally does, we simply have to lie in the water.

Then the work began, for there has to be something behind the trails to prevent the gun from running back too far, so we had to dig, bale out

Gerhard Gurtler, German Field Artillery

A smashed house, probably in the village of Wytschaete.

Opposite: German artillery shells in their distinctive wicker covers.

water, and drag tree trunks into position. That went on all day and all the next night.

Towards the afternoon the fire increased noticeably until it developed into a regular barrage. And then came what is the worst thing of all in our life here – the lugging of shells. In themselves the baskets aren't particularly heavy – 70 to 80 lbs – but when you have 100, 150 or 200 of them, it's no joke. The ammunition columns usually arrive at night so that one had to be as quick as possible, because of the English fire and one's anxiety about the horses, and what with the darkness and the slippery ground, it isn't easy.

By midday the communication trenches were impassable. The bombardment raged with undiminished intensity. We reported to Von Mall: twenty-seven dead so far, all mutilated horribly; there were very few wounded.

By the evening the parapets had disappeared. We reported to Von Mall: forty-one dead, all blown to shreds – we shuddered to look at them.

Leutnant Georg Bucher, Platoon Commander, German Infantry

Waiting for the enemy's next move: throughout 1917, German soldiers fought on the defensive, which required its own brand of courage and comradeship.

All through the night the soil of Flanders was lacerated by most furious shellfire. In the morning we reported to Von Mall: fifty-nine dead, all unrecognizable. More than twenty severely wounded men were lying in the dugouts. The company's stock of iron rations was divided among us – we snatched at it and devoured it greedily.

At midday, when I was about to take my report to Von Mall, the ground heaved and rocked: somewhere close at hand hundredweights of explosive must have penetrated. I staggered out of my shelter and worked my way along the ruins of the trench while shell splinters hummed around me. Where the Company Commander's dugout had once been, twelve steps deep and reinforced with balks of timber, was

now a huge smoking crater not less than 10 yards in diameter. What had caused the explosion I didn't know – it must have been a shell the size of a small balloon. There was nothing to be seen in it but wreckage and a little blood-soaked earth. Young Von Mall had been no coward, I said to myself as I stood before his open grave, wherein no trace of him was to be seen or found.

'I'm in command of the company now,' said Bart, who had been second in command. I remembered him at Lorette – a cool customer in a scrap. Bart was wiser than his predecessor: he didn't inquire how many were dead, but was concerned only with the number of the living. That number became smaller and smaller. We were as cut off from the rear as if we had been a colony of lepers. How could a message have got through to us? It was as if we lived in a different world, in the abyss of death, where there were no longer telephones, signals and runners – only shells, gas, blood, agony, and death.

Nothing is so trying as a continuous, terrific barrage such as we experienced in this battle, especially the intense English fire during my second night at the front – dragging shells and dragging shells, and then the actual artillery duel in the rain and filth.

Gerhard Gurtler, German Field Artillery

Darkness alternates with light as bright as day. The earth trembles and shakes like a jelly. Flares illumine the darkness with their white, yellow, green and red lights and cause the tall stumps of the poplars to throw weird shadows. And we crouch between mountains of ammunition (some of us up to our knees in water) and fire and fire, while all around us shells upon shells plunge into the mire, shatter our emplacement, root up trees, flatten the house behind us to the level of the ground, and scatter wet dirt all over us so that we look as if we had come out of a mud bath. We sweat like stokers on a ship; the barrel is red-hot; the cases are still burning hot when we take them out of the breech; and still the one and only order is, 'Fire! Fire! Fire!' – until one is quite dazed.

And now came the most dangerous time for me. It was just getting dark when suddenly our bolt jammed: 'Gurtler, you must go to the other section and fetch the battery-artificer' [a skilled technician responsible for gun repairs]. Through the darkness, through the enemy barrage of 6

Gerhard Gurtler, German Field Artillery: 'The whole place is in the middle of arable fields reduced to a sea of mud, churned up … by the daily barrage of the English 6, 8 and 11-inch shells.'

[and] 8-inch shells, to No. 2 Section. I leapt from shell hole to shell hole while fresh shells fell to right and left of me, in front and behind. The nearest one burst only 3 yards away, but I escaped the splinters as I was lying deep in the mud of a crater. The mud I naturally did not escape! Thus I proceeded for half an hour into the void – not knowing the way, not knowing the position, but only the direction. In one crater I found a wounded infantryman, and crouched beside him for quite half an hour. It is not pleasant to await the arrival of an 8-inch in the slimy yellow water of a shell hole! Will it get you, or will it not?

Then on again. Sometimes I thought I should get stuck. Once when I dragged my foot out of the mud, my thigh boot remained behind! At last, I reached the battery, delivered my message, and then came the journey back! And once more the bringing up of fresh ammunition, hauling shells, making up and collecting cartridges, removing empty cases, until the artificer arrived and we could go on firing till the end of the English attack. Then the gun emplacement had to be cleaned up and aeroplane camouflage procured – that is to say, grass mown and branches cut.

The third night had come. The enemy gunners were still working furiously, turning the shattered ground into an indescribable wilderness of shell holes.

The ashen faces of the youngsters who crouched in the dugouts were distorted with terror. Their lips asked hopelessly for bread, for iron rations, for water – I would have conjured it from the clouds for them if I could. Eight men had tried to get through to the second line in order to bring food back; not one of them returned – they must have been killed.

We laid the remains of our eighty-four dead in the huge crater – I had known every one of them. Not for a moment did the shells leave them alone – they were tossed up, flung about and blown to pieces.

It was going to be like Lorette over again – I recognized the signs, the inflamed, blinking eyes, the trembling lips; the shrill, overwrought voices. The worst of it was that there were badly wounded men in nearly every dugout – the sight of them in their agony was almost unbearable. My dugout had been wrecked while I was with Bart, and I quartered myself with my friends in turn. Gaaten shared Sonderbeck's shelter.

Leutnant Georg Bucher, Platoon Commander, German Infantry

Riedel and I were very anxious about Burnau, who already gave every indication that as soon as the terror of being in a dugout got hold of him we might expect a typical outbreak of madness; Riedel kept some leather straps close at hand as a precaution. I did whatever I could to make things easier for Burnau. I took his place for a spell of sentry duty; within a minute of my going up into the open air he followed me and clung to my shoulder. 'Let's die together, Georg,' he stammered. I saw how his lips trembled, saw that he was completely unnerved and demoralized. I needed all my strength to remain calm, to keep the mastery of myself, of a body famished and thirsty, exhausted and miserable, exasperated and

buffeted. We stood like two helmeted heroes of old times, my arm resting on Burnau's shoulder while annihilation raged around us. So Riedel found us – he used to creep out of his hole every five minutes to keep an eye on Burnau.

The hours went by. We had almost ceased to speak to one another, but the slightest word seemed to give Burnau the courage to hold on. 'I'm not a coward, Georg, but …' I understood: another day and then another … yet Burnau would hold out. I would compel him, would beseech him, would give him all I had to give. …

At midnight there was a direct hit on our ammunition store – the effects of that shell were indescribable. Towards morning one of the youngsters got up and left our dugout; Riedel, Burnau, three others and myself averted our faces, but a shudder went through us. The youngster stood for a couple of minutes at the top of the dugout steps, threatening us with two grenades from which the safety pins had been withdrawn, and telling us what he thought about the war – words so impressive and affecting that I couldn't have raised my pistol to protect myself. That youngster was going to climb out of the almost flattened trench and run with a crazy smile to meet his death before the enemy's lines. He had told us where he meant to go to the English. To attempt to stop him was out of the question – someone would have been badly damaged – but perhaps I ought to have tried.

We crouched side by side in the dugout. I wondered what the others were thinking. 'There was nothing to be done, Georg – he would have blown us to bits with the hand grenades,' Riedel said hoarsely. 'Our last candle' – he pointed with a dirty, trembling finger at the wretched light that shone unsteadily upon our misery and helplessness. Perhaps our lives were to flicker out like that candle. It would have been all the same to us if only there could have been some end to that incredibly furious bombardment – an end, any end – or I should soon have become a maniac.

'Georg!'

I jumped up at Gaaten's resounding cry. He rushed down into the dugout, blood running from his mouth.

'You're hit!' I cried hoarsely.

He burst into wild laughter, spitting blood and fragments of tooth.

'Nothing – a tiny splinter! But outside …' he hesitated and then broke into horrible curses. The signs were so unmistakable that Riedel quickly grasped his arm and held it like a vice. Gaaten broke free from him with a wild cry.

'Keep your hands off me!' he shouted fiercely, and gripped his trench dagger. 'Sonderbeck is finished,' he added in a choking voice. 'Left leg off nearly to the stomach – he's asking for you …' Gaaten's voice sank to murmured curses. We rushed after him out of the dugout. For us at the moment drumfire didn't exist.

We found Sonderbeck to the right of the huge crater. Blood was streaming from him. He did not shriek – but his hands were clutching a ghastly fragment of himself, his severed leg, which still wore a wide-shafted talisman boot. It lay across him – he held it to him as a mother might hold her child.

*A large bell taken
from Wytschaete
Church and used
as a gas gong
in the German
trenches.*

A shell landed close by and covered us with dirt, but I scarcely noticed it as I knelt by Sonderbeck. He recognized me in spite of his agony.

'My leg, Georg, my leg, my leg!'

Riedel knelt down beside me. 'Kurt ... mate,' he said hoarsely. Sonderbeck turned to him his deathly pale, distorted face: 'My leg, Riedel ... O God!'

I couldn't bear to look at the dead limb in his arms – I tried to take it away from him, but he held on to it so fiercely and moaned so imploringly that Riedel pulled me away. 'Leave him alone, God damn you!' he shouted.

Burnau had taken Sonderbeck's head in his lap. We cared nothing for the drumfire, for our comrade was lying there, bleeding to death – I saw that nothing could save him – he would bleed to death, for there were no stretcher-bearers and no suitable bandages. None the less, we used our carefully hoarded field dressings – we had to do all we could for him; I would have snatched handfuls of clay and plastered it on the wound if that could have held back the blood. Our efforts to stem the flow were in vain. Fate was against us.

Suddenly the fire lifted from our trench – the enemy guns had lengthened their range. Zero hour had come. Had my father or my mother lain bleeding to death in that trench I should have done what I did do, what Riedel, Gaaten and Burnau did: I jumped up with a shout, helped to drag open boxes of hand grenades up from the dugouts and ran around the trench bellowing orders.

There were only forty of us left. We stood waiting in the devastated trench, our strained eyes peering from beneath our steel helmets. We had nothing but our rifles and hand grenades – the machine guns had all been smashed – nothing but rifles and hand grenades!

Gerhard Gurtler, German Field Artillery

Half the morning had already passed, and now came the sequel which follows every battle: a long file of laden stretcher-bearers wanting to get to the chief dressing station; large and small parties of slightly wounded with their field service dressings – some crying and groaning so that the sound rings in one's ears all day and takes away one's appetite, others dumb and apathetic, trudging silently along the soft, muddy road in their low, heavy boots, which look like nothing but lumps of mud; others again quite cheery, knowing that they are in for a fairly long rest: 'For at home, for at home, we shall meet our friends again!'

Their thoughts wander back into their past lives like stray birds that do not know their way. Some figure appears before their mind's eye: perhaps a little old mother, holding a tattered letter close before her eyes – a fresh young girl stroking the narrow gold ring on her finger – a boisterous small boy 'presenting arms' with a stick.

And those men who are still in the front line hear nothing but the drumfire, the groaning of wounded comrades, the screaming of fallen horses, the wild beating of their own hearts, hour after hour, night after night. Even during the short respite granted them, their exhausted brains are haunted in the weird stillness by recollections of unlimited suffering. They have no way of escape, nothing is left them but ghastly memories and resigned expectation. . . .

My gun is the only one which has had no casualties. 'Haven't you got a bullet for me, Comrades?' cried a corporal who had one leg torn off and one arm shattered by a shell – and we could do nothing for him. Of us new ones from Juterbog, two have already been killed – a one-year man and a bombardier – not to mention sick and wounded. And we have no news of the other batteries, all communication being cut off.

We could expect no help from the rear. The artillery wouldn't put down a barrage to save us – everything had been destroyed by the bombardment. The second line, the third line? Probably a few men still remained alive in them – a miserable handful who could give us no support, no covering fire from their machine guns. We were cut off and alone, isolated in the trench where we gasped and cursed and shouted. We forty had been shelled without respite for three days and three nights, demoralized inch by inch, tortured by hunger and thirst, driven crazy by seeing men blown into shreds of flesh or bleeding to death in agony. Surely there was nothing more in the world that we could have suffered, nothing that could have been added to what we had endured. The enemy advanced carelessly towards us in groups followed by packed waves. Evidently they thought we were all dead. They were less than a hundred yards away.

Leutnant Georg Bucher, Platoon Commander, German Infantry

We fired about three clips of cartridges – within a minute we forty, firing at that beautifully compact target, had accounted for more of the enemy than the number of our casualties during the three-day bombardment, for the Tommies hadn't expected to meet with any resistance. No longer were they wandering carelessly towards us – their advance had become a wild rush.

'Hand grenades!'

We hurled them furiously at the advancing foe – then we snatched up as many as we could hold and made for the waste of shell holes behind us, hurling grenades as we ran. The enemy followed us, tumbling into the abandoned trench where little Sonderbeck was dying.

Few of us fell, for our running forms were difficult targets. The garrison of the second line were blazing away with machine guns and rifles. They

A German Maxim MG08 machine gun with a belt of 250 rounds ready to repel any onslaught. The gun had a fearsome reputation and could fire seven rounds a second.

left a lane open for us and we joined in the defence of their position. But all in vain – the groups and waves still advanced, becoming thinner and thinner, though fresh waves pressed on from behind. For a little while we fired with deadly effect into the advancing mass; then we and the garrison of the second line took to our heels and ran back to the last line of defence between us and our smashed-up artillery positions.

Joining the men in the third line, we turned on the enemy, firing our rifles and hurling hand grenades. Then we resumed our flight, a miserable remnant of 200 or 300 men, followed by thousands of khaki figures. The enemy barrage was falling far to our rear.

Our retreat was no uncontrolled panic. Again and again a thin chain of us dropped into shell holes and lashed the khaki horde with our bullets, fired a few rounds and then retreated. Not every man rejoined the flight, for the enemy could shoot, too. Those who fell were left where they fell, although they shrieked for help. We couldn't help them – we had no choice, for behind us were murderous bayonets, hand grenades, rifle butts, spades.

Along the mile-wide front of the attack we were in retreat. Nowhere did I see a division preparing to counter-attack – there was nothing but breathless flight with the slender chain of rearguards. We felt no shame in this mass retreat – it was, rather, an episode which offered us salvation after three nights and days of shellfire and horror, an opportunity for escape from the zone of terror. We had almost a sensation of being victorious when, as the rearguard, we dropped into a shell hole and shot down men in khaki and flat helmets – it seemed to put new strength into my weary body when I saw one of them fall. A bunch of them rushed at us. Riedel threw his last hand grenade, which exploded just as it touched one of their bodies. Four of them instantly crumpled up; our five rifles barked – three more of them lay twitching on the ground.

Then, shouting wildly, we rushed to join the retreat. We were intoxicated with blood.

We ran past a smashed-up battery – the smoke-blackened gunners joined us. Away away! That was all that mattered!

We reached a ruined village – white-faced cooks were trying to mount horses which were kicking out in all directions. They left the horses to

Right and
opposite: *A
smashed wood
in the salient.
While the trees
have been shorn
of their branches,
the foliage still
appears dense.*

go to the devil and joined us. Away – away! The roads were choked with crowds in utter confusion trying to get away. Batteries galloped across the open fields – infantry, pioneers, brass hats, signallers, wounded, all mingled. Away!

Enemy aeroplanes reaped a horrible harvest, mowing down men and animals by the hundred. Those who escaped continued the flight, while German Fokkers swooped down from the clouds to take vengeance on the English fliers. In the middle of a village which had been shot to bits stretcher-bearers were loading wagons with the severely wounded. They glanced at us with weary eyes and then at their doctor, an old grey-headed man who bandaged and bandaged unceasingly; he did it calmly and professionally. The shattered leg which he was tying up seemed to

interest him far more than our flight. He remained at his post – so did his assistants. In a few minutes the Tommies would arrive – but he remained, bandaging, giving morphia, as he would continue to do during the first hours and days of his captivity. The greatness of that non-combatant restored me to sanity. A feeling of shame came over me – my brain began to function with hateful clearness.

We had been running for nearly 2 miles and were almost exhausted. The next half mile was littered with corpses, the harvest of the English aeroplanes. But with this horror discipline returned – our orders began to be obeyed, men clustered around us and proceeded to put themselves into a state of defence on the outskirts of a village. We were all infantry – the other branches of the army continued in full flight – and we stuck where we were. It was the turning point, at least for me.

I found Riedel, Burnau and Gaaten not far off – their hunted eyes were ablaze as they shouted hoarsely for ammunition. From somewhere on our right packages of cartridges were flung across to us – someone had found a boxful. We snapped open our rifle – magazines, pressed into them clips of cartridges and scattered the rest within reach behind a low, tumbledown garden wall. Our rifles took aim at the advancing foe.

There were dozens of us firing, unhurriedly, for ammunition was scarce and every shot had to tell. 'That's for Sonderbeck!' Riedel growled through his teeth as he knocked a Tommy over. Gaaten too was taking vengeance. We killed and killed, spurred by the memory of a dead friend, conscious that in a few seconds we too might meet death by bullet, bayonet or rifle butt. There were some sixty of us in that group, all shooting and killing. The Tommies were falling fast, but more and more came on, drawing ever nearer until they were only 30 yards away. In their excitement their hand grenades fell short of us.

'Run for it?' Gaaten asked coolly.

My muzzle moved towards a Tommy on my right. 'Not I!' I hissed.

Riedel hastily reloaded and took aim. 'Nor I,' he said – his voice was as hard and dry as the crack of his rifle as he blew out a Tommy's brains. Burnau said nothing, but he was shooting, shooting – as we all were.

The Tommies were working forward – their hand grenades were actually coming over the garden wall. Then I saw the khaki mass hesitate, turn and stampede away from us.

A trembling hand pointed to the right. There a compact mass of our men, advancing across an open field, overwhelmed the attacking waves and took them prisoners. From the left, too, men from our division were moving forward.

'The "old man" is leading them!' Riedel bellowed, flinging his rifle away and unbuckling his spade from his belt. Yes, it was the Colonel, leading in

Opposite:
Putting a brave face on matters: these men were living under extraordinary pressure.

person the assembled remnants of his men. How he ran and shouted and waved! We jumped up – when our 'old man' led us we would follow him into the mouth of hell.

Forward we went, bellowing, swinging our rifle butts and spades. Everything in khaki was struck down – we killed as we ran – retaking the ground as far as the old artillery positions.

More than that was impossible – a belt of country 1½ miles deep remained in the hands of the enemy and we should have to fight desperately if we were not to be flung back by a new attack. Once before we had fought with a like bitterness and ferocity. That had been at Lorette; there the French foe had been in vastly greater numbers, but had not possessed the furious, superhuman courage of those English Tommies, whose bravery compelled my admiration.

We dug in with all speed beside the gun pits. Our 'old man' had relieved us of the necessity and the responsibility of making our own decisions: now he could do much more for us from the rear than if he were with us in person – he would be able, as always, to send help to us if we were at our last gasp.

The panic behind us was over. Hastily collected reserve batteries, put into the gaps in our line, replied vigorously to the enemy's vastly superior gun power. The broken threads of the staff were joined together. The front held firm. All through the evening and the night shells screeched over us but our front remained unbroken. We gorged ourselves with bully beef, drank brandy flavoured tea from khaki water bottles, smoked *Gold Flake* cigarettes and examined our new English ankle boots. Their former owners lay dead.

Gerhard Gurtler, German Field Artillery

The battlefield is really nothing but one vast cemetery. Besides shell holes, groups of shattered trees and smashed-up farms, one sees little white crosses scattered all over the ground – in front of us, behind us, to right and left. 'Here lies a brave Englishman' or 'Bombardier – 6.52'. They lie thus, side by side, friend beside friend, foe beside foe. In the newspapers you read: 'Peacefully they rest on the spot where they have bled and suffered; where they have striven; under the eyes of the dear comrades with whom they marched to war; while the guns roar over their graves, taking vengeance for their heroic death, day after day, night after night.' And it doesn't occur to anybody that the enemy is also firing; that the shells plunge into the hero's grave; that his bones are mingled with the filth which they scatter to the four winds; and that after a few weeks the morass closes over the last resting place of the dead soldier, and only a little crooked, white cross marks the spot where once he lay …

Gerhard Gurtler was killed on 14 August.

Overleaf: *A limber belonging to the 1st Scots Guards stuck in the Ypres mud.*

7 Blood and Mud

'Never shall I forget the sight which greeted my eyes when the battalion was eventually relieved. I looked around and began to laugh, one of those crazy moments when one laughs at tragedy, for it was not men I was looking at but mud figures. Not a button could be seen on a tunic, in fact a tunic could not be seen either, the only particle on any man which had not a thick coating of light-brownish mud was the actual eyeballs, even the faces were coated.'

Anonymous, 31 July 1917

———

On balance, the first day of the offensive had been a success for British troops. Yet there had been no emphatic advance as seen during the year's other 'first days' at Arras and Messines. There were early, encouraging signs. Within thirty minutes of the men going over the top, German prisoners could be seen in the half-light of dawn streaming into British lines, while many more, their compatriots, could be seen heading the other way in flight. The British guns had hammered German artillery, whose spirited, albeit patchy, response was remarkable, given the accuracy of the British counter-battery fire. North of the Menin Road, troops surged over the ground, in some places beyond the furthest avowed objective. Success was not, however, consistent. Immediately south of the Menin Road, it was much more limited. In places, the second but not the third enemy line was breached, and where the ground proved more treacherous, the gains were negligible and, in places, not even the first enemy line was tenable.

In the afternoon, drizzle turned into pouring rain and British casualties increased as they met with stiffer resistance. The Germans had learnt to keep troops in immediate reserve and not to overload the front line with men. As the day wore on, the concerted advance broke up into localized fighting. The poor conditions made signalling difficult and telephone cables were repeatedly cut. Even visual communication between neighbouring units proved impossible

Opposite:
The battlefield
immediately after
the advance
on 31 July. For
much of the
next two weeks
the rain severely
hampered
operations.

A German soldier, possibly of 240th IRR, is found wounded by men of the 8th East Surrey Regiment, three days into the offensive.

at times. Further back, attempts at consolidating the ground taken – extending communications, mending roads, constructing tracks and establishing dumps – was hindered by accurate enemy shellfire and an increasingly quagmire battlefield.

The tanks had mixed success: some did sterling work, but many arrived late to their starting line or became hopelessly stuck. Those tanks that did well had relied in some measure on luck, as where ground conditions were dryer, they were able to keep broadly on track, trundling forward at a slow, steady pace. Two-thirds of those deployed were eventually bogged down and many were gradually destroyed as they floundered.

The weather and stubborn German resistance had compromised the day's early promise. Nevertheless, important ground on the left flank of the attack had been won. The issue was: could the offensive be maintained with rain coming down in torrents? It seemed unlikely.

Major William Watson, D Battalion, Tank Corps

It began to rain, and it rained until 6 August, and then it rained again. We, who were in Corps Reserve, had nothing to do except to wait restlessly in our camp – we might receive orders to move up at any moment, if the enemy line gave any indication of breaking; but, although on our corps front we had successfully reached our first objectives, and the

Tanks stuck or knocked out in the mud close to the Menin Road, 31 July.

Pilkem Ridge, from which we had been driven by gas in April '15, was once more in our hands, the German defence remained intact. It was clear that the enemy, who, like us, had made every possible preparation, must once again be thrown back by sheer force. And the continual downpour made the task day by day more difficult. The more it rained, the more necessary a prolonged preliminary bombardment became, and a lengthy bombardment made the ground increasingly unsuitable for the use of infantry and tanks. It was an altogether vicious circle.

We had very great trouble with the guns, owing to the difficulty in pulling out when switching onto a fresh line, or when the top traverse on the guns became exhausted. This was caused through the ground being wet, and the soil very clayey. The trails, after firing a number of rounds, would become very deeply buried, necessitating much digging with pick and shovel and strenuous heaving to get them out – thus some time was unavoidably lost, and the full allotment of rounds on each target could not always be got off in the time. The fact that the guns had been placed in dugout pits was, to a large extent, accountable for this....

To give some idea of the mud, I need only mention that I saw a horse, harnessed to a French wagon, with its hind legs so deeply sunk in the mud

Lieutenant Edward Allfree, 111th Siege Battery, Royal Garrison Artillery that it could not move. Its hind legs were buried right up to its haunches, so that its stomach was level with, and lying on the ground, with its front legs stretched straight out in front of it along the ground. It had to be dug out. The mud was absolutely terrific, and it rained without ceasing the whole day. I simply loathed it.

It was critical that the ground taken was properly consolidated. The land swarmed with men whose job was not to fight but to help facilitate those who would. Fresh drinking water had to be brought up and clean water wells located. Streams had to be bridged for the movement of artillery, roads mended, tracks laid. New accommodation had to be found, cleaned up and protected. The wounded were searched for, and the dead buried, graves marked and personal details recorded. Just servicing the front was a huge logistical effort exacerbated by the conditions. The stretcher-bearers in particular were worn out.

Lieutenant Edward Allfree, 111th Siege Battery, Royal Garrison Artillery

Boesinghe [village], today, was in a ghastly state! It seemed hopeless to find any place to live in, and the idea of having to live here was most depressing. The place, however, was no longer deserted. The Hun, as a result of yesterday's battle, had been pushed back to beyond the ridge the other side of the canal; the street had been cleared of debris, and transport, ambulances and muddy, rain-soaked guardsmen and RAMC men and stretcher parties thronged the place and dabbled about in the rain and slush. Everything was wet, dirty and miserable. Stretcher parties were bringing in wounded from the shelled, desolate mud swamps the other side of the canal, where the fighting of yesterday had taken place, and putting them on motor and horse ambulances, which were prevented by mud from getting further forward than Boesinghe.

These unfortunate wounded men had been lying out there since yesterday, in the rain and half buried in the mud. The shell-churned mud was so bad that it took a stretcher party of six, four hours to bring in one wounded man. They worked valiantly, these Red Cross (RAMC) men. Having safely delivered their burden, back they went to the mud fields to recover another poor fellow; and it continued to rain on them all the time. It was cold, wet, miserable and dreary beyond my powers of description. . . .

Some of the most evocative images are of men in danger and completely unaware of the camera's eye.

Two officers of the 8th East Surrey Regiment, Acting Major Charles Place DSO MC (left) and Captain Charles Holms MC in trenches near Sanctuary Wood. Both men would be wounded in October.

I paddled around with my party in search of cellars. Most of the more suitable ones were now occupied by infantry, who had lighted fires, where possible, and were trying to dry themselves. They were all moving out tonight; I stuck notices on the doors of those I selected, to indicate that they were appropriated by 111th Siege Battery. Others which were not now occupied, I set parties of my men on to clean out as best they could. We found a fairly dry cellar, and there I left Bombardier Brierly with one man to take charge of, and to keep off intruders from those habitations I had appropriated. I think he soon had a fire going and some hot tea and grub.

2 August: It rained all last night and the whole of today, with the natural result that everything was beastly wet, and the mud was muddier than ever. Our move is postponed on account of the ground being too soft to move the guns. We fired most of the day on the Hun back trenches.

3 August: Still raining. Great difficulty experienced with the guns owing to the trails and wheels sinking so deeply into the soft, wet ground. The whole battery had to heave on one gun every time it had to be pulled out to switch. Every conceivable means was adopted to try and prevent the trails sinking so deep, but none were very successful.

4 August: Still raining, and still firing.

5 August: Still raining this morning, but it cleared up later.

A beautifully observed image of men of the 8th East Surrey Regiment standing in Jeffrey Trench. Behind, a working party crosses the battered landscape.

The rain put paid to offensive operations, for the British had to cross a morass largely of their own making. Meanwhile, the Germans launched a series of small counter-attacks but the conditions hardly suited them either and all attacks were beaten off. For ten days both sides wallowed in the rain and mud. All the divisions that had launched the offensive were relieved by fresh troops, and preparations were made to reboot the offensive as soon as weather permitted. In the meantime, supplies were brought forward by any means possible.

Lance Corporal Archibald Davis, 419th Field Company, Royal Engineers

All work done in the front line such as making trenches, gun emplacements, barbed wire, etc. were carried out by working parties consisting of infantry in [under the] charge of engineers. Certain of these parties were detailed as 'carrying parties', and their duty was to indent for and carry the necessary material from the RE dumps to where the work was to be done. It was a hard task, I did some of it, and very dangerous. These dumps were dotted about in various places amongst the trenches and REs were put in charge. The dumps not only became depleted of the materials used, but were the targets for bombs and shells, and much of the material was blown up. Also the men in charge suffered a great deal from gas attacks. These forward dumps were fed from larger dumps behind the line, which, of course, were in turn fed from dumps still further back.

Each of the forward dumps had always to have in stock a certain fixed quantity of every material that might be required, and I was given the job of inspecting the forward dumps from day to day, ordering materials from the rear dumps, and seeing that whatever might be required was always available.

In the course of my work, it so happened that the Major told me he must have certain material on one of the dumps by a certain date. I indented for the material, but could not get it sent up. I reported my failure to the Major, who told me to use whatever means I liked, but the material must be got up. Consequently I wrote a stinging letter to the officer in charge of the rear dump saying that he was to send me the material without fail, and that I could accept no excuse for the material not being delivered by a certain time. I signed my letter A.H. Davis, L/C, RE. I received a very apologetic letter per return by runner expressing deep regret at not having been able to let me have the material before, but that it was being sent up that very night. . . . He had taken me for a Lt Col.

Had a tough business to get up the rations this evening. We met the transport at the brickstack and found that in addition to the rations was a very large quantity of stores, which would mean us making three or four journeys. The transport drivers are generally content with dumping the stuff off whether we are there or not and then getting back out of it at a gallop. I can't blame them for this is a most 'unhealthy' spot and Fritz has got the roadway taped to a nicety. However, this evening, Driver Ashford ASC offered to try and get his GS wagon over the shell holes up to the sap entrance. It was some game but in crossing a mixture of trench tramway lines and shell holes, one of the horses fell, the front of the wagon slithered into a shell hole, the rear got caught up in a broken tram rail and one of the wheels came off, while the rations and stores spread themselves about the country. This was cheerful as Fritz was bumping us pretty merrily. We set to and emptied the wagon and unharnessed the horses; then lifted the wagon up onto fairly level ground, replaced the wheel, turned the wagon around and put the horses in again. It was useless trying to get the wagon up any further so it set off back again. I admire Ashford for attempting what none of the other drivers would think of doing. It was raining all the time and we were soon wet through. Before we came out I took the

Sapper Albert Martin, 122nd Signal Company, Royal Engineers

Above: A carrying party with rations crosses the shell-swept ground near Ypres, August 1917.

precaution of removing my shirt so that I should have something dry to put on when I returned. I fell into a shell hole with a heavy box of rations and the bacon got covered with mud.

Driver Aubrey Smith had a delicate operation taking up ammunition in a convoy of limbers. Men of the Queen's Westminster Rifles (QWR) and the Queen Victoria Rifles (QVR) had been delegated to help unload the boxes of bombs on arrival at a dump, but they were nervous and not keen to stay with the convoy for one minute longer than necessary. The horses too were frightened and in Smith's team, 'Jumbo' and 'The Grey', reliable in most circumstances, were as twitchy as the men about to lead them.

Driver Aubrey Smith, 1/5th (City of London) Battalion, London Rifle Brigade

One's legs began to tingle, and a longing to turn back, or, at any rate, abandon the horses and fall in the ditch, was no doubt present in every man's mind. We clapped our helmets on tighter and had trouble with the digestion of our breakfasts; a tight feeling gripped one round the chest and a craving for a stimulant arose, varying according to different tastes. ...

The track we were following was not only muddy, but dotted with shell holes, and only the fact that we kept moving prevented us from sinking dangerously and perhaps getting stuck. However, [Lieutenant] Pocock unfortunately had to halt us while he located the exact spot for dumping the bombs, and the limbers before me suddenly pulled up short, leaving my back wheel in a shell hole. Knowing Jumbo's failing, my heart sank within me as rapidly as the rear half sank into the ground; the mischief was done. When the two front limbers moved on again, sure enough, Jumbo's heart failed him, and he leant back hard in his breeching while The Grey, finding it impossible to shift the load, just stood rooted to the spot, petrified with fright. The Queen Vic's man was in a similar dilemma several yards behind, but I couldn't see him.

Endeavouring to coax the horses forward with endearing names and tugs at their nosebands was no more efficacious than sitting on top of them – using spurs and whip. Standing broadside on to the firing line, they preferred to offer themselves up as a sacrifice and resigned themselves to their fate. Their driver was not so heroic, his one desire being to get back home again, and the wild swear words he used revealed the full extent of his wind-up. His heart now left his boots and leapt to his mouth; would that the phlegmatic horses had shown such animation! The Grey, instead of putting forward a supreme effort, inspired by panic, had gone right past that stage to one of utter helplessness, terror-struck with the noise.

The most obvious solution is not necessarily the first that comes to one's mind when excited, which possibly explains why for the moment I took the idiotic course of trying to dig the wheel out. The spare-men had gone on, but I borrowed a shovel from a man behind a barricade and frantically worked on clearing away the sticky mud around the axle of the wheel, knowing that the horses could not run away in the meantime. But its futility was soon apparent, for after a few minutes' labour the wheel looked as firmly embedded as ever. Just then, the other two limbers cantered by, empty, on their way home, the drivers grinning at my plight and shouting advice to unhook the horses and depart. The dump was 100 yards ahead.

Only then did the saner course of unhooking the rear half and taking the front half forward alone suggest itself to me; relieved of the incubus, the horses leapt forward with delight and reached the dump in a series of mad plunges, The Grey setting the pace of the war dance, to which Jumbo somewhat reluctantly conformed. There was not a soul at the dump. In various dugouts ahead, some poor wretched infantry were crouching, awaiting a dead-hit on their thin roofing, but they could hardly be expected to come out and assist a driver who was, after all, but a temporary visitor up there; they had got to endure it for the rest of the day. The two QWR men were nowhere to be seen, and as for the NCO of the convoy, it transpired that he had already packed off to the rear with an attack of nerves. Lieutenant Pocock, it is only fair to add, had his hands full elsewhere – helping the QVR driver, I believe. Therefore, down with the tailboard and out with the forty-five boxes of bombs into the nearest shell hole, 'beaucoup' wind-up on the part of the unloader, who had never worked so frantically before, and many curses directed at the heads of the fatigue men who had quitted the scene so abruptly.

The horses cantered back gladly to the rear half, but it turned out to be a sheer impossibility to hook it on again without assistance, though Jumbo and The Grey consented to be 'backed' several times in making this

A dead German lying in an enemy trench taken on 31 July.

attempt. It therefore became necessary to dump the remaining boxes by the shell hole where we had stuck, and although the horses could easily have bolted with the empty front half during their process, by a lucky chance they stood perfectly still. One of two shells had come very close to us, and as soon as the unloading was complete I went round to look at the horses, both of whom, I was sick to find, had been wounded. Jumbo's wound was slight, but The Grey was smothered in blood from his shoulder to his foot; the blood gushing out so quickly that it became imperative to get him away at once to a place where the wound could be bound up. A minute later, fortunately, Pocock arrived, and I was therefore able to get the rear half hooked on. It was his first transport trip up the line and he prayed God it would be his last, but this in no way implied that he wished to be struck dead on the spot. He bade me flee the benighted place, and, needless to say, I fled.

Despite their wounds, both horses pulled the empty limber back out of the general slough, although The Grey began to limp badly and Smith had to halt and endeavour to bandage the horse and lighten its work as far as possible.

Driver Aubrey Smith, 1/5th (City of London) Battalion, London Rifle Brigade

For the remainder of the journey Jumbo pulled the weight of the empty limber, enabling The Grey to limp along beside him without working. It was a pathetic sight to see the old horse, of whom I had grown very fond, bleeding profusely and suffering pain, and my conscience smote me for having spurred and sworn at the poor creature when he had stood petrified with fright a quarter of an hour before. Jumbo, too, in spite of his previous jibbing, was at any rate working hard now and seemed to know that something had happened to his companion, who required his assistance.

The sight of the old grey was hardly a good advertisement for the state of the roads ahead of the artillery convoys that passed by on their way up the line, as a good many drivers' faces testified. The officers' faces were set, and the men looked fed up to the hilt, for shells had to be taken up by day and night. Many passed remarks such as 'You'll lose 'im, mate', 'He's going fast, chum', 'Mych shelling up ther?' etc.

But the query I remember most clearly was that of a Labour Corps man in Dickebusch, where I watered the horses.

"as 'e bin 'it, choom?' asked the idiot.

On 10 August, the weather relented, permitting an attack close to the Menin Road where successes had been slim on 31 July. Once again, the attack was a disappointment and over 2,000 casualties were sustained for a maximum gain of 400 metres. With casualties strewn across the ground, supreme acts of comradeship and courage were commonplace, some to the point of death. Private Thomas Hope, the 16-year-old signaller with the 1/5th King's Liverpool Regiment, chanced upon one injured man in a shell hole whose last unseen act of self-sacrifice was heartbreaking.

We come across a sergeant. Poor fellow, he has lost both legs above the knee and has a nasty wound in the stomach. At first we think he is dead, but a movement of the eyes assures us he still lives. With strands of wire we circle both thighs and twist each one as tight as possible; this stops the bleeding. The puncture in his stomach doesn't look bad but makes it impossible for us to move him without a stretcher. His glassy staring eyes follow our every movement, not a groan escapes his lips. We talk encouragingly to him, but cannot tell if he understands or not. There is something uncanny in the way he follows us with his eyes. His look seems to be one of antagonism: I almost believe he resents our presence. I suggest to Naylor that we should get stretcher-bearers, we can't possibly move him without, or the hole in his belly would kill him. It is then I think I understand the look in his eyes. I wouldn't want to live myself without my legs; to have to crawl on my stomach like a worm; that isn't life but a living hell. Ahead of him he has months of agony lying on his back, providing the hole in his stomach allows him that chance, months

Private Thomas Hope, 1/5th The King's (Liverpool Regiment)

of gnawing pain, months of stabbing pain, years of mental pain – pain and misery all the time.

Just now he is all numb-drowsy, as if he was slipping away into a void. If we take off those strands he'll just fade away. But following on these thoughts come my own when life has been a matter of seconds or inches. Yes, life can be very very sweet when we feel it slipping from our grasp.

'Come on,' I urge, 'let's get the stretcher-bearers, Naylor, this fellow is about all in.'

We haven't far to hunt for them. In a shell hole we find two RAMC men, a broken stretcher lying between them. The supports are splintered in several places; it could never bear the weight of a man. We learn they have been sniped at for the last half hour, and are not keen to leave their present shelter. However, after a little persuasion they follow us towards the shell hole in which the wounded sergeant lies. The last few yards we crawl on our bellies as a machine gun sweeps the ground.

The orderlies are soon at work. They put the professional touch to our amateurish job, but even they can do little more than we have attempted. 'Besides,' one remarks, 'he can't live longer than a quarter of an hour, he's lost too much blood already. Even if he had a chance we could never get him across the open in the daylight. When it's dark, we'll have a shot at it.' Then as an afterthought: 'If he still lives, poor blighter.'

There's nothing else to be done. We have seen too much of this forced callousness to worry about it. Our own turn may not be far distant. Naylor and I carry on with our job.

It is late afternoon, now, and I have visited the shell hole in which the sergeant lies many times; I dread whenever I have to approach it. His staring eyes haunt me. Why the hell did Naylor lay our line to that particular hole? Next time, I'm going to haul it out; I won't look at that poor blighter again. It isn't so bad when he is unconscious, but when his eyes follow me, when they stare at me when I crawl into the hole, stare at me when I tell him they'll soon have him out of this, stare at me as I test the line and are still staring as I crawl out again, I feel as if I had been intruding, almost as if I had been violating the sanctuary of the dead and been caught in the act. Yes, I must shift that wire; to hell with Naylor and his systems.

As the day wears on, our little part of the front gradually becomes more unpleasant. Casualties keep on mounting and we are forced to patrol the lines single-handed instead of in pairs.

The shelling is so intensive that our signal lines are never unbroken for more than a minute or two. The Boche counter-attack is expected at any time, and we are still out of communication with battalion headquarters.

Naylor, who is outside on the line, hasn't reported for almost forty-five minutes. He should tap in and do so every half-hour if possible. If there is no word from him in five minutes I'll have to go out into that hell and try the impossible. I watch the minute hand of my wristwatch tick round, while the signaller taps away unsuccessfully on his buzzer. The corporal signaller gives me a nod, and grousingly I get up, loop my field telephone over my shoulder and make towards the entrance of our captured pillbox. Before I reach it the SOS comes in from our advanced posts, and I hesitate

Left: 'Returning after laying a line.'

Right: A communication trench photographed by Signaller Sidney Banyard.

at the entrance before bracing my nerves to go out amongst the general upheaval. I hear our operator's excited voice:

'I'm through, I'm through to battalion, corp.'

I return into the Signal Office shouting: 'Good old Naylor,' while to myself I think: I won't have to go out now, after all, I'll be able to stay here where it's safer.

I watch the operator send through our messages for more artillery support and a request for bombs to be sent up, and congratulate myself on having escaped a nasty job.

'How do you find the signals?' enquires the corporal.

'Pretty weak,' answers the operator, 'can hardly read them at times, seems as if there's a "short" somewhere.'

'Jock.'

'Hello,' I reply. 'Better go out and give Naylor a hand. Look for a short circuit and use plenty insulating tape. By the way' – as I make for the entrance – 'tap in when you find Naylor, and let me know how things are.'

'Right-o.' As I leave the pillbox the Boche barrage falls with surprising suddenness on our support lines. Picking up the wire outside I trail it through my hand as I stumble along in the gloom, mending numerous new breaks as I go. The barrage has lifted and is now falling on our reserve lines, and I hear our Lewis and machine guns joining in the argument and know the Boche is attacking.

I am nearing that accursed shell hole. I don't recognize it from the hundreds of others, I can't even see it from the hundreds of others, I can't even see it through the gathering dusk, but I know I am almost on top of it. Yes, as surely as if it was the only one here. Those eyes will stare at me again as I slide down and stop for a breather, stare as I crawl out.

This is it, no, it's not. That's not the sergeant; another occupant. My God, it's Naylor.

I am beside him in a second.

'Naylor, Naylor, old man, where've you got it?'

I shake him, but it's not good. A gash in his neck tells its own tale; blood is still trickling out of his mouth. Poor old Naylor, suffocated in his own blood. I shake him again, and feel for his heart, but already I know that dear old Naylor, with all his schoolteacher airs, has gone. I'm glad now that I let him have his own way so often. His fads annoyed me at times, he was always so particular about the little things, but after all he wasn't a bad spud, far too good for a death such as this.

Old Naylor's turn, I reflect. I wonder who will be next, there aren't so many of the old crowd left. Hell, mooning like this won't get me anywhere.

I unstrap the telephone, fix the leads, and calling up the company headquarters, find that part of the line is in working order and my signals getting through.

'Hello, that A Company? Jock speaking. I've found Naylor. Yes, hit in the neck. Oh, he's got it all right, certain. You'll send somebody out for him? Right, can't miss it, the line runs right up to it. I'll bring in his pay book.'

Then: 'Hello, d'you hear me all right? The fault must be forward, so I'll tap in as soon as I find it. Cheerio.'

I unfix the telephone, insulate the scraped wire where I have tapped in, and turn slowly towards Naylor. I've never quite mastered my natural shyness of touching a dead man, but, after all, this was Naylor, he wouldn't mind me going through his pockets. I undo the buttons of his tunic pockets, take out everything I find, gingerly slip my hand into his trouser pockets and do likewise. The lot I cram into my own already bulging pockets. A last glance just to make sure I am not mistaken about my old comrade, then grasping the line I start off.

Twenty yards further on I stumble over something. Curse it, the line is right underneath. Why the hell must they come to my line to die? But perhaps he is only wounded, so I look closer and turn him over – the sergeant. Yes, it must be him, there can't be two sergeants with their legs shot off and a wound in the belly within 20 yards of each other. Damn it, but that's strange. How did he get here? What does it matter anyway, he's dead.

I stoop over him and grope around for the wire. It's not there. I return and pick it up a yard or two on the other side of the corpse. I trace it back to the dead sergeant, but lose it again on the other side of him. I roll him over and the wire goes with him. Grasped in his hand I find it and begin to understand. I go round to a circle and soon discover the other end of the wire, then I repair the break and once again we are in communication with headquarters.

I can only surmise what must have taken place in that shell hole between the wounded Naylor and the dying sergeant. It was obvious that the sergeant had crawled those 20 yards with the broken wire in an endeavour to find the other end. How he managed it, crippled and maimed, I cannot tell. The fact remains he had got far enough with one end of the broken wire in his hand to allow the signals to pass through the earth to the strands of the other part. The break was joined and our SOS message had got through.

An unselfish act of a dying man – just a gesture of true comradeship.

With the weather predicted to improve, the next push switched to ground north of the Menin Road and a multi-divisional assault, with the German village of Langemarck in the centre of the advance. The day, 16 August, would be a warm overcast day and, mercifully, no rain was expected.

Recently commissioned from the ranks, Second Lieutenant Henry Foley was preparing to take his men forward for the assault opposite Langemarck village. The responsibility for those under his command, the knowledge that many would not survive the next two days, was in stark contrast to the corresponding prospects of Private Hugh Quigley. His battalion, 12th Royal Scots, was now occupying a quiet part of the line, to the south, in Picardy, close to the old Somme battlefield. Their juxtaposed recollections are a poignant reminder of the varying but simultaneous fortunes experienced by men as they served in the trenches.

Second Lieutenant Henry Foley, 6th Prince Albert's (Somerset Light Infantry)

Ypres, 14 August

At 7.00 pm we fell in, preparatory to moving up nearer the line. My platoons were in line one behind the other with a gap of about 30 yards between each. I had just left the centre platoon, and was walking towards the front of the company, when a 5.9 shell screamed down apparently just over my head, and burst with a deafening crash behind me. I swung round, and saw that where but a second before had stood some thirty men, chatting and joking as they slipped on their equipment, there was now nothing but an appalling shambles. The shell had landed right in among them. Many men were simply blown to pieces. Those who still writhed on the ground we carried into an old trench nearby, and tried to dress their wounds. The poor fellow I was carrying, Liddon's servant, kept saying 'It's no good, Sir, you can leave me. I know I'm done.' He was terribly hit in the back and soon died. All told, this one shell cost us twenty-six casualties – practically a whole platoon gone.

At least eight of the casualties were killed outright and a further two died of wounds from this one incident. Seven of those killed were carried back and buried together in one plot at the nearby Duhallow ADS Cemetery.

Royaulcourt, Somme, 15 August

I am writing this from a dugout made by cutting a square recess in a sloping bank and covering it with corrugated iron and earth. A rabbit existence, sleep all day, and a modicum of work at night. Entrance is gained by crawling on all fours through a low opening, slithering painfully over legs and bodies to a fixed place. War appears to be a matter of listening to a few whistling shells exchanged at long intervals, of marking out minute figures on a dull-brown hillside crowned with trees and a phantom-like hedge of poplars. Not a movement anywhere; even the sun lingers more drowsily here than elsewhere, and the grass bends but seldom to uncertain winds. The old conception of a violent strife of combatants or even the modern of an inferno of bursting shells dies down to quiescence, and there dwells a sober touch about the whole landscape, as if it were alone given to droning bees, fluttering butterflies, and flitting swallows.

Private Hugh Quigley, 12th The Royal Scots (Lothian Regiment)

Ypres, 15 August

At 10.00 pm we trailed across the canal and started on our long tramp to the assembly point. Provided there was sufficient room, this was to be just east of the Steenbeek, and just north of Pilkem Road. Luckily the night was comparatively quiet, and we reached the marshy ground west of the little stream without mishap. Here I left my company sheltered in shell holes, and went forward to find out the best way across to the other side.

Our outposts had been pushed forward 60 yards beyond the stream, so that there was just room to assemble my company behind A [Company], who were to lead the attack. To our right, however, a pillbox on the road had held out, and was still in enemy hands, so that on two sides of us we had a vigilant and very nervous enemy, who kept up a continual rifle

Second Lieutenant Henry Foley, 6th Prince Albert's (Somerset Light Infantry)

fire, and who was ready to send up his SOS rocket at the slightest sign of movement in our lines.

Private Hugh Quigley, 12th The Royal Scots (Lothian Regiment)

Royaulcourt, Somme, 15 August

Last night the desolation received a quiet haunting beauty, the moon dreaming through haze from a dewy earth, mist lying in long swathes in every hollow and below the trees. There dwelt no foundation in anything, a barred nocturne of pearl-gray with dark shadows of foliage floating uncertainly like weed on water. The Very lights gleamed but faintly, and shells fell only after hours, as if unwilling to disturb a great peace. Along the road, emptiness, except for a visionary sentry motionless, like a statue or a tree stump frozen into harmony with the surroundings: several ghosts were bending and rising to the right, a working party laying out wire. They seemed to be digging their own grave.

In that junction of mysterious man and nature rests the unique interest of this type of war, the only feature of a monotonous life. And this junction is not confined to night, but to day also; men living and working on a hillside so completely screened by adaptive colour that only movement betrays; a deserted village housing unnoticed a whole brigade, or even half a division; or a farmhouse, almost completely ruined, covering a company. Trenches may be occupied in daylight by a battalion marching along sunken roads for miles, or through communication trenches, and the observer may look across country, see nothing whatever, and report no movement anywhere.

Second Lieutenant Henry Foley, 6th Prince Albert's (Somerset Light Infantry)

Ypres, 16 August

To reconnoitre the ground east of the stream with any success, movement was, of course, essential. I was hardly surprised, therefore, after I had been looking round for a few minutes, to see a beautiful shower of golden rain shoot up from the German lines, and to hear next minute the swish of shells overhead.

East of the Steenbeek we were so close to the enemy that we were immune from his shells, but back where I had left the company they were falling thick and fast. Back I went, therefore, to lead my men into comparative safety. So heavy was the barrage, however, that for some time we had to wait. I sat in fearful discomfort in the bottom of a tiny trench half full of liquid mud. During the half hour, on an average, we missed death by inches about once a minute. Knowing that this storm was too violent to last, and as we had plenty of time before Zero, which was fixed for 4.45 am, I chose to wait, rather than risk the chance of total annihilation in attempting to get the men across the boggy ground while such a tempest was raging.

As soon as it had slackened, however, I got them on the move, and one by one they staggered across the flimsy plank bridge, which was the only means of crossing the Steenbeek.

Royaulcourt, Somme, 15 August

I have taken a new interest in beetles, especially when wakened at midnight by an inquisitive gentleman exploring my chest. They crawl up and down the walls of the dugout, strange jet monsters dear to Scarabeaus, shaped to inspire terror in a child soul. Caterpillars are very constant with their attentions, dear little playfellows escorted by earwigs and huge spiders. Ladybirds preen themselves on your knees and go to sleep in boots; ants delight to scamper up one leg and down the other, get lost sometimes and emerge at your neck in a great state of bewilderment. Greenflies and bluebottles utter dulcet melody all day long, strange buzzers hover on the face and tickle the ears and nostrils. There is a constant interchange of courtesies between the grasshoppers on the banks, and crickets rattle lugubriously by the roadside at night. Strange bedfellows always seem the most romantic, and we have enough of them here to inspire. ...

Private Hugh Quigley, 12th The Royal Scots (Lothian Regiment)

Ypres, 16 August

Once in position there was nothing to be done until the fateful hour of Zero. The exertion of the last few hours had given me a frantic thirst, and to save my own supply of water I took a bottle from the side of a poor fellow nearby who would need it no more.

The CO and his HQ were established behind a ruined cottage right in our foremost line. For a long time I sat with him, and we talked of the former shows we had been through. At times like this he was at his best – perfectly self-possessed, ready with shrewd advice in all our little

Second Lieutenant Henry Foley, 6th Prince Albert's (Somerset Light Infantry)

Second Lieutenant Rolland Franks (centre), 8th East Surrey Regiment, during a pause in the fighting. He was killed on 12 October near Poelcappelle.

difficulties, eager to go through every danger and discomfort with his men. Before I left him, as Zero time drew near, he told me that A Company had been weakened by casualties, and might be slow in starting, in which case I was to do my best to get them on the move myself.

Four-thirty-thirty-five-forty; how many anxious eyes glanced in the first blush of dawn at watches so carefully synchronized that they beat as one? And then, like a clap of thunder above the raging of a storm, burst out the deafening roar of our opening barrage, that curtain of flying steel and smoke which was to creep slowly forward across the unknown before us. The excitement of that moment was intense. In a twinkling I was on my feet, urging on the men of A Company. So thin was their line that my own leading wave soon overtook and intermingled with it.

Hermies, Somme, 16 August

The army does not study individualities, but it has indulged a fondness of mine. We have a unique opportunity of viewing sunrise and sunset in the trenches owing to the degree that men must stand-to at daybreak and nightfall. Perhaps without this one would forget, or lack resolution, to study the sky on one's own initiative. I have felt sometimes that there was nothing really worthwhile, and lethargy overtook me when one of those far-flung sunsets flaming over the hill reminded me that I had something more to live for than sleep in a muddy trench, that the everlasting beauty was still alive, even when least expected. …

This morning the sun has stolen like a lance along the ridges and beneath the trees, cutting adrift the white mist hanging over them, and sprinkling the lower sky with filmy blue. The clouds mount above it in a beautiful mackerel; their wings are broadened for flight, pearl-lights dwelling in the hollows and opal shadows like an army of angels fleeing from night to day. I have never seen such glorious vistas of sunset or sunrise as in this country. … Strange that this should be the whole of life, yet how satisfying it is! The mind or memory cannot turn its full face to the materials of war and forget all else.

Private Hugh Quigley, 12th The Royal Scots (Lothian Regiment)

Ypres, 16 August

I had hardly gone forward 50 yards, when I felt a sharp pain in my left arm. At the moment it seemed nothing and I ploughed on. In another minute, however, the gauntlet glove I was wearing was full of blood; I pulled it off, and found that blood was pouring down my arm. I saw that this must be stopped at once, and went over to Battalion HQ where Rich soon had the wound bound up with my field dressing. The CO was most sympathetic, and said that I had better wait there for a while. This seemed at that point almost intolerable, when I thought of what we had been through in preparation for the show, and I determined to go on if I could.

The attacking waves had now passed almost out of sight into the smoke ahead. I had not gone very far when a fit of dizziness swept over me, and I had to tumble into a shell hole. On regaining consciousness I realized that reaction, following the bleeding and the strain, I suppose, of the last few days, had thoroughly set in; I felt like nothing on earth, and about as much

Second Lieutenant Henry Foley, 6th Prince Albert's (Somerset Light Infantry)

use as a sick headache. In a dazed, idiotic way I looked around for some convenient refuge, and eventually wandered off towards a large pillbox [Au Bon Gite]. The one thing my soul craved for at that moment was sleep. Outside the pillbox were several Tommies. I remember wondering why they stayed outside, instead of taking shelter inside. The reason was soon apparent – it was full of Boches. My actions now were those of a drunken man. I felt perfectly furious with these inoffensive Huns for being in the pillbox. I called loudly through the low doorway for them to come out.

Private Hugh Quigley, 12th The Royal Scots (Lothian Regiment)

Hermies, Somme, 16 August

We are busy cutting a road for transport between two high banks, sun glistening on dry earth heaps, and men, recumbent, shading eyes from the glare. There are only two colours, light purple and dark blue-grey; the purple grows warm and luminous, living as a reflection on water, and the shadowed faces shine nevertheless transparently, with a mat light along nose and eyes, just sketching the features. Even dark objects – boots or equipment – are bathed in the luminance and lose contrast to become merged in the whole. The heat is so great that no real light and shadow remain, just a difference of form, not of colour, shadows clearly projected but not silent. The sky comes forward over the hill, not the infinite azure sea, where clouds float at a vast distance, but a fine screen with white patches of cumuli rising slowly to the zenith.

Strange flies born of the sun, flit along the path; huge bees whizz past uncannily; butterflies rise and settle again on the hot clay, there is a multitude of greenflies and bluebottles buzzing noisily in the shadows. There dwells a fineness in it all, a sultry beauty of contour untouched by association.

Second Lieutenant Henry Foley, 6th Prince Albert's (Somerset Light Infantry)

Ypres, 16 August

The thickness of the walls made it impossible to see into the interior. At the sound of my voice the babble within only grew into a roar. I tried them in English, French and German but with no effect. At last a brainwave seized me, and I yelled '*Kamarad*' at the top of my voice. The result was magical. A perfect shriek of joy came from the lusty defenders, and one after another they bolted out, while I leaned against the wall of the pillbox, revolver in hand, dizzily trying to count them.

I next remember waking up on a chair inside the pillbox, and finding that my wound had been re-dressed. I think this must have been about nine o'clock. I had a splitting headache, and felt absurdly weak, the wound throbbed, but otherwise the sleep had refreshed me and there was now no feeling of faintness.

I observed that the pillbox had become a temporary dressing station, and was filled with wounded, some of who slept, while others, more badly hit, were groaning and cursing. A strange scene. Across the entrance lay a dead German. News of the attack trickled in, and with joy we heard that all had gone well, and Langemarck had fallen.

A Lewis gun team, photographed by Captain George Birnie, the Medical Officer attached 8th East Surrey Regiment.

Langemarck had fallen but this was the one highlight in an otherwise dismal day. As was so often the case, there was great heroism displayed by the men who attacked, and four Victoria Crosses were awarded for valour to those directly involved in the assault. It is noticeable that two of the four medals won were given for actions directly in front of Langemarck and a third adjacent to the village: awards were more prevalent in a winning than a losing cause, even if the courage on display in both was comparable.

The battle, as so often before, was disintegrating into a grinding, attritional struggle, with line-straightening assaults after limited gains. There was no prospect of a breakthrough, just the slow wearing down of an enemy who could least afford the losses.

Private Thomas Hope, 1/5th The King's (Liverpool Regiment)

Soaked through and sweating like horses we plough our way in the darkness backwards and forwards through the wilderness of mud. Running the [telephone] wire through the hands, we flounder in and out water-logged shell holes, stumble over foul-smelling heaps of putrefying flesh, or, as machine guns sweep the ground, crawl over the more recent dead of the morning's advance, which emit strange noises – half groan, half sigh – as the weight of our bodies presses the air from their lungs.

When we find a break we scout round on hands and knees in a circle to try and pick up the other end, which may be anywhere within 50 yards, but at last it is found, the join made, then insulated, then we go on.

Shells, machine guns, the nearness of these still forms, and the darkness, all add to our misery and fear, but the line must be kept clear. As soon as one break is mended another is made; the task seems hopeless. Physically we are beat, but the boys in front rely on us to keep going and we cannot let them down.

And so on throughout the night, we trudge to and fro, seldom meeting a soul, although there must be thousands all around us.

The road to our right is alive with transport, but here between the captured Jerry first and second lines, we seem to be the only two living beings amongst the dead. Away from the roads and tracks a battlefield can be a very lonely spot.

Towards dawn the usual Jerry hate increases until we find ourselves just within the limits of a truly terrific barrage. A wall of smoke and upflung earth blots out all landmarks, but just ahead of us should be an old trench, and we make a dash for it. Loaded with equipment and field telephone I stumble on after Webster, my legs sinking up to the knees in mud at every step, until the stumbling gradually becomes a slithering and floundering amongst the vindictive morass.

Occasionally I come across a yard or two of firmer ground and try to sprint over it, bent double as the shell splinters and clods of earth whizz around me, then, without warning, down I flop into another stretch of squelching mud. I try wading through it until at last I can go no further and drop exhausted into a newly made shell hole, where the explosion has unearthed fairly solid clay, which I don't immediately notice, being only faintly surprised that I am not sinking gradually down and down into its churned-up slimy depths.

The ground beneath me is in a continual state of trembles. Fifty yards further on I can see the comparative safety of the edge of the barrage, but I have ceased to worry over these things. Utter exhaustion has made me indifferent, and I care not whether I live or die as, unconcerned, I watch the inverted cones of earth soar skywards and wait for the clods to clatter

The caption merely states, 'After heavy shelling, August 1917.'

'A dugout Jeffrey
Trench.'

down on top of me. The blasts of hot air and lyddite fumes, the hiss and smack of flying splinters have lost their power to send me scampering for safer quarters: I am brave beyond my wildest hopes. It is a feeling I have never experienced before, this calm indifference of exhaustion.

I see Webster dodging between the bursts and smoke on his way towards me and try to wave him back, but he carried on until, with a rush and a jump he is in the shell hole beside me.

'Hurt, Scotty?' he yells.

'Not me. I'm just all in. I'll come along after I've had a breather.'

'Breather be damned, let's get to hell out of this.'

Snatching up my heavy drum of wire and telephone, he hauls me to my feet, and with a final 'Come on,' leads the way.

The short rest had given me back my wind and, relieved of my heavy baggage, I somehow manage, with Webster's help, to pull my weary legs along, and drop down beside him into an old trench just clear of the barrage.

'Phew, that was hot.'

'Bloody hot,' is all Webster replies.

From the safety of the trench we watch the landscape changing, then as suddenly as the barrage dropped, so it lifts, and once again we climb into the open and the eternal break in the wire.

The shelling has cut our signal line in so many places that it could never be repaired, so we decide to run out a new wire from the extra drum I have lugged about all night. Before we can get started, however, our relief, Mac and Streaky, arrive, and are rather surprised, I fancy, to find us still on our feet. We slip into a hole and swop the latest rumours, then, with a cheerio, Webby and I make for the captured pillbox, which is now our battalion headquarters.

The entrance, facing the Jerry lines, has had a direct hit but has withstood it well, only a slight crack being visible and proving beyond doubt that whatever the Germans have been forced to find substitutes for, concrete certainly isn't one of them.

As we enter we notice the walls are splattered with blood and fragments of flesh, while on the narrow floor lies an artillery man with a badly mangled leg, and beside him a comrade holding a rosary in his hand. As gently as possible we step over the wounded man, but the passage is only 2 feet wide and is lined on either side with men. Our effort is rather clumsy and evokes groans from the figure on the floor and curses flung at us from his pals, which we treat with true soldierly indifference.

In the Signal Office lie what is left of three more artillerymen and one of our runners. We are told they were standing in the passageway when the shell burst and were blown there. We merely glance at the gruesome sight as we pass by, knowing that shortly somebody will cover up the pieces with sandbags.

On reporting to the sergeant we are told to go and lie down in the rear compartment, and with visions of a sleep, we grope blindly along an alley, eventually stumbling down four steps into a square emplacement with machine-gun slots in each wall. The last step down lands us into a foot of water, and our curses are answered from the semi-darkness with: 'Don't disturb the goldfish,' and 'Watch your head on the doormat' – all of which we ignore, as we scramble back onto the last step above high-water mark, and view our bedrooms with mixed feelings.

A solitary candle, stuck at a perilous angle on the wall, throws a half-hearted flickering glimmer of light round the place, revealing, perched along each wall on a narrow ledge – for all the world like hens gone to roost – the usual miscellaneous mixture which comprises the normal headquarters staff. Occasionally someone's foot slips off the 6-inch ledge,

and down he comes with a splash which is greeted with loud guffaws by those who have already undergone the experience.

The game seems to be to cling to the ledge as long as possible and thereby keep your legs dry, but once you have slipped you adopt an air of utter contempt for dryness, and with the exception of lying full length in a foot of water, disport yourself in the most uncomfortable and wettest way possible, and feign sleep.

The stumble at the last step had decided the matter for Webby and I, so we wade over to the only vacant space on the ledge, light a fag, fling a few queries at a couple of optimists who are attempting to bale the water out with empty cigarette tins, then with our equipment and rifles over our knees, we settle down for that well-earned rest.

In those far-off civilian days such an experience would have laid us on our backs for weeks, but the exposure and discomfort now only seems to harden us for worse things ahead. Somehow I manage to doze. The exploding shells and the rattle of machine guns outside are vague muffled sounds in the background as my head drops further forward. Sleep is coming at last, the only sanctuary I ever find up at the front.

Sapper Albert Martin, 122nd Signal Company, Royal Engineers

It was a gaunt and haggard party that straggled across the duckboards and past our old dugouts at Burgomasters Farm but it was a merry withdrawal, for we were moving in the right direction. The farm is now in artillery transport lines and an Observation Balloon is tethered in the field behind the house. On the whole we look more thoroughly done up than ever before. Even the robust Brady is pale and wan, while I shudder to see myself in the glass. Still, we are out of the line now and it is really wonderful how quickly Nature picks herself up again if she is given only half a chance. In less than a week we shall be looking as fit as ever.

The lorries put us down only a few yards from our billets that are the same as before. After getting settled I removed my socks for the first time in three weeks. All the time we were in the line we were not supposed to take off even our boots and puttees but we generally got these off each night. My socks have been soaked through time after time with rain and mud and perspiration so that it was impossible to take them off in the ordinary way. I had to cut them and tear them and remove them from my feet in pieces; the soles were as hard as boards. Washed my feet as well as I could in water from the pond and now, being sleepy, I lie me to my blankets and slumber.

We do not get uneasy at feeling little creatures crawling about our bodies; we are well used to them, but last night after lights out I felt a large body of them proceeding in regular order up my leg and the left side of my body. It was a rather unusual sort of crawling, and putting my hand round my side I caught hold of something large and soft and somewhat slimy. Aitken struck a match and I extracted a young green newt about five inches long – harmless but unpleasant as a bedfellow. I quickly lifted the flap of the tent and threw him back towards the pond from which he came.

Opposite:
Two officers'
servants, 11th
West Yorkshire
Regiment, outside
an enemy pillbox
at Stirling Castle,
mid-September.

A disabled tank,
stuck fast since
the first days of
the offensive.

CQMS William
Andrews, 1/4th
The Black
Watch (Royal
Highlanders)

We quarties [Quartermasters], waiting on the road at Bus House, had tea, rum and bread waiting for the men, and had to get them away as fast as we could in motor wagons to Epsom Camp, Westoutre. The poor wretches, though near exhaustion, were still in that extremely talkative stage which follows a dread experience. As an old reporter, I knew the state of mind well, for I had found that if you could only get quickly to the scenes of colliery explosions or railway disasters the survivors would tell you everything you wanted, but if you got there some hours after, a reaction had set in and they were reluctant to say a word; they just wanted to forget....

Every man was eager to tell me of his own adventures. There was one oldish man whom I never hitherto heard say a single conversational word. He was one of those poor fellows who did their duty but had no joy of companionship and took their misfortune with dumb fatalism. I always pitied such men most, for they seemed to have so few resources. So I listened whilst he told me in full detail, and in tones of astonishment and almost incredulity, how two gigantic Germans had made for him, and he had stood his ground, run his bayonet through one of them, and smashed the other in the chin with the butt of his rifle. He told me this again and again, following me about as I got hold of little groups of men and persuaded them to hurry with their food. I had, at length, to be severely regimental. Of course, I hated to be rough with these poor fellows who had been fighting for their lives whilst I was in comparative comfort, but it was for their own safety that I cleared them as quickly as I could from the fast-filling road, on which the Germans might open out with shells at any moment.

Just as men would crave the moment of relief when they could finally leave the trenches for a well-earned rest, so others would sullenly, reluctantly, make their way forward through jammed communication trenches to take over front line duties. Private Thomas Hope left the trenches at almost the same time that Lieutenant Edward Alfree was going the other way, up to an Observation Post, seemingly as far from human life as it was possible to be. The deep difference in these men's emotions can only be guessed.

We have been relieved at last – by an Irish division. Everything has been handed over to the incoming troops, even to the quarter-of-an-inch stub of my last cigarette. Poor devil, he looked at it so covetously that I had no option but hand it over. His 'Thanks, mate' rewarded me. After all, they are just coming into this nameless thing of mud and death, while we are gladly leaving it for a spell. I can afford to be generous to the extent of a well-fingered stub of a gasper. We tarry a little over the handing over, as there is a good deal of shelling going on down the road we must take. Assuring ourselves that the new signallers are comfortably settled, we have another look at where the shells are falling, and with a final cheerio, hitch up our packs and start down the trench.

Private Thomas Hope, 1/5th The King's (Liverpool Regiment)

It was a long and unpleasant walk. We started at 7.30 am, going as far as Boesinghe in the sidecar, which we left at 196 Battery's position. We then had to proceed on foot over the canal, over the ridge the other side, past our old OP at Captains Farm, down the slope towards the river Steenbeck, over an improvised bridge, past the Wiggendrift (which was a strongly concreted building the Boche had occupied, and which we had fired at on former occasions), then over a wide, flat, open expanse, pitted with shell holes, wet and marshy in places, with dead bodies lying about (both British and Boche) in various attitudes as they had fallen, some half in shell holes and half out. We then reached what had been a Boche communication trench, but which was now no more than a battered bank of earth. We followed this forward, taking advantage of such cover from observation as it afforded, till the telephone line, which was guiding us, led us to a Boche concrete pillbox erected in what had been the trench. This was the OP – officially known as 'FA' (I do not know what 'FA' stood for, but every OP had some official reference number or letter)....

Lieutenant Edward Allfree, 111th Siege Battery, Royal Garrison Artillery

Perhaps the worst feature about FA was that it was so isolated and far from home. It seemed far out into the Interior of Hell. So far forward over those miles of desolate battlefield, now so swept by shellfire, that neither tree nor house nor blade of grass was left – nothing but brown shell-pocked earth, with here and there some bare splintered tree trunks, which had once formed a wood, or a few bricks, which had been a farm. You might stand in the ruins of Boesinghe, and look across over this

A corner of Inverness Copse, photographed by Lieutenant Colonel Graham Seton Hutchison, 33rd Battalion, Machine Gun Corps, after capture, 25 September.

barren land to the top of the ridge, where shells might be bursting (they so often were), sending up fountains of earth and smoke, but the OP was far beyond that. You might get over the ridge to Captain's Farm and look across more barren land to the valley of the river Steenbeck, where shells might be bursting (they so often were), but the OP was far beyond that. You might get over the river, and look across another equally desolate, but muddier, expanse towards a ridge of earth, along which shells might be bursting (they so often were), and the OP was there, far along this earth bank that had been a trench.

Private Thomas Hope, 1/5th The King's (Liverpool Regiment)

At every bursting shell we duck down, and wait until the upheaval has settled itself. As Webster remarks: 'There is no damned use in hurrying and running into a packet; we'll take our time and make use of every bit of cover.'

We seem to be more often on our bellies than on our feet, but finally we file out of the trench and onto the road. For a minute or so we watch the shelling. They are coming over in threes at about half-minute intervals. One learns to take note of these things; they mean all the difference between life and death. Accordingly we wait for the first shell to burst, then make a dash past the crater. They drop at almost 50 yards' distance; so we regulate our runs to be well clear of the second and third shells, then of the third and the first of the next series of three; and so we repeat this manoeuvre until we are practically out of range. This will be our last run. Another 60 yards and we shall be clear of the stretch of road under fire, but we are so anxious to be on the safe side that we delay our rush just a fraction too long, and have hardly covered 10 yards when we hear the shell approaching, at first like a giant hissing which gradually gathers in volume and takes on a more menacing tone, then like a rushing steam engine coming straight for our backs.

So far from life, and, as it seemed, so near to death. So far from your friends and from assistance should you need it. It was a long and tedious walk over those interminable duckboards, winding between shell craters; and as you plodded along with various impedimenta suspended around you, it was hard to exclude from your mind that at any minute and at any stage, that fateful shell might burst in your path. Some part of this area, over which our route lay, was always being shelled. It was just luck if you were to happen to be on that particular spot at the time or not. At times, of course, you could see in advance where the shells were falling and make a detour to avoid that particular spot.

Lieutenant Edward Allfree, 111th Siege Battery, Royal Garrison Artillery

I am undecided whether to follow Webster or drop where I am. My skin tingles and my breathing almost stops as, with a hurtling roar, the demon arrives, and I fling myself clear of the road onto a mess that gives way beneath me, something which feels cold and slimy as I sink into it, and gives forth a suffocating stink. A disturbed rat scuttles away, and I press even closer to this nauseating couch as the ground beside me shudders and heaves. The clods of earth and paving-stone are still falling as I jump up, and, with Webster and Mac, finish that last dash down the road, the stench of dead mule still lingering in my nostrils.

Private Thomas Hope, 1/5th The King's (Liverpool Regiment)

Above: *The Lille Gate, on the southern edge of the Ypres Salient, photographed by Colonel R. Perceval-Maxwell, 13th Royal Irish Rifles. Note the hessian screen to obscure direct observation.*

Right: *Transport moving through a shell-swept Ypres.*

Each step now takes us father away from the shelling and our spirits rise accordingly, until, as we turn off the road and make for the outskirts of what had once been the thriving town of Ypres, we are as happy as schoolboys. We cross the moat and through the Menin gateway in the ramparts. Every inch of this road we know, and yet, as we enter the ruined city, everything seems different; it is so quiet, so ghostly. The rattle of a limber on the cobblestones is all we can hear. It gives us an uncanny feeling and accentuates in glaring relief the desolation that surrounds us.…

We go in search of our battalion and are formed up in pitifully small companies and marched to a field on the other side of the town, where we are halted for an hour until dusk.

No sooner do our heads touch the ground than we are dozing off, but only seem to have settled ourselves comfortably when it is time to move again. On we trundle along the country roads, practically sleeping on our feet, past farmhouses, through villages, silent and shuttered, alongside beet and hop fields and still we carry on, continually pushed into the muddy ditch at the side of the road to allow transport and army wagons to pass. Big country houses loom up inhabited by soldiers, which, we guess, are divisional or corps headquarters. Where we are, or where we are going, nobody seems to know.

'Why the hell can't we doss by the roadside?' wearily shouts Webster, but everybody is too exhausted to answer even that enquiry.

On arriving at FA, we find it consists of a concrete pillbox – pretty strong and massive, giving one a distinct sense of safety. It would probably stop a direct hit from a 4.2 shell. There is an inner chamber about 3 ft 6 inches or 4 ft high inside. The outer chamber is a bit more lofty and has an aperture in the roof. Probably the Boche used this in some way for observing, but the aperture is useless to us for that purpose. The entrance is in the left-hand side as you face the Boche, and around this has been erected a low barricade of sandbags, forming a low wall, over which, by standing outside the pillbox, one can observe without exposing oneself to the view of the Boche.

After the walk there, it seemed a little haven of refuge, but it was not a savoury spot. Just the other side of the sandbags, about 2 yards from

Lieutenant Edward Allfree, 111th Siege Battery, Royal Garrison Artillery the entrance to the pillbox, was a dead Boche, lying with his face in a shell hole; a few yards down the trench behind us was another, and just in front of us was a dead British Tommy. They never got buried – it was not worth exposing oneself to the enemy to perform the task. Each time I went to the OP I saw them rotting away – getting thinner and thinner – till at last they were actually skeletons in discoloured uniforms. In the meantime great green-bodied bluebottles swarmed over them, and it was only with difficulty that one kept them off one's bully beef or sandwiches, when partaking of lunch. I suppose they rather fancied a change of diet. At night, I think they went to roost in our pillbox.

Private Thomas Hope, 1/5th The King's (Liverpool Regiment)

Night is giving way to dawn when at last we are marched off the road and into a field. A halt, some instructions are given in front, then a figure carrying a hurricane lamp counts us off in sections and leads us to a darker patch on the dark landscape, which blossoms into an erection of some kind. There is the creak of rusty hinges and we find ourselves in a barn of sorts. Our entry is greeted with the cackling of awakened poultry and the grumbling of shocked pigs at this barbarian intrusion of their nocturnal privacy.

We sort ourselves out into our own particular groups, fling off our packs, and with a 'to hell with the war, I'm going to sleep' feeling, stretch ourselves out on the straw which covers the floor of the barn, and we are soon vying with the dislodged occupants for musical honours.

Lieutenant Edward Allfree, 111th Siege Battery, Royal Garrison Artillery

The interior of this pillbox was not exactly enticing. It swarmed with these flies, and probably with other things as well. On this first day, we found inside numerous Boche effects. There were two dirty old mattresses down on the floor; a number of machine-gun cartridges; some hand bombs; a rifle and numerous empty tins containing putrefied remains of food.

The Major gave orders to have this cleared out, and the next time I visited the OP, I found it in a vastly improved condition, thanks to the efforts of the telephonists. But on this first day, in spite of its unsavoury condition, we were glad to take refuge in the innermost chamber on several occasions, as periodically, the Hun did a shoot on us, and dropped his beastly shells all along the trench. He probably suspected that his old

Above: *Captain Birnie's camera captures the desolation of his battalion's surroundings. His images of the battlefield are exceptionally rare.*

Left: *'Boche retaliation', according to Captain Robert Perry's caption.*

concrete dugouts were being used by us as artillery OPs. The view from FA was fairly extensive. On our left front was Houthulst Forest, on our right front was Poelcappelle, and to our right flank, and fairly close, was the remains of Langemarck.

Private Thomas Hope, 1/5th The King's (Liverpool Regiment)

The next thing I remember is the opening of the barn door and a stream of sunshine on my face, while a leather-lunged sergeant invited us to show a leg. With much grousing and cursing we sit up and stretch ourselves, then realizing how chilled we are, jump up and stamp some warmth into our bodies.

Breakfast puts us into a better humour, and we jostle and joke around the solitary biscuit tin of water which constitutes the communal bathtub. Razors are brought out and there is the usual scrimmage for odd pieces of scented soap and broken mirrors, but, thank Heaven, I am still spared that little bit of torture. A razor over my face once a month is all I find necessary to comply with King's Rules and Regulations.

Spit and polish becomes the order of the day, and we scrape and brush until there isn't a vestige of the mud of the trenches left. Then bathing parade. With our towels over our shoulders we march singing down to the bathing-shed. The guns are only a rumble in the distance, and our spirits revive according to the number of miles we put between ourselves and their death-dealing nearness. It has become such a custom to live without a future that the knowledge we can now talk of tomorrow with some measure of certainty makes us light-headed. Pleasure is now derived from the common things in life that at home would have passed unnoticed. The sun, the trees, the birds, green fields and the country people going about their daily labour; how peaceful it is, surely life as we were meant to live it. …

Opposite: *Out of the trenches after a stint in the line and waiting for the rations to arrive.*

The chance to live again, even if for a short period, was greedily grasped by anyone far enough from the front line to lose that gnawing fear of trench life that death was just an instant away. Senses were heightened to 'normal' summer life that in a previous existence, as civilians, would have passed most of these men by. Not any more. It was a time to enjoy the sun, reflect, and try to ignore the future.

To me, a squalid village, a dusty street, a dirty child, seemed things of beauty and of worth, and the sun setting behind the slagheaps and smoke-hung air, a thing to call forth a psalm of praise. To see the country around one, to feel its freedom, and the air on one's face, to throw aside one's equipment and, greatest joy of all, to live on the level revelling in the daylight – only those exiles from earth's beauty, released for a time, can know what these things mean. Prisoners freed from prison! …

Lieutenant George Brown, 9th The Suffolk Regiment

Lying in the long grass of the meadows, the sun beating down on our already tanning features, we idly smoke and yarn away the hours between parades.

My thoughts seem to come and go as quickly as the tunes from Webster's mouth organ … a grasshopper clicks noisily somewhere near my

Private Thomas Hope, 1/5th The King's (Liverpool Regiment)

ear, a couple of butterflies flit to and fro above my head, while as far as the eye can see runs the straight poplar-lined road. A peasant trundles along it leading a horse and cart. Time to him seems to be of no importance. The very atmosphere breathes peace.

I try to shut out the past and forget there is a future. If only this could last forever. That is all I ask. A quiet countryside unknown to war, with green trees instead of splintered stumps, clean earth that hasn't been tortured and poisoned by explosives, a task like that peasant's to justify my existence – and peace.

Lieutenant George Brown, 9th The Suffolk Regiment

Those in England cannot realize what a company commander's life is like – even out of the line – its trials and worries and the awful responsibility of it all. Some 200 men, most of whose education consists in the ploughman's daily round, looking to him for every little thing. Grievances to be settled, justice to be weighed out, financial matters to be adjusted and the great responsibility of life and death, for on his orders men go to meet certain death or wait in comparative safety. When life is cheap it isn't one's own that counts, it's those lives that are dependent on you, and behind them the lives at home in England.

I had two pathetic letters today, one from the fiancée of a man to whom I had to break the news of her loved one's death, thanking me – oh, so piteously! – for my kindness, and asking if I could tell her how she could get some souvenir to take with her down the empty years that lie ahead. The other more pathetic still, and yet more touching than any I have ever received.

Let me quote a little of it to you. The writer had lost both husband and brother. This is what she wrote: 'Please don't laugh at me, but I am a lonely woman now, and if there is in your company a lonely soldier who would be glad of letters and cigarettes, do me a kindness and let me have his name.' Somehow I found tears in my eyes as I read it, it was so infinitely sad and yet so beautiful.

Oh, the many sides of life that lie in these soldiers' letters! The pathos of the men whose dear ones are lying ill at home; messages to children they have never seen and may never see; words of comfort and hope to mothers, fathers, sisters, brothers, wives and sweethearts.

Now upbraiding, now consoling. Now joking, full of humour and cheerfulness and never a real complaint against it all, only a devout wish that it may be finished soon. Truly one dips below the surface of life, and we who have seen all this can never be the same careless pleasure-seekers again. . . .

War is far distant tonight, the dull boom of the guns is muffled and lost in a hundred and one murmurs of the night. Within, I sit alone in the farm; alone, and yet from the next room comes the laughter of young voices, finding cheerfulness now that the day's work is done – such is the eternal heritage of youth. Let me try and paint the scene for you: a long wooden table covered partly by oilcloth, partly by a stained tablecloth which has seen better days. A couple of black bottles, some dirty glasses, papers and a scattered pack of cards, a vase of flowers, drooping their heads as though protesting against the sordid ugliness of it all. The daily paper and *Comic Cuts*, that summary of yesterday's news that reaches each company in France. A couple of enamel water jugs and an untidy pile of books and a smoking oil lamp. On the opposite walls hang a row of files of papers, a crude coloured picture of the Madonna and Child, and two of those framed certificates without which no house seems to be complete. On the left two windows open into a garden and orchard, and through these steals the heavy perfume of night-scented flowers; between the windows another certificate. Behind is a large cupboard, smelling of damp, and foul from prolonged disuse. A fireplace and overmantel with a huge cracked gilded mirror, and two hideous vases of artificial flowers.

The mantelpiece is covered with a litter of books, papers, shaving tackle and toilet necessaries. Beyond is my wooden bed, over which is another Madonna. The fourth wall is bare, save for two more certificates and a pair of spurs. Against this stands my washhand stand, a wooden box on which stands a green canvas bucket, and a sponge bag and my valise, while in the further corner, in solemn splendour, rests my tin hat. Scattered about the room are eight wooden chairs. The uneven red-tiled floor is covered with crumpled paper, tobacco ash and the corpses of flies. Boom – a distant gun breaks the silence and suddenly the meaning of it all is borne upon one. A 'runner' enters with countless orders, and sleeping men are wakened

Catching up on much-needed sleep.

and dispatched with messages to outlying billets. For here one's work is never done, by day or night. Such runners enter, breaking into meals or disturbing one's hard-earned sleep, until one prays just for a few hours to call one's own, to read or write or dream of the home life that seems so very far away.

No more than a week's rest precipitated preparation for the next tour in the trenches for Thomas Hope and his comrades. They would remain in the countryside for the time being but they would undertake mock assaults that meant only one thing: they would return to the line in September.

Battlefield orientation was somewhat easier in back areas.

Field days and intensive training are now the forerunners of another spell at the front, and each morning finds us on the march to some rendezvous. The new drafts, oblivious to what is in store for them, treat these outings like a picnic and their good spirits certainly are infectious. We thoroughly enjoy playing at war.

On arrival at the appointed spot we find the whole division assembling, and with much banter and good-natured chaff, are directed by a guide to a farmhouse commandeered as our headquarters for the occasion. The battalion is halted outside, and the signallers and staff noisily take possession of the two front rooms, while the plans are briefly outlined to us by platoon sergeants.

Private Thomas Hope, 1/5th The King's (Liverpool Regiment)

Our trenches are the ditch at the side of the road, our objective the second or Jerry back line, the battalion objective a strongpoint in the shape of a quarry, a thousand yards in front.

Flag-waggers denote the barrage, and woe betide the man who treats the scheme as a joke and sits down instead of flinging himself flat at the sound of the whistle.

Our officer emphasizes the fact that his training must be taken seriously. Every man must take advantage of cover wherever possible as if actually at the front, and we must deport ourselves like seasoned troops of a storm division going into action, not like a host of schoolboys at a Sunday school treat. A hint is also dropped regarding the likelihood of an honoured visit by the Commander-in-Chief, who is desirous of personally thanking our division for splendid work done in the last attack. I have the feeling that we are expected to swoon from sheer delight at this piece of news, but strange to say it seems to leave us older soldiers, at least, quite cold and unmoved.

We take up our position in the ditch and wait for the flags to start waving, then over we go, and move forward to the attack. The flag-wagging comes to a stop in front, the barrage is stationary, whistles blow, and down we flop. This is the first imaginary strongpoint. Our phantom guns will no doubt put it out of action in a few minutes, leaving no time for a snooze.

'Something like a war this. I could stick it for duration.'

'So could I. Oh, damn that whistle.'

Up we get and advance into a field of ripe corn. In the centre the stalks stand so high that we are completely hidden, and certain unpopular sergeants and corporals are bombarded with tufts and lumps of earth. Much shouting ensues but the corn is thick and friendly, and nobody knows from which direction the missiles came. A hare springs up and threatens to stampede the whole formation, but authority at last brings us back into line, and our chances of hare soup for dinner are gone.

When we emerge from the cornfield, it is a sorry mess, with dozens of beautifully trampled paths running right through it, but Monsieur Le Farmer stands by and smiles – the English pay good compensation.

Once in the open we are under the critical eye of the headquarters staff, and the business develops into a well-drilled field day. The rests during the gunners' shoots are very acceptable, and allow Mac to take potshots with a catapult at the opposing troops, composed of men of our own brigade made up for the occasion as Jerries with white bands round their hats.

The sound of beating hoofs draws our attention to the field we have just left and an exceedingly smart cavalcade, glittering with gold braid and red tabs, with lancers in front and behind, canters past – the Commander-in-Chief has honoured us.

'Don't think he noticed us, Jock. Won't he be annoyed when he finds out' – and Mac lazily stifles a yawn.

Some say 'Good old General'.

The rest of Mac's observations are lost in the general noise that accompanies the rush to our last objective, the quarry. This we capture in grand style, yelling ourselves hoarse and putting the fear of death into its occupants, who begin to wonder if we really have gone mad, and not realizing we are just making the best show we can while the General is about.

Imaginary counter-attacks are repulsed with ease, and having won this bit of the war we return to the field kitchens in the rear for our midday meal of stew.

A practice battle may be good training for those in authority, but to the ordinary private soldier like myself, who receives the minimum of information as to what it's all about, it means merely another outing to be made as enjoyable as possible.

Overleaf:
Captain Cross
with two runners,
33rd Battalion
Machine Gun
Corps at Tyne
Cot pillbox.

8 Bite and Hold

Opposite:
*A captured
German pillbox
photographed by
Signaller Sidney
Banyard. Note
the rum jar.*

'A rather interesting screed has been sent round by the II Corps giving some information about the artillery work from 27 June to 31 August. During that period 2,766,824 rounds were fired, weighing 85,896 tons! This is the equivalent of 230 trains of thirty-seven trucks each and one of twenty-nine trucks, each truck holding 10 tons.

**Lieutenant William Bloor, 146th Brigade, Royal Field Artillery,
9 September 1917**

A ugust had not been a success, nothing like, so hopes would have to rest on September. There was one obvious upside: the weather was improving rapidly, and other than one very wet day on 6 September, the rain that had so benighted the previous month disappeared and, as the temperature rose comfortably over 70° F, the ground dried, and dust rather than mud would be the issue.

Haig's concerns over the prosecution of the offensive by his commander, General Gough (5th Army), were brought into sharp relief when he handed the decision-making reins to General Plumer (2nd Army), who would be responsible for the furtherance of the offensive and a major assault planned for the second half of the month. Overwhelming firepower, artillery and machine-gun barrages would be deployed in an elongated operation that would culminate in the British and Empire troops pushing the Germans back beyond the Passchendaele Ridge, still 2½ miles away, not in one over-ambitious move, but in a series of assaults or 'steps'. The Germans would be methodically bludgeoned into giving up ground that would be consolidated and made impregnable from counter-attack. The only issue was that Plumer needed time to plan, and meanwhile the fighting abated. No one could miss the rather obvious fact that nothing was happening at precisely the time when, climatically, the weather was nigh perfect for an offensive. In the interim, as further consolidation of the ground won was undertaken and supplies were brought forward in vast quantities, so there was a simultaneous encouragement to salvage materials from the battlefield. In early September, Major Neil Fraser-Tytler became aware that his new divisional commander was – to the point of distraction – a stickler for recycling the artillery's spent shell cases.

Major Neil
Fraser-Tytler,
149th Brigade,
Royal Field
Artillery

We heard that we had once more changed our divisional RA [Royal Artillery] commander, and that the new arrival, whose name is General B., was coming to inspect the brigade in action. He is an individual well known for having a 106 fuse temper and 'non delay' [i.e. an immediate and violent temper] language far in advance of any other general in the regiment, and worst of all, it was reported that his pet mania was the immediate clearance of all empty cartridge cases from gun positions.

The careful return of shell cases is no doubt very necessary, but on some positions it must pay the taxpayer best to let them lie till the next advance. Casualties to horses and men while performing the slow job of loading them up in wagons may thus be avoided. But this was no excuse in the General's eyes, and he slated two batteries of our brigade unmercifully on account of them. It was to be our turn next day. Just behind our guns were two huge craters filled to the brim with shell cases, at least 10,000 of them. All seemed lost; however, that night came inspiration. At dawn I arose, found an old notice board, and swiftly the battery painter covered its face with the following legend:-

The walls of the Cloth Hall in Ypres are propped up while a plea to men to 'Eat Less and Save Shipping' was likely to be ignored.

'C. 28. C. 53 Dump
All 18-pdr. And 4.5 cases to be dumped here.'

Result, much kudos for our very neat position and a broad smile on the face of our colonel, standing behind the General.

12 September: This morning the Colonel summoned the whole battalion to the concert hall, a ruined house with a roof of yellow tarpaulin. We knew perfectly well what was coming. A fortnight's training in bombing, firing or rifle grenades, shooting at disappearing targets, and practice of assault formations going in waves over a hill, gave us an inkling of hot work in front of us. He told us of the traditions the division stood for, the high position it held in the regard of the Army Commander, appealed to the courage of an army which had triumphed at Messines, Vimy, Arras and Ypres; recalled to us the German treatment of our prisoners, and of harmless Belgian and French civilians, violation, seduction, murder, until it appeared a sacred duty to die fighting for such a cause. At the last he warned us solemnly of the penalties attached to cowardice in the field. 'If the Hun shells too heavily, side-slip, but for God's sake don't go back. We have him by the short hairs, and it only remains for us to make a finished job. We have all had a fierce time punishing him and making him pay for those desecrations of human hearths and hearts; by the grace of God, we shall give him so much of his own hell that he will wish he had never created such misery.'

When he had finished and we went out into the clear air, into the quietly smiling sunlight, a feeling not exactly of pain or even fear overtook me: a dim sense of exaltation, as if a definite vocation in life had been assured, a definite reward, a final gathering of all forces of soul and will to answer the great call, an obliteration of every quavering and hesitation. ... This was the real thing at last, not a mere toying with life and fate.

Private Hugh Quigley, 12th The Royal Scots (Lothian Regiment)

The solemn penalties for cowardice were all too well known, and hardly needed repeating. The exponential growth in the ferocity of artillery bombardments was enough on its own to drive any man mad, but it depended on the individuals, according to Company Quarter Master Sergeant William Andrews, and how, in many cases, they might have been wounded before.

There were not many of the veterans left. Even the best of all soldiers, though not hit, could not go on fighting year after year. We had a very good NCO, who, after an action, when details were being collected for official descriptions of the battle, began to cry, said he could not remember

CQMS William Andrews, 1/4th The Black Watch (Royal Highlanders)

doing anything, and supposed he would be shot for cowardice. I have not the slightest doubt that he behaved with his accustomed coolness and gallantry, but towards the end got some sort of shell shock. He plainly would not be of any more use, and he was found a staff job. Many of our men had been wounded once and sent back to the line, and we could not expect them to be as trustworthy as before. If a man had been wounded by a machine gun he would generally be panicky when there was machine-gun fire. Similarly, a man who had been wounded by a shell was unsteady in shelling. We were getting many conscripts, whose fighting value, inevitably, was less than that of the old volunteers. For one thing they were often sent straight into the most frightful experiences, whereas we veterans had been trained by a gradual process into self-control under stress.

Whether CQMS Andrews would have considered Private Quigley as a newcomer is hard to say. Quigley had been on the Western Front a little over two months but had been fortunate enough to have soldiered in what were backwaters in comparison to the salient, which he now entered for the first time prior to the assault timed for 20 September. His curiosity about the landscape was piqued and he wrote home in alarming candour of this new world he was now immersed in.

Private Hugh Quigley, 12th The Royal Scots (Lothian Regiment)

17 September: The country resembles a sewage heap more than anything else, pitted with shell holes of every conceivable size, and filled to the brim with green, slimy water, above which a blackened arm or leg might project. It becomes a matter of great skill picking a way across such a network of death traps, for drowning is almost certain in one of them. I remember a run I had at the beginning of this week – for dear life, if you like. Five of us had spent the night patrolling and were returning to Brigade HQ when the enemy sighted us and put a barrage along the duckboard track we were following. Early dawn broke in the east, and a grey light filtered eerily through dim cloud masses to a desolate world of brown, touching the skeleton woods strangely, and blackening the edge of the ridge where the German trenches lay. First one shell dropped 10 yards behind us, then one came screaming so close that we dropped in our tracks and waited for the end. I got right under the duckboard track, and the hail of shrapnel

and mud on it was thunderous enough to frighten the most courageous. Then we stood up, all safe though muddy, and with a 'Run like hell, boys', went off in a devil's race, with shells bursting at our heels, for half a minute, dropping at last in complete exhaustion in a trench out of range.

It is quite the usual thing to stand about a hundred yards away and see some poor devils getting chased for their lives. Our artillery has an interesting habit of putting up a specially warm barrage when the line is being relieved, with the result we get a very thorough shelling in return just when we cannot shelter. When we left the Menin Road and took to the duckboards at a time when the enemy placed a barrage on them, the most careless of us cursed the man in front of him if he happened to pause a minute. It seemed the best solace for excited nerves to keep going, no matter whether in or out of danger. Yet, luck stood by us; in spite of our over-zealous artillery, not a shell dropped near us until we reached our trenches, and then we had it stiff. A sergeant and two privates were blown to pieces 20 yards from me: all night and early morning we lay in the shallow trench, trying vainly to keep knees from shaking and teeth from chattering, with a deadly sick feeling in the stomach as bits of shrapnel hit the side of the trench with a dull thud and earth was shaken over our face.

In the morning, through a glorious clear sky of pale blue, we watched our own aeroplanes and the enemy's circling slowly and dropping outside our range of vision, heard the constant rattle of machine guns and the crack of high shrapnel, white and black. All we could do was to lie motionless on our back and pray that the enemy had not seen us. I tried to sleep, but nervous excitement kept me awake all day until night, when we dug out a new trench. While plying the spade, I encountered what looked like a branch sticking out of the sand. I hacked and hacked at it until it fell severed, and I was picking it up prior to throwing it over the parapet when a sickness, or rather nausea, came over me. It was a human arm.

Private Quigley's ordeal was far from over. That evening, he was sent from their improvised trench on patrol and, after being spotted by the enemy, he took refuge in a deserted pillbox.

Private Hugh
Quigley, 12th
The Royal
Scots (Lothian
Regiment)

This pillbox had been used at one time as a charnel house; it smelt strongly of one and the floor was deep with human bones. From there we watched the Very lights flickering outside, and casting a weird light through the doorway, the red flash of bursting shells. Occasionally a direct hit shook us to the very soul. While sitting there, the odour overcame me and I fainted. Waking up an hour afterwards, I found myself alone, without the faintest idea of my whereabouts, uncertain where the enemy's lines were or my own. Some authors practise the description of fear, but nothing they could do could even faintly realize my state. It went beyond fear, beyond consciousness, a grovelling of the soul itself. For half an hour I stood inside, wondering whether to venture out or stay in at eminent risk of daylight coming to disclose me to the enemy. At last, bravery returned, and I went out only to stumble over a derelict wire a hundred yards further on, and find my hands clutching at a dead man's face. But on the other side of it lay our trench, and I was able to calm down in readiness for the morning barrage.

A brigade bomb store in a former German-occupied pillbox. Note the effect of several direct hits on the bunker. The percussion of a direct hit from a heavy shell could often kill the occupants.

It is extraordinary that Private Quigley was able to regain his composure to such an extent that he was able to write anything as detailed as this letter. The trial of his courage had been immediate and unforgiving, and devoid of the 'gradual process into self-control under stress', as described by CQMS William Andrews.

They have a curious way of finding direction in Belgium. The landscape had no salient features of its own; everything blasted to mud – railway embankments, woods, roads, confused in shell holes and mine craters. Trees are only skeletons, and masses of obscene ruins mark farms and houses. You look in vain for a wood where such is marked on the map. The only way at night is to bend down close to the ground and gaze at the skyline for black shadows of pillboxes; by those shadows you find your way. Or, to remember a road once seen, the oddest details must be noted – a solitary length of rail or wire, a 'dud' shell, three stakes together, a fragmentary hedge, a deserted waterlogged trench, dead men lying at various angles, and the position of pillboxes in relation to the track followed. The most exciting time I spent was in hunting B Company headquarters across this monotony of mud and water. I think I must have visited the whole division before finding it, artillery as well as infantry; had to lie through a pretty fierce barrage, too.

Private Hugh Quigley, 12th The Royal Scots (Lothian Regiment)

Tower Hamlets opposite Inverness Copse, 26 September, on the day Lieutenant Wilfred Bion took his tank into attack at Hill 40.

Of course, we had our recompense. It was night when the two of us set out to find our company and midday when we finished. About eleven o'clock we saw a light bobbing up and down to our left, and going to it met an artillery officer, who, on being asked, directed us in the wrong direction. Being absolutely dying of thirst, we waited till he had gone and then prospected for his dugout. There, we were almost drunk on soda water and lemonade, dined royally off his table, and came out better men.

The concentration of British guns for the offensive was the greatest of the war, although by their numbers they were vulnerable to counter-battery fire directed by enemy observers still strategically on (marginally) higher ground. Meanwhile, enemy aircraft attempted to search for the vast dumps of shells needed by the British artillery as well as bombing rest camps, harrying tired men who had thought they were temporarily out of harm's way. The effects could be devastating to both life and morale. Not four weeks earlier, the 10th Queen's (Royal West Surrey Regiment) had lost nearly a hundred men, over forty of them killed, in one speculative evening raid, as the men slumbered amongst the trees in a camp over 10 miles south-west of Ypres.

Private Henry Russell, 10th The Worcestershire Regiment

Before this attack was made we were to be treated to a spell in the trenches for a preliminary look round. Accordingly, we left the lorries at Hill 60 and found much evidence of what was to be expected in the course of a few days. As at Messines, so here, were guns in countless numbers, with their ugly noses pointing in the direction of Klein Zillebeke, while stacks of shells were encountered everywhere we walked.

The front line, which was on the crest of a ridge, gave a splendid view of the immediate country in the possession of the enemy. With the naked eye several churches could be seen quite distinctly and far-distant chimney stacks were smoking furiously. I looked many times through field glasses at apparently sleepy villages a few miles away, but never did I see the slightest sign of life, only the smoking stacks and the flashing of guns.

The targets set by Plumer were attainable, with the troops leapfrogging each other. In a new strategy, each successive wave that attacked the enemy would be increased in strength so that the effect would be to amplify the pressure on the enemy rather than the reverse, when attacking forces were badly thinned just as they met stronger and fresher enemy reinforcements. A quarter of those to be committed to the offensive would also be held back as an immediate reserve to be deployed where the situation required support. This methodical general had given much operational thought to this latest assault.

It was the night before we moved to the trenches for the 'push', and the divisional band had arrived to entertain the troops. The sergeant majors and sergeants possessed a barrel of beer, and they formed a boisterous party in a corner of the camp. I strolled away from the tents for I felt moody and wished to be alone.

Private Henry Russell, 10th The Worcestershire Regiment

The band was playing *When you come to the end of a perfect day*, and the tune seemed particularly affecting. I felt strangely apprehensive and not a little homesick. For a full year I had been escaping death by inches and I wondered how long it would last. I wanted to shake the hands of those I loved. How good it would have seemed if someone from the homeland could have passed by then. No matter if he had been a one-time enemy, I could have fallen on him and embraced him.

I tried to concentrate my thoughts on the distant future when war should be no more and the accursed trenches were only a memory, but I could see no future. I could not look beyond the next two days. My life, and the lives of thousands of other men, were but the playthings of the moment. In a couple of days, perhaps less, the acres of Klein Zillebeke would be stained with the blood of those who were now listening to the music of popular melody. In forty-eight hours their fresh young bodies would have started to rot. It was no idle premonition, no exaggerated view of what might be. It was a stark raving fact that 20 per cent of the men were not expected to be living in two days from now.

For a long time I mused thus. The band had completed their programme and had played *The King*. The raucous laughter of the sergeants came echoing across the ground. The bugles rang out the weird notes of the Last Post. It was time to return.

Sapper Albert Martin, 122nd Signal Company, Royal Engineers

This morning I came up out of the tunnels and had a wash in a shell hole. Then I went to the top of the bank and had a look round. It was not safe so I didn't stay long. Looking towards the enemy (the front line is about 400 yards away) the land dips down into a slight valley and on the hill beyond stands Gheluvelt, which at this distance appears hardly to be touched. Tower Hamlets, our objective, is this side of Gheluvelt but on the other side of the valley. I counted a dozen derelict tanks and we call this neighbourhood 'Tank Cemetery'. Looking backwards over Zillebeke Lake, Ypres stands out grisly and white like a ghost of a city, and really that's all it

Scots Guardsmen manning Gully bombing post, Mills bombs ready to hand.

is. This spot is certainly a vantage point. No wonder Fritz pays it so much attention. With the exception of short bits of trench at the entrances to the saps the only shelter is to be found in shell holes, and half of these are filled with water. The horses with the rations cannot get right up here, so each night all men not on duty have to form a ration party and go and bring them up. Returning, I got into the trench and was almost up to the door of the sap when a shell burst on the parapet and I was covered with mud and dirt, one piece giving me a nasty whack on the top of the shoulder. I thought no more about it until later in the evening when something caused me to put my hand to the spot and I found a long scratch, no worse than a kitten would give. I am rather surprised because all I felt at the time was a thud as if a heavy clod of earth had struck me. Thank God it was no worse, though at times the strain of this existence makes one long for death.

The troops filed into the trenches and, once again, the weather mockingly began to drizzle, dampening the clothes of men who already had more than enough to cope with.

Three quarters of an hour before Zero! The steady drip, drip of water from the roof of our cubicle has almost lulled me to sleep. Half our battalion is packed away in this dugout, a typical British one, damp, stuffy and cramped. It has only one thing in its favour – depth, and that to us means safety.

Private Thomas Hope, 1/5th The King's (Liverpool Regiment)

The thud of the searching shells can be heard, the dugout trembles with their violence, but we are too far down for them, they cannot touch us here. What matters it that the walls are thick with slime, or that the roof leaks like a sieve and we sit huddled together on a floor of thick, sticky mud? Down in this burrow we know we can live and that truly is heaven. A few more minutes of time and we'll have to leave this sanctuary and then ___. Those who can, stop thinking, and like myself try to find respite in fitful oblivion.

The rum ration is brought round, a spoonful to a man, and as usual Mac and I give ours to Webster. So far, I have never taken it, as personally I can't see what good a spoonful is going to do me, but, on the other hand, neither can I see the harm, for, as Mac often says, it isn't enough to keep one's stomach from turning; but I have been brought up in a temperate home, and have no desire to break the old faith even to help win the war. French beer and wine I have learned to place in a different category to alcohol, but army rum is to me strong drink, a belief which Webby stoutly encourages.

After much swearing and good-humoured chaff, the sergeant with his orderly, jar and spoon departs to the next cubicle, and we are left alone with our thoughts. My own I try to make a blank, as it is the easiest way. I know what is before me and am fast becoming a confirmed fatalist. I look round at my comrades: Webster and Taffy are talking in low tones, both very serious looking. Mac is lying across my feet; his eyes are closed, but by this time, like myself, he is very much awake. Two of the others are scribbling on a field postcard and exchanging confidences, while yet another new recruit is reading a letter, evidently his last from home, and appears to be the most unconcerned of the lot.

Try as I like, however, my mind will dwell on the folks at home, and I wonder if I will ever see them again. Such morbid ideas are foolish, however, and I try to concentrate on other things, but home seems to be uppermost in my mind and I recall with tender thoughts the day my brother and I crawled into the dog kennel to smoke our first cigarette, mother's surprise at seeing what she thought was the kennel on fire and the smoke escaping from every joint in the woodwork, the pail of water which came splashing in on top of us as she attempted to extinguish the flames, then the sorry spectacle we made as dejectedly we crawled out, sick and wet, and _____ 'Fall in on top at the double' brings me back to the present and makes home seem very far away.

Lieutenant Edward Allfree, 111th Siege Battery, Royal Garrison Artillery

I was called at 3.00 am to relieve Barraclough, and to start off another barrage at 5.40 am. A rather curious mistake occurred in starting off this barrage. I had gone onto the guns with my watch carefully set to the second, clearly understanding that I was to give the order to fire when the time arrived. I had left the Major in bed, but awake with the telephone beside him, as he always had. Presumably it occurred to him, after I had left, that he had not given me sufficiently definite orders to open fire, and

'M.G. Barrage Dugout 46.' Lieutenant Colonel Graham Seton Hutchison took this image of Captain Faulkner (left) and Lieutenant Charles Stokes, 19th Battalion Machine Gun Corps, just before going into action, 25 September. The next day, Faulkner was severely wounded and Stokes was killed.

that I might wait till I got the order from him. So to make certain that I should fire at the appointed time he rang up the telephonist at the Section Commander's Post, immediately behind the guns, to say, 'Tell Mr Allfree to fire when it is time.' The telephonist did not wait for the end of the sentence and having heard 'Tell Mr Allfree to fire', he yelled out to me 'Fire, Sir.' It was still about two minutes to time, so I said, 'What the Hell do you mean?' He said, 'The Major is on the phone, and he says "Fire".' I said, 'Check that message back – it's not time yet.' The Major again repeated his message in exactly the same words, and again the telephonist thought the message complete when he got to the word 'fire', and again yelled out to me, 'Yes, Fire, Sir! Fire!' I thought to myself 'Well I don't understand it, but I suppose my watch has suddenly gone wrong, and the Major is wondering what on Earth I am waiting for – anyhow, an order is an order, so I gave 'Fire', and the barrage started about two minutes before time. The other batteries, hearing us start, at once blazed away – probably thinking they were late. I don't suppose my first shell had got halfway on its journey before all the other batteries had fired.

The Major at once called me to the phone, and said, 'My dear Allfree, what on Earth have you done?' I explained that I had fired on his order, after first checking it back, and getting it repeated. I then handed back the receiver to the telephonist for him to receive a few words from the Major. We never heard anything further of the matter from any higher quarters. If the Colonel troubled to look at his watch, when he heard the barrage open, he probably thought it was his watch that was at fault. But more probably he was asleep.

Private Thomas Hope, 1/5th The King's (Liverpool Regiment)

Outside it is pitch dark, but all is bustle, while innumerable figures flit to and fro like ghostly shadows. On our side it is fairly quiet for this part of the line, but the Boche seems a bit restless and is searching with his heavier guns, Very lights sweeping up reveal us to each other as moving silhouettes marching over the uneven ground to our assembly trench.

The fifteen minutes before 'going over' have a peculiar eeriness all their own. One's heart seems to thump a little louder, while a pulse in the throat keeps beating in unison with it. There is a subtle air of expectancy. Everywhere is activity, a muffled ghostly activity. Orders are given and passed on in a whisper, thousands of troops to right and left of us must be on the move, but our vision is confined to the back of the man in front of us, the sides of the trench and a slice of cloudy, almost obscured moonlight.

We arrive at our assembly point, a hastily dug trench in the rear of our front line from which we go over with the third wave, just in time to get across no-man's-land before the Boche recovers from his surprise, providing the attack is the surprise packet we trust it will be, and nicely placed to catch all that comes our way if he is expecting us. ...

I find myself wondering if the others are as much afraid as I am. It is the waiting that unnerves a fellow, the waiting and the uncertainty of it all. If only I could escape from it I'd willingly do cookhouse and latrine fatigues for the rest of my life, nothing would be too menial, I'd give my soul in bondage to live my life in peace. ...

A machine gun rattles away to our left, while an occasional shell whistles over our heads and bursts in front or rear. A Very light shows me Mac on one side chewing away at a piece of gum, for all the world like a cow contentedly chewing the cud, and Webster on the other, calmly fixing his equipment, while over all hangs a vibrant stillness as if the very atmosphere was charged with the overwhelming activity shortly to be released. I can't help wondering if the Boche, 200 yards away, cannot sense the tension.

Five minutes to go – our platoon officer slithers along the trench repeating as he goes:

'Wait for the whistle now, boys, and keep in touch.'

The waiting is over; our heads thump away as loudly as ever, but our mental fears have vanished. Unconsciously we make sure our bayonets are properly fixed, sling our rifles over our shoulders, and with a shrug to settle our equipment more comfortably, file towards the opening in our trench. For a full minute not a sound can be heard, and then, as if by the wave of a wizard's wand, the air is rent by a million screaming, hissing devils of death. It is Zero.

Out of the trench we scramble and form into some semblance of order, then move forward rather anxiously knowing that if we can reach and cross no-man's-land before the Boche counter-barrage drops, we are in comparative safety for the time being. Our own wire holds us up for a

The effects of a direct hit on a German gun, Widjendrift Road.

second or two, but at last we are all through the prepared gaps. Here we re-form, and after watches have been consulted, advance again. Everything is done to time. We advance so many yards in so many minutes. We take cover for so many more minutes while the artillery deal with a machine-gun nest, then we advance again, providing the guns have done their work in the approved manner.

Sapper Albert Martin, 122nd Signal Company, Royal Engineers

I was awake when the attack started at 5.40 am so I went up on top to watch it, but the barrage on both sides was so heavy that it was impossible to see any movement because of the smoke, but along the line of attack, shells were bursting in dozens at a time … I shaved and washed in a shell hole and about eight o'clock climbed to the top again to have another look at the attack. It was evident that things were not going so well as anticipated – the line had moved forward but it was still far from the final objective, and there was no doubt that Fritz was putting up a very fierce and stubborn resistance. The battalions making the attack were the Hants [Hampshire Regiment] and the KRRs [King's Royal Rifle Corps] followed up by the Kents and the Surreys. On our left is the 23rd Division and on our right the 124 Brigade. I have been on duty in the Signal Office a good deal during the day and little bits of information have been trickling through regarding the progress of the attack.

Putting them all together, the situation seems like this. Fritz had occupied some of the derelict tanks lying in no-man's-land and had made strongpoints of them. He fought desperately and disputed every inch of ground, and his snipers remained at their posts, hidden in tree trunks etc., and even after our troops had passed them continued to shoot our men from behind. One of them was captured badly wounded, and Colonel Carey-Barnard coming up, raised his revolver to kill him but, seeing his terrible wounds, refrained, and the wretch then pointed out where one of his sniping comrades was hidden. A machine-gun post in a pillbox held our men up for a long time. Our artillery played on it but could not get a direct hit. The Hants could get no further. They had lost all their officers and a great many men. Colonel Corfe of the Kents tried to rally the men but was soon hit by a bullet in the shoulder, but he held on until the post had been outflanked. Then he collapsed.

The succession of horrors was confusing my mind. I was cool, yet had a strange idea that the end was near. The roar of the batteries was unceasing and a stream of enemy shells were passing over us to burst on the trench we had just left.

Several hundreds of yards away the barrage was creeping steadily and remorselessly over the enemy lines, and the first two companies of the battalion could be seen following in its wake. Columns of earth were rising behind them, for the Germans were concentrating on preventing the arrival of reinforcements. The scene was impressive. That men can advance through such a hell when their very instincts must be shrieking out for safety! But there is no turning back. Discipline will ever conquer fear.

Even as we were watching the progress of the battle a huge shell burst near the entrance of the gun pit, and when the smoke had cleared and I had recovered my wits, I found that my two patrol partners were lying dead. This occurrence filled the remainder with panic and we dashed from the gun pit and sought shelter in holes and bits of trenches. I was relieved to find Tanky sitting in a corner smoking a 'Woodbine'.

Private Henry Russell 10th The Worcestershire Regiment

A shell burst over Inverness Copse. Note the rolled-up stretcher in the foreground.

'Where you bin?' he asked quietly. …

In this small piece of trench were three gunners, several company men, and an officer who had only lately joined the battalion after seeing service in the east. The officer confessed that he had lost his batman, who was carrying his rations, so I opened my emergency tin of bully and shared it. This warmed up his confidence.

'Should you call this affair hot, or merely ordinary?' he asked.

'Red hot,' I replied. 'If it gets any hotter we're done.'

'I'm glad to hear that, for a repetition of this every day would be a little too much,' he answered.

Private Thomas Hope, 1/5th The King's (Liverpool Regiment)

The Boche wire is crossed before we see any of our own dead or wounded, while evidence that our gunners have done their job well is apparent. The 'Jerry' front line is no more. In its place there is a jumble of ploughed-up earth interlaced with timber and iron sheets, and an occasional concrete emplacement still standing, battered but indomitable. These constitute our greatest source of worry.

Now we meet up with our first and second waves who are digging in, and we carry on through them. Webster and Mac are still on either side of me. So far, we have been very fortunate, but the machine guns begin to take toll, while shells commence dropping amongst us. Our own barrage in front forms a wall of spouting earth and death between us and the Boche. The din is terrific.

A machine gun suddenly spurts out right in front of us, and automatically we drop flat. Some I notice drop clumsily and lie still; others clutch frantically at limbs. The gun rattles again and is easily located in the semi-darkness by its flashes streaming from a concrete pillbox still defiant. … The shrill sound of a whistle is heard above the noise of bursting shells and machine-gun fire, and our company officers sign for us to work round the flanks and rear of the pillbox. We crawl on our stomachs from shell hole to shell hole, as our Lewis gunners engage the Jerry garrison and keep their attention fixed to their front. At last we have wormed our way round, and are now to the rear of the emplacement where we form in a semi-circle with bombers a few yards in front. There is a sudden rush, and it is all over. Regardless of uplifted hands three of the occupants are bayoneted as they emerge from the narrow entrance, before we realize what we are doing. It is not that we are brutalized, but we are so keyed up to killing, that our minds can't relax quickly enough. We rush forward with the one intention of beating down all resistance; we must, to save our lives. Little wonder then that when men surrender, they are sometimes too late to stay our hand. The slightest movement in the heat of close combat can often be misrepresented. It becomes natural to make sure first.

The delay has left our wings in the air, but we soon regain touch with our right and left companies, and plod on behind the protecting screen of our barrage.

Prisoners emerge from dugouts, their hands in the air, fear and bewilderment expressed on their faces. Still dazed from the terrific bombardment, which has passed over them like a scourge, they are almost childish in their desire to show friendliness, dreading the unknown future, yet eager to leave behind the hell from which they are escaping. We pass them by; they are safe enough, and our moppers-up will herd them together and escort them to the cages in the rear.

A barbed wire pen for German prisoners, erected by men of the 33rd Division.

We were lying in a dreary position. The attack was finished, but the attackers could no longer be seen owing to the contour of the ground. Nearby was a stagnant pool containing a dead German, and the murky water was stained a crimson hue. I kept looking at him and wondered how long he had been there and if he was married, and whether he had been thrown in or had crawled there to die alone. Twenty yards away lay a man with both legs torn off below the knees. He was an officer's servant, a quiet, inoffensive sort of chap, well liked by everyone, and perhaps a little above the average type of infantryman. I had passed him coming to the trench and he had asked after the stretcher-bearers, but I had not the heart to tell him that they were overwhelmed with cases, and that he had little hope of being carried away for many hours.

Private Henry Russell, 10th The Worcestershire Regiment

Just before midday the long-expected runner came from the advanced line. We were to take the place of a gun team which had been wiped out. Thereupon Tanky commandeered a couple of riflemen to bring up the team to a respectable strength, and we followed the runner to the new line.

I was amazed to see that no attempt was being made to keep under cover. Men were walking about the top as though they were miles behind the lines. A considerable number of holes had been dug haphazard, but there was no communication between any two of them. A thousand yards away was a ridge which limited the vision, and I presumed that for the present the Germans must have retired well beyond the ridge, otherwise we should have been heavily fired upon. A few pillboxes were scattered about in front and the land seemed marshy midway to the ridge. On the left were the dwarfed stumps of a once not inconsiderable wood, and beyond that the country seemed opened out to permit of a wide field of fire.

Sapper Albert
Martin, 122nd
Signal Company,
Royal Engineers

It is now apparent that the attack has fallen considerably short of what was expected, but what can you expect from men who are tired and hungry and wet through? To say nothing of the fierce opposition they have had to face. Our Advance Signals when they went up last night tried to establish themselves in a dugout but were peremptorily ejected by Col Carey Barnard who wanted it for himself. So they settled themselves in a little lean-to shelter behind the dugout. A stray dog that had somehow or other got up the line also tried to get in the dugout. He wouldn't stop in the shelter because it was only covered with corrugated iron and a few handfuls of dirt to camouflage it. During the morning Percy Mayne was wounded in the arm while bringing a message to Brigade HQ. He delivered it and then had to be carted off to the dressing station and so down the line. An American doctor who is attached to the Kents performed the operation of amputating a man's leg in the midst of the attack. I expect that tomorrow the English papers will be shouting the news of a great victory, but has been a ghastly and murderous failure. A reinforcement arrived for us this evening – a young fellow just out from England. It's ridiculous to send a new recruit up to a place like this. I was surprised to see some Military Police in these tunnels. They are the warriors who infest the rest areas and spend their time in 'running' poor unsuspecting Tommies who leave cycles unattended for a few seconds. Their business up here is to prowl round the tunnels looking for men who have taken shelter when they ought to be outside. A miserably ignoble trade!

The drizzly night had given way to a bright, warm day. Plumer's divisions, including the 1st Anzac Corps, achieved most of their objectives in the centre of the assault. Yet success was rarely total and the 41st Division, where Sapper Martin was serving, was badly cut up in difficult, boggy conditions. His view of the results was very limited and hardly typical of the battlefront as a whole. The award of twice as many Victoria Crosses in comparison to 16 August was indeed indicative of that greater success. German counter-attacks failed miserably, both on that day and during the days following.

Stretcher-bearers at work: battlefield conditions meant that it could take several hours to extricate one wounded man.

In the early morning the mail and rations arrived. It was remarkable how letters and parcels followed us to the most inaccessible places; but, of course, where men are sent, food must follow, and the post generally came with it.

Private Henry Russell, 10th The Worcestershire Regiment

I received from home the local newspaper, and opening it, found underlined, in a column devoted to those local men who had made the great sacrifice, the name of a friend who had met his death somewhere near Ypres. It was strangely incongruous that I should have my attention drawn to it just at a time when I was not at all sure but that my own name would, in the course of a week, be included in that selfsame column.

For twenty-four hours we had existed on nothing but our emergency rations, and it was with very great satisfaction we noted that today's issue was abnormally large. This was rather puzzling at first until we remembered that the company had suffered many casualties. How many we did not know, but judging by the amount of food sent to us there must have been very few other mouths to feed.

The hole which Tanky and I occupied was too small to accommodate more than two and allow for freedom of movement, so the remainder had settled in a piece of trench that ran at right angles to ours. About 6 feet of earth separated the two holes, and communication was kept up by shouting across. Early in the afternoon a German aeroplane, flying very low, appeared over our position. He was obviously observing the formation of the new line. From some distance away an officer cried out to us to open fire, and somewhat reluctantly I disposed of a magazine, but apparently without effect, for after circling the immediate front he made a detour to his own lines.

Some hours later the enemy artillery became active and a whizzbang battery commenced, directing the fire of one of its guns unpleasantly near our little trench. At first we did not take a great deal of notice, but it gradually dawned on us that the shots were being observed and that we were the target.

Every two or three minutes we could distinguish the report of the gun, followed immediately by a crash in our vicinity. One burst near enough to smother us with stones and earth, and it began to cause serious anxiety.

'This is through firing that perishin' gun,' shouted a voice from the other trench. ...

We piled the rations about us to ward off pieces of shrapnel which flew into the trench. ... Tanky had a tin of Maconochie over his heart and bully beef and jam alongside, while I balanced half a loaf where I guessed my lungs were. It was ridiculous but might reduce an otherwise mortal wound to a superficial one. ...

'What are you doing, Tanky?' I asked.

'Only praying, mate. Don't seem much else left; do you?'

'Do what?'

'Pray.'

'I've been praying ever since that gun opened,' I replied.

'Perhaps he's praying to hit us.'

'Good Lord, Tanky, what a thing to say.'

Despite continued heavy shelling, both Russell and Tanky clung onto their precarious slither of trench until nightfall when their battalion was relieved and they could finally make their way back. Overall casualties had been heavy, more than 20,000 in total, with some battalions faring much worse than others.

Once out of the danger zone I felt wonderfully cheerful. The joy of having passed safely through such a crisis was intoxicating, but back at the camp I suffered a relapse, for the tent which had formerly accommodated nineteen was only required for three.

Private Henry Russell, 10th The Worcestershire Regiment

The following night I strolled away from camp as I had done before the 'push'. The divisional band was not playing; neither did the boisterous laughter of the sergeants echo across the ground. An atmosphere of tragedy overlay the camp, and well it might, for I had heard, unofficially, that the battalion had sustained 375 casualties; and I had no reason to doubt the assertion.

Some of the newspapers named it the battle of the pillboxes, others the Menin Road battle, and all of them acclaimed it a great British victory. I suppose it was, if measured in the term of square yards gained, but I rather thought that if every unit engaged had fared as disastrously as ours, the victory was purely illusory.

There would be little let-up for the enemy. Although the Germans pummelled the forward area, hoping to disrupt British planning for the next step, they were only tinkering around the edges of the inevitable: Plumer's next assault on 26 September.

Second
Lieutenant
Wilfred Bion, E
Battalion, Tank
Corps

We were going into battle. At least, my section was going into action – not battle. A division of infantry, a section of tanks, simply to clear up a couple of pillboxes.

We were urged, ordered, to reconnoitre. This was exciting, frightening. Soon, we felt, we should *know*. Our section commander, a young, bespectacled captain, addressed his officers and men. The talk was designed to tell us of the nature of the operation, and, I suspect, enthuse us with the lust for battle.

'As you all know, we shall shortly be going big-game shooting.' He sounded as if he was talking from the bottom of a heavy cold. 'The red line on the map' – here came a crackling of papers as officers, four of us, with the crews craning their necks to see the shared papers – 'marks the starting point. We have to take Hill 40. Got it?' More rustling. 'And the village behind.' Gunner Harrison, our cockney, looked serious, which usually meant a witticism was coming, but none came.

'Bion, you take Hill 40 and patrol it till the infantry have consolidated. You must watch the sunken road – marked just to the north-east – because our intelligence have told us that the 'umptieth' Division have just moved in. You will see on *this* map, which is secret and must not be given to you,' – he held it up for us to see – 'the sectors held by the individual units are marked and will probably remain unaltered for three or four days – that is till after your show.… The village [Zonnebeke] no longer exists, but Quainton, you and Cohen have to take it and hold it. You can tell when you are there by the brackish stain of the mud. Any questions?'

'The pillboxes, Sir!' It was my tank sergeant, O'Toole, speaking. His large protuberant ears, red, shiny face and permanently indignant expression suggested that an officer should have asked the question. Perhaps he was blushing for us.

'Ah yes; I nearly forgot those. Well, you know they have usually six or more men in them – some people say a dozen. As they are solid concrete and over a foot thick, all you need do is fire at the gunslits and go round to the back door. The gunners are concentrating on them so don't go too near. If you fire at the gunslits you may stop the Boche firing.'

Twenty-year-old Wilfred Bion, of the Tank Corps, had arrived on the Western Front in late June and this would be his first action – and his first time in the salient. The action in which his tanks would serve was a little bigger than he imagined and would include several divisions of men attacking over a wide front.

Time was pressing, the weather was sure to change and the nights were already cooler, the mornings more misty; autumnal weather was not far away. The success on 20 September spurred Sir Douglas Haig into believing that a breakout from the salient, and deeper objectives such as attacking key enemy supply hubs, were possible, but a surprise and partially successful German counter-attack on 25 September, with enemy battery fire potent, appeared to blunt any idea that German strength was spent. The assault would be several divisions strong. Second Lieutenant Bion's description of the preparation and execution of his part in the attack is illuminating and powerful.

The sky for once was blue and cloudless, the land a glistening ochre. There were in the distance some scattered stumps which we decided was a wood, since one was marked on the map. We were walking down a slope supposedly to the Steenbeek from which the ground rose to a series of

Second Lieutenant Wilfred Bion, E Battalion, Tank Corps

Map reading proved problematic in a devastated environment, as Lieutenant Wilfred Bion discovered.

gentle rounded slopes, one of which was Hill 40. The enemy line between us and the hill which was to be my objective was clearly marked on the map as a series of trenches in great depth, redoubts and machine-gun posts, all in red and dated the previous day. It was meticulous and a marvel of the work done by the Royal Engineers. We walked on a duckboard track, shattered here and there by a recent shell burst. Otherwise there was nothing to be seen; no trenches, redoubts, fortifications or machines.

We stopped and sat on a piece of duckboard to study the map. As I fumbled with it I found my hands were trembling: I was exasperated to find I could not control them. I was grateful to [Second Lieutenant] Quainton that he seemed not to notice them. A sudden scream and almost instantaneous explosion made us both flatten out. The enemy had fired a salvo of three. We picked ourselves out of the mud as we realized the burst was some hundred yards away, in no sense dangerous. Then we noticed a group of three men between us and the shell bursts. They were

The flooded Steenbeek.

standing; their teeth shone white in a mirthless grin; our reaction had been observed. I was too obsessed with fear of cowardice to avoid flushing with humiliation. We walked on with as much swagger as we could muster.

And now a fresh anxiety – where was the Steenbeek? At this time it was as deeply graven and marked in our minds as the fortifications were clearly delineated on the map. … We looked at the maps again. They were exact and clear; the cursed place where we stood was not. As far as one could see, even in the direction from which we had come, was a rolling desert of mud where shell holes intersected shell holes. We were in a hollow from which the ground sloped upwards; water trickled from one shell hole to the next, or lay at the bottom. Quainton asked one of the party of men with whom we had now drawn level where the Steenbeek lay. Still grinning inanely he pointed down to the quag where we stood. So, that was the Steenbeek. …

'One of those lumps,' said Cohen vaguely indicating the horizon, 'must be Hill 40. The German line is between us and them, about a hundred yards away.' The slow quacking machine-gun note and some whining bullets were at once answered by a burst of rapid fire. 'Lewis guns; too damned close for my liking. Come on, let's get out of it.' Cohen with his wound stripe could dare say this, but neither Quainton nor I could. The working party had disappeared. We had not seen them go and this intensified the sudden sense of loneliness. The sky darkened. 'What about Hill 40?' I asked. 'Look for it tomorrow,' said Quainton sarcastically.

My anxiety to be gone made me particularly guilty about not having identified my objective. The ochreous slime, glistening, featureless, stretching for mile after pock-marked mile, scared me.

Bion and his fellow officers left the area as fast as they could, hurrying 'in short, quick, staccato steps', as the Germans began yet another harassing bombardment. The next morning they would meet up with their tanks.

In the darkness we could just distinguish some remains – possibly they had been sheds. English Farm they called it. This is where our tanks were to rendezvous for the battle. The timing was exact and we went on without having to wait for each other, but not before some German bombers

Second
Lieutenant
Wilfred Bion, E
Battalion, Tank
Corps

unloaded. Meant for us? Did the enemy know of our impending attack, or was it just a routine raid on English Farm because it was there? Then a star shell fell on our route. We stopped instantly, or so we liked to think; no man moved. The entire line of tanks, eight of them, was glistening, brilliant metal against the velvety blackness of the night. The star shell burned on and on. What an age they took to open fire. Bayliss, at my side, suggested they were just having a good laugh as they watched us, standing to attention there like a lot of military dolls. We had not recovered from our first bombing; dread of the immediate future weighed heavily on our attempts at being carefree. Suppose, though, the presence of the tanks had given away the impending attack? It is difficult now to believe that our anxieties were of so little substance.

The route we were pursuing became jammed with traffic; suddenly without warning troops came from nowhere. We waited. Nothing happened. I ordered Allen to switch off the engine. On that packed road no one spoke. Occasionally a mule whinnied or harness jingled.

'If the Boche start shelling we shall be for it.' It was Quainton, whose tank was some 30 yards behind mine, who had come up to see what was the matter. He had always had that kind of initiative and I envied him his easy, uninhibited way. 'I think I'll go forward to see what's up. After all, they told us this road would be kept clear for tanks.'

Infantry, gunners, ammunition limbers were all stuck in a solid mass in the silence and darkness. Every so often a red spurt of sparks and an explosion marked the fall of an enemy shell. It was a quiet night, but for how much longer? I had vision of a chaos of plunging mules, overturned ammunition limbers, and above all, tanks with their 90 gallons of petrol aflame.

There was a sudden disturbance; a young staff officer had appeared. 'You!' – he was speaking to me – 'What the hell – is this your tank? What the devil do you think you are doing? Get on man! You should be at your starting points by now!'

'I can't sir …' I started to explain.

'Good God, man!' he cut me short. 'Drive through them! Push them off the road!' I realized I had fallen into some peacetime form of manners. 'This is *war* – get on!'

With sinking heart I told Allen to start the engine. We edged and pushed. A gun limber went over amid the curses of the team. 'You fucking bastards!' they swore at us. I felt they were right. I tried to get off the track but the tank began a fearful slither into the mud. Allen stopped the skid with difficulty and we pushed, surrounded by curses and hate every foot of the way. ...

Suddenly our guns opened up their preliminary barrage. All around us the mud became alive with the white flashes of our artillery. These were not field artillery – they were 6-inch howitzers in position 50 yards behind our front line. In a moment or two the enemy counter-barrage started. Our 'road', inevitably, was the target of their fixed lines, calibrated over the weeks, automatically registered. The nightmare was now fact. I signalled Allen to turn at right angles off the road. The shelling was now uniform, as heavy off the road as on it. Yet it was a comfort to feel we were not now a pre-determined target. At least I did know what was happening on that road.

Ascertaining whether the line is cut or not; a signaller with 215 Siege Battery, Royal Garrison Artillery.

I judged we had reached our starting point, signalled again to Allen and pointed our tank towards the 'hill' which somewhere in shell-illuminated night was our objective. The tank commander's private fear now possessed me – that I would fall wounded, unobserved by the crew and so be driven over by the tank. Just as I reached our side door a shell burst blew me over. The door opened and my crew pulled me in and slammed the door to. 'I thought you was a goner, Sir,' said Richardson. I worked my way to my seat in front next to the driver, Allen. We shut off the engine; we had another forty minutes to go before Zero.

With the engine's roar silenced we could appreciate the racket outside, like an inferno of slamming doors. And now

I was aware of a novel sensation; the tank with which I was familiar as a solid mass of steel was shaking continuously like a wobbling jelly. No protection more solid than a figment of my imagination. I was not aware of being afraid, which, from the point of view of comfort, is as good as not being afraid. The tank continued to wobble and the doors to slam; sometimes the slam and the wobble were instantaneous. When I realized that both violent slam and wobble occurred at intervals which were rhythmically connected, I knew we were very near the bursting point of a heavy shell. I felt we should move; there was nowhere to go.

Since it was dark the enemy was firing blind on their established barrage lines and, so far, we had not been hit. Could a shell fall short or over? It could – so I gave up thinking about it, thus taking shelter instinctively in mindlessness. Gunner Allen had nothing to do, but I could order Hayler and Allen, a youngster whose face I could see by the dim interior light of the tank to be glistening with sweat, to get out with me and release the pigeon reporting our arrival at our starting point. I recorded the time and Hayler stolidly fixed the message to the container on the carrier's leg. With only five minutes to Zero Hayler tossed it into the air. It promptly settled on the edge of a shell hole and began to walk about. Exasperated, frustrated, we watched its deliberation. 'If it's going to *walk* to HQ it will bring very stale news.' 'It's not daylight yet, Sir', Hayler reminded me. We started to throw clods of earth at the bird as if that would disturb a composure which could not be shaken by the now intense shellfire. 'I wish I had its bloody wings …' shouted Allen. 'You want the best wings: we have them', it seemed to say.

It was nearly time. 'Get in and start up,' I ordered. The crew began to swing the starting handle. Nothing happened. Then, just as despair began to settle on us, the engine sprang to life with a roar.

Dawn; and we were moving into battle.

The tanks were moving forward towards the heavily fortified village of Zonnebeke. The fighting would be ferocious, the Anzac Corps to the immediate south, V Corps directly in front and to the left of the village. Bion's objective, just on the fringes of the western edge of the village, was barely discernible through the limited observation gleaned from the necessarily small aperture at the front of a tank.

Through the front flap I could see the contours of the 'hills' and that was all. We were in low gear; even at full power we could only lurch at a mile an hour from shell hole to shell hole. The tank began a list to the right. We could not correct it and the 6-pounder gun filled with mud as it ploughed through, not over, the ground. The flying earth made it impossible for Allen or me to open the front observation flaps more than a thick slit. When I tried to use the periscope it was shot off.

Once, to our right, I saw the stumps of trees. It was a great relief as the wood was marked just to the right side of Hill 40. So far so good – if only the tank would right itself, but it would not. We were on rising ground, but with drainage gone the higher ground was a morass worse than the Steenbeek.

It was time to try to check our direction. Opening my flap wider I was relieved to find the shattered trees more or less where, according to my guesses, they should have been. Bothered by chunks of earth each time I opened the flap at all widely, I found it difficult to make my fleeting glances cohere. 'Shells seem very close, Sir,' screamed Allen in my ear. He was right. With the increasing daylight the rhythm of shells I had noted before we started had given way first to the drumfire of Zero hour, and then to something more discriminate. The enemy could see us and his artillery were aiming concentrated fire at us. He could not miss. Yet miss he did, and this contributed to the delusion of safety. And then I realized, in one of my repeated glances in the direction of the trees, that they were not trees but our infantry advancing in line with their rifles slung on their shoulders. I had imagined that infantry used their rifles for shooting; not so – not in Ypres Salient. Imaginary security; imaginary aggression? Yet men died.

With sinking heart I pulled out my map and looked at it. It was the same map so it was hardly surprising that it looked the same. But what the devil had it to do with the mud bath in which we wallowed? My hands were now trembling although I was certain of death, probably the whole crew, but certainly for Allen and myself. What happened in the back of the tank I left to Sergeant O'Toole, that brave, ugly man with red face and protruding eyes and the biggest protruding ears I have ever seen issue from the sides of a man's head. The first time he introduced himself to me as assigned as second in command to my crew he had stood as rigidly

Second Lieutenant Wilfred Bion, E Battalion, Tank Corps

Overleaf: *A tank stuck fast in Inverness Copse, 25 September.*

to attention as a knock-kneed man could and announced defiantly, his habitual expression, that he was an orphan.

Something heaved up in the middle of the tank with a grinding noise. I signalled O'Toole. 'Get out with Colombe and fix the unditching beam.' The two clambered out – to certain death I thought. The huge balk of timber, iron shod, had to be belted to the tracks so that they were locked to revolve together carrying the beam round under the belly of the tank and giving the track additional purchase.

They did revolve but the tank did not budge an inch. The beam scooped the mud out from under the tank; we were digging ourselves deeper into the mud. A louder, more raucous grinding than before – 'Transmission has gone,' shouted Allen. The engine was racing, free-wheeling. He shut off the power. 'Get out!' I ordered, and the whole crew tumbled into the mud. O'Toole yelled and pushed me away from the door. A bullet spattered, missing my head.

As I looked at my map and hands in the tank I felt I was floating about 4 feet above myself, Allen an interested and unfrightened spectator. This disassociation, depersonalization, was a way of achieving security – spontaneous, automatic, but potentially costly as it involved not knowing of the imminence of death.

We formed, according to our training, a 'strongpoint'. We scattered in a rough line between the tank and the position in which we thought the enemy lay. We had our Lewis guns and ammunition. If I knew where the enemy, or even Germany, was we could have fired in that direction. I got out my compass. I could hardly believe my eyes when I saw we were facing in the wrong direction. Luckily for us I retrieved some capacity for scepticism; it delayed me enough for suspicion to ripen into certainty that the compass was disturbed by the mass of steel of the tank. We crouched in our shell holes, fiddled with our guns to see the mud had not clogged them. Morning passed to golden afternoon; the sun came out, the gunfire seemed less and our tank, now winking out of sight without help from the unditching beam, no longer attracted gunfire.

Bion's tank was stuck fast and they were helpless to assist the attack, to the point that one man, Richardson, 'the grandfather of the crew' – aged thirty-eight – produced photographs of his family to show Bion. Bion had no idea what to do and so they waited, watching from the tank apertures as, at one moment, a flurry of British troops appeared to retire then, soon after, witnessing a British barrage break up a German counter-attack. Eventually an officer appeared by the side of the tank and shouted orders for Bion and his men to retire.

'Oughtn't we to stay – Lewis guns, plenty of ammunition?'

 'Do what you bloody well like – I've told you the orders.' He was cross. So was I. Why the devil start arguing? I wanted to be cleared out. The officer had gone. I knew – I still know – I should have stayed, orders or no orders. Even junior officers are supposed to show initiative. 'Come on chaps!' I yelled, waving them back. Breathless, hot, worn out, we got back to the Advanced HQ in a German pillbox.

Second Lieutenant Wilfred Bion, E Battalion, Tank Corps

Bion was never quite sure where he had finished up in relation to Hill 40, but at the end of the day, while Zonnebeke had fallen, the small mount remained in enemy hands. Bion was interviewed next day by a Brigade Intelligence Officer.

The Intelligence Officer sat on one side of the table and I sat facing him. 'Can you show me whereabouts your tank got stuck?' It sounded simple, but though it was early afternoon I seemed incapable of thought. I said it was a bit to the right of Hill 40, that is, east of it – or was it west? It could be …

 He waited patiently. 'Here, show me on the map.'

 Obviously it could not be west – it would be in German lines. Not east, because we would not have got into action. But, come to think of it, I was not sure we *had* got into action. I kept thinking of my shell hole which I shared with a corpse from a previous engagement.

 'Here,' I said with a wobbly finger.

 'Or,' he said with scarcely concealed sarcasm, 'possibly here, perhaps?'

 I agreed it was very likely. …

 'You say the tank sank out of sight?'

 I considered this. 'No, it sank level with the ground. You could probably see it if you stood up.'

 'But … didn't you *look* at it before you went?'

 'Not standing, Sir. I had nearly been shot through the head just before.'

Second Lieutenant Wilfred Bion, E Battalion, Tank Corps

'Well, yes, I suppose there is always the risk of that … in battle I mean.'

I was getting cross. 'This was supposed to be a battle … sir.' I added.

He looked at my face for a moment and then studied his map. At last he said, indicating that the interview was over, 'Well, thank you very much. I think that will do. … Oh, by the way, did you see any infantry?'

I said they had been falling back when we left – a small bunch of them under counter-attack. 'Here, pretty well on the top of the hill, a bit to the left I should say.'

'Ah! That's very interesting.' It must have been my only intelligible remark. I saluted and left.

Intelligence, of a more comprehensive nature that was given to Haig, continued to insist that the Germans resolve could break at any time and so the impetus to continue the fight remained. The offensive was driven on throughout October, regardless of the worsening weather. Reserves were kept close to the battle line, to be brought up the moment the German line was seen to fail comprehensively. It did not rain on 1 October but it did for the next week, and for twenty-four of the thirty-one days that month. This was no surprise, as October was almost the wettest month of the year in Belgium. Conditions that had bedevilled the start of the campaign, returned with a vengeance.

Lieutenant Edward Allfree, 111th Siege Battery, Royal Garrison Artillery

Immense gunfire all day. An attack was launched at early morning. Went up to top of the hill about 11.00 pm to have a look at the guns at Ypres. I had the extremely wonderful sight of an SOS call as it is attended to nowadays. I saw the rocket go up, and it is actually true to say that before the rocket had burst and fallen, the guns had started, and in ten seconds there was a line of flashes along the whole of the 19th Division front. The gunners must have been actually standing at the guns waiting. The counter-attack, I heard the next day, was completely smashed – and I should think so! No words of any writer could convey the majesty and thrill of the dreadful sight and sound. Perhaps I am more impressionable than some, but there are so many things in the war that I think beyond measure wonderful, and which affect me greatly, but it is quite impossible to even endeavour to try and describe them. There is no doubt that I see and feel and am appealed to by the grandeur, romance and immensity of it all, and it has a very exhilarating and uplifting effect on me, and I am able to take immense pleasure sometimes in doing a job or perhaps being in a place which to the other type of mind is simply and very wholeheartedly just 'The Beastly War'. I have been as frightened as a man can be, many a time, and have had 'my heart in my mouth' very often (as nearly as that can be done literally) and the experiences are unpleasant, but up till now, thank God then a thousand times, I recover from it at once and feel no more. To lose one's nerve must be the very worst Hell there can be for a soldier in this enlightened 20th century. We have a case in the battery now, and I only hope I am blown to shreds first. I seem very like a badly bitten spring poet trying to write what I have never even breathed hitherto, but in a word, I have never been as happy in my life as I have whilst on active service – utterly foolish and impossible though that must seem to everybody else.

Our nightly game of bridge in the mess was sometimes disturbed by shellfire. I remember we were having a game one evening, between tea and dinner, when the shells began coming over. No one took any notice or said anything for some time, though, I am sure, each one was feeling somewhat anxious. It was most distracting, when considering whether to double 'three no trumps', to be, at the same time, wondering where the next one was coming to. Then you would hear the scream overhead, and down it would come with a crashing roar, and the splinters would whistle over the shed. Someone might murmur 'Seemed a bit closer, that one' and someone else would say, 'Two hearts', and over would come another one. But no one seemed to want to be the first to move. At last I decided to stick it no longer. It seemed too silly to be sitting there, playing Bridge, when, at any moment, a shell might fall through the roof, and despatch all the officers of the battery at once. So I said, 'Look here, I don't think this is good enough – they are coming too damned close – I'm going to clear.' The rest readily agreed that it was time we went. And so, to the trenches at the flank, we adjourned, and there waited till Jerry saw fit to leave off. They were certainly falling very near the mess and when we returned we found that two splinters had passed through the wooden side of the shed.

Lieutenant William Bloor, 146th Brigade, Royal Field Artillery

CQMS William
Andrews, 1/4th
The Black
Watch (Royal
Highlanders)

I had now had two and a half years on the Western Front, and had gained a very fair idea of how the German artillery mind worked. I could tell from the map – or I thought I could, which was just as cheering – on what points Jerry would fire. Thus, if you had a crossroads on a ridge with a high contour line, you might be certain that he had guns trained on it. All high ground, however peaceful it looked, if it was open towards Jerry's line, was dangerous. We old hands knew from the noise they made his different kinds of shells, and reckoned how many he would fire in one series. Armed with this knowledge, such as it was, whether accurate or not, I had no hesitation in halting my party before crossing a danger point and in rushing them over it as soon as I thought I could count on a lull in the fire. Some officers thought this a panic plan. They were like an officer who to show his contempt for danger, walked one night on our front line parapet. As he was shot in about two minutes, he taught us not the lesson he meant.

Lieutenant
George Brown,
9th The Suffolk
Regiment

Life here, in spite of all, has its humour, and to see others laugh and join in their laughter, although shells are bursting within 100 yards and often within 20, and bullets are whizzing round one's ears or splashing at one's feet, seems strangely natural. I would like to go to sleep, and for a while at least forget, but two of my platoons are out, and I am not going till they get back. Things are a little quieter now, though not much.

From tomorrow for five days or so I shall be in command of my position, shut off as it were from the outside world. Still, I expect the time will pass quickly. It's a great responsibility, and it's that that tells. It isn't as though I'd worked up to the position and had experience behind me. I plunged straight into it, walking before I can crawl. Still, I hope and expect to come through all right. Imagination on these occasions is rather a handicap. Don't think that I am depressed, I'm not, but these letters are more or less pictures of the moods I am in, and my time for writing is during the lonely vigils of the night, when depression holds its strongest grip on the tired mind and body; this and the never-changing scene of desolation around one, the waste, wreckage and carnage of war, must tinge one's mind towards gloom. One's pictures are set in sombre colours, and one's pen reflects mainly their darker hues. The cheerful moments here are too precious to lose. Cheer-oh!

'A Boche Company Headquarters', according to Captain Robert Perry. Perry is trying on a German helmet for size.

There were further advances on 4 October and again on 9 October, with further bites out of the German line. These included the low-lying but strategically important ridges and spurs that ceded not just local battlefield supremacy, but privileges of observation, protecting British troops, guns and transport passing through Ypres and into the salient, and also, east, views over German-held territory and Passchendaele village. The next step would be taken on 12 October. Private Hugh Quigley of the 12th Royal Scots would go over the top for the first time.

11 October: At sunset the battalion set out, each company with its set of pipers and drummers. The sky, from being a wonderful mauve-purple of great brilliancy where white balloons hung ghostlike and smoke from distant shells hovered mysteriously dim, grew dark almost at once; trees crept back into shadow, and the road, from a golden continuity, sunk into nothing. No outline lay on anything – ruins, hedges, fields, ditches, disappearing in an intense darkness. . . .

As I peered into each face to find my section, the harsh unnatural look was in all, that strange repellent tenseness of feature and expression caused by intense emotion – emotion not only of nerves strung to the utmost pitch, but of body, for almost every man had a dose of rum. The platoon

Private Hugh Quigley, 12th The Royal Scots (Lothian Regiment)

officer, usually a quiet retiring lad, not over-confident, surprised me with a mouthful of curses for being late. It might appear bravado, but I think I was the only cool one among them, actuated by a sense of wonder at so much excitement. After all, the business had to be done, and there was no use bunking it or flying into hysterics. The lucky chosen men would come back, the others would not.

Battlefield conditions now precluded any further use of tanks, which had been deployed on 9 October to little effect, the empty carcasses of which littered the battlefield, like Bion's machine, with no chance of retrieval. Quigley's battalion, part of the 9th (Scottish) Division, would be in the centre of the attack, known to posterity as the First Battle of Passchendaele.

Private Hugh Quigley, 12th The Royal Scots (Lothian Regiment)

The rifle grenadiers – I was one – slipped on their makeshift bags of bombs, bags made of sandbag with bands of split puttee. If there is an agony comparable to that strain on the shoulder caused by a dangling weight of a dozen grenades, when the pins and rods project and dig into the ribs at every step, I would accept it with wonder as being something unearthly.

Passchendaele had its own particular brand of exhaustion: British prisoners captured in in the Ypres Salient, October 1917.

Then the beastly puttee-band broke in two and I had to fasten it round a corner of the bag. I have lost count of the times that band was fastened. At every jolt it would drop with a thud, and at every irregularity the whole weight would shift forward and bow me down like an old cab horse unable to see the ground. With a groan I would pitch the ghastly thing back and then the band flew loose. Thus the rotten game started again. The man in front was palpably nervous; he lost trace of his forerunners time and again, and the whole company would stop till he made good. Every hole in the duckboard track seemed to put the fear of death in him, for he spent valuable minutes gingerly picking his steps, while the men behind cursed and swore. At last I drew my bayonet and told him the next time he stopped he would stop on its point. That cured him; he didn't lose connection again.

The dramatic entered into the business. After going about 8 kilometres, across a road where a transport lay shattered with men and mules scattered about, the work of a shell not ten minutes before, we entered the salient. Then no one could have told from what direction the shells were coming; they whistled and screamed behind, before, beside, until one thought the air so full of them that the mere matter of putting up a hand would be a sure way of encountering one at least. We passed a crowd of ambulance men carrying away wounded men who had been lying out for days. The shells began to burst very close; one dud almost hit me on the toes. ...

Graham Seton Hutchison's view across the morass at Polygon Wood, November 1917.

Overburdened with the weight of ammunition, and falling down as they staggered forward, Quigley and his three friends took the first opportunity that presented itself to jettison their bombs into a shell hole. It was an extraordinary act, given that these men were about to go into action and underscored the level of stress and exhaustion they were already feeling. The grenade-filled sacks disappeared into the mud without making a sound.

Private Hugh Quigley, 12th The Royal Scots (Lothian Regiment)

Then rain came down, the true Belgian blend. Like the others, I carried a spade between the pack and back. I never knew how thoroughly soaked one can be in a few minutes on account of this arrangement. The spade shank led the water nicely to the very small of the back. In a trice a river was running inside my trousers and over every part of the body. A strong wind blew, and the feeling of cold was so intensified that the bravest of us longed for a shell to come and end our misery. We stood for six hours in that blinding rainstorm, in battle position, before the order came to get into shell holes. This was no easy matter, for every hole appeared a veritable quagmire, where one sank to the knees in glutinous mud. I found a fairly dry one, and had just scooped out a nice comfortable recess where I could shelter from the wind when the barrage began.

Then, with rifles slung, and great trepidation in our hearts, we scrambled up, in any formation at all, and went forward into the heat of the flame....

None of us knew where to go when the barrage began, whether half-right or half-left: a vague memory of following the shell bursts as long as the smoke was black and halting when it changed to white. It was all the same to me: I was knocked out before I left the first objective, a ghastly breastwork littered with German corpses. One sight almost sickened me before I went on: thinking the position of a helmet on a dead officer's face rather curious, sunken down rather far on the nose, my platoon sergeant lifted it off, only to discover no upper half to the head. All above the nose had been blown to atoms, a mass of pulp, brain, bone and muscle.

Apart from that, the whole affair appeared rather good fun. You know how excited one becomes in the midst of great danger. I forgot absolutely that shells were meant to kill and not to provide elaborate lighting effects, looked at the barrage, ours and the Germans' as something provided for our entertainment – a mood of madness if you like. The sergeant's face struck me most, grey and drawn, blanched as if he had just undergone a deadly sickness. There was death in it, if ever death can be glimpsed in the living. A fat builder, loaded with 500 rounds, acted the brave man, ran on ahead, signalled back to us, and in general acted as if on a quiet parade. The last I saw of him was two arms straining madly at the ground, blood pouring from his mouth, while legs and body sunk into a shell hole filled with water. One highlander, raving mad, shouted to us, 'Get on, you cowards, why don't you run at them?' As if running could be contemplated with a barrage going 25 yards a minute.

Then the enemy put up a counter-barrage, something to make the hair stand on end, shells tripping over each other, gas sending out a horrible smell of mustard, shrapnel whirring just over our heads, and a strange explosive which ran along the ground in yellow flame for yards and took the feet from us. We rested in a shell hole for a minute, just to give our nerves a rest and escape the machine-gun bullets which pattered thickly on the ground all round us. I saw one gentleman going through the pockets of a dead German, very careful to unpin the Iron Cross colours on the breast. May he have good luck for his thieving.

The lightening effect appeared in great glory, superb in a word. The enemy knew exactly when the barrage would begin, for at 5.30 he sent up long streamers of green stars and a strange arabesque of yellow, red, and crimson lights; Very lights hovered all over the sky already paling in a grey bleak dawn. Then with a continuous drumming our shells burst on him; before us the country seemed a mass of crawling flame, wave after wave of it, until the clouds were blotted out, and our men advancing into it grew nightmarish, as if under a cliff of fire.

Vaguely, in the distance, several dark forms could be seen running over a ridge, the enemy retiring to be out of range. I had seen a dark blotch to the right, and was going towards it, thinking it a machine-gun post in our advanced line, when the enemy counter-barrage surrounded it and spread in long lines behind us. Thus we were shut in, and the only thing to do was to advance. Some of our shells fell short and exploded in isolated groups of men. But when the mud and smoke cleared away, there they were, dirty but untouched. The clay, rain-soaked, sucked in the shell

A wounded German is helped back during fighting near Polygon Wood. Few enemy soldiers were as fortunate as this one.

and the shrapnel seemed to get smothered, making it useless. One [shell] from the enemy fell behind me and made me gasp as if someone had poured cold water down the back. A man beside me put his hands to his ears with a cry of horror, stone-deaf, with eardrums shattered.

We got the first objective easily, and I was leaning against the side of a shell hole, resting along with others, when an aeroplane swooped down and treated us to a shower of bullets. None of them hit. I never enjoyed anything so much in my life – flames, smoke, lights, SOS's, drumming of guns, and swishing of bullets, appeared stage properties to set off a great scene. From the pictorial point of view nothing could be finer or more majestic; it had a unity of colour and composition all its own, the most delicate shades of green and grey and brown fused wonderfully in the opening light of morning. When the barrage lifted and the distant ridge gleaned dark against the horizon, tree stumps, pillboxes, shell holes, mine craters, trenches, shone but faintly, fragmentary in the drifting smoke. Dotted here and there, in their ghostly helmets and uniforms, the enemy were hurrying off or coming down in batches to find their own way to the cages. They knew our lines better than we. Nothing fulfils the childish idea of a ghoul more satisfactorily than those prisoners, mud-befouled, unshaven, terror-stricken, tattered, and heavily booted, with their huge helmets protecting the head so closely.

Then going across a machine-gun barrage, I got wounded. At first I did not know where, the pain was all over, and then the gushing blood told me. The problem now lay in front, how to get through the double barrage of machine guns and shells the enemy had out behind our advancing columns. I decided to make a run for it, but knew not where to run, and followed a German prisoner to an advanced dressing station, where four men carried me on a stretcher down the Passchendaele road, over a wilderness of foul holes littered with dead men disinterred in the barrage.

The attacking troops, British, Australian and New Zealanders, all failed to make any useful impression on the enemy positions, barely reaching the first objective and in many cases ending up back where they had started. Artillery support had been poor but it was not the fault of the gunners: their guns were sinking axle deep into the mud, some deeper. Indeed, before the battle was over, the position of some guns was known only by a fluttering flag on a pole. The action was called off.

The battle dragged on into November, the Germans desperate to close down the offensive, transferring two divisions from the Eastern Front to Flanders in order to shore up the defences. But what the Germans required most was persistent bad weather and it was being granted in bucketsful. Had the weather not intervened, perhaps Haig would have witnessed the breakthrough he had craved, but it was not to be. The fighting continued, Haig bringing down troops of Sir Arthur Currie's Canadian Corps to help push the line onto the Passchendaele Ridge, as much to get the troops onto dryer ground as to finally take this long-term objective. The offensive was finally halted on 10 November.

No troops who fought in the salient, on either side, had been more tested in battle. Major George Wade, an officer serving in the 20th Light Division, captured that sacrifice and undoubted heroism as well as anyone when he wrote about conditions near a duckboard track not far from Langemarck.

It was a terrible thought as one passed each of those stiff, chilled soldiers, that he had once been dear to some mother, wife, sweetheart or child, who had known him only when he was warm and full of life and who now could have no conception of what had happened to him on that fatal track.

Finally, as it grew dark, the track reached *Drop House* – so called because projectiles of various kinds were always dropping on it. It was a captured German structure of immense strength and it was now used as a

Major George Wade, OC, 172nd Machine Gun Company, Machine Gun Corps

Machine Gun Company HQ. In spite of the tremendous thickness, it had one fault – the entrance was on the enemy's side and was protected only by a huge mound of sandbags. Around it lay dead men, mules, broken limbered wagons and wheels, ammunition boxes, grave mounds and little wooden crosses.

Here were the guides, waiting to lead the various sections to the men they were to relieve, and here the duckboard track went off in different directions. From then onwards, the way was indicated by signposts of all kinds; some standing at various angles, others just lying on the ground.

There was no front line; just an irregular chain of shell holes seldom in touch with one another, each occupied by men whose faces were blue with cold and whose teeth chattered and hands shook. All were wet to the skin and crouching in mud and water sometimes up to their waist, not daring to raise their heads for fear of enemy snipers. Here and there, lying behind mud heaps, lay our own snipers, watching for a glimpse of the enemy. A feeling of intense misery pervaded the area – and always that smell of decaying flesh, which one could not ignore or forget.

Curiously enough, the most poignant memory of the front line was just a tiny piece of army biscuit. In a large shell hole there was a machine gun and its team. It was sandbagged one side and water had to be bailed out continuously. On the sandbagged side, a rubber groundsheet was hanging down. The sergeant asked in a hopeless way: *'Can anything be done about this man?'* He lifted up the groundsheet which was covering a niche in the wall in which lay a soldier. His face was waxen and his eyes were closed. His tunic was covered with bloodstained mud and he was breathing very faintly. He had been hit four days before and there had been no possibility of evacuating him in any way. The machine-gun crew had done all they could, bandaging him and rubbing his limbs to stop them becoming frostbitten. It was obvious that the wounded man was nearly dead, and when spoken to made no reply; but on his half-opened lips were little bits of army biscuit. That was all his fellow machine gunners had had to offer a mortally stricken man.

At that time there were a number of wounded men lying about on the knee-deep muddy battlefield and conditions were so impossible that no stretcher-bearers or carrying party of any kind could rescue them.

They lay dying in icy shell holes or in the open. It was so bitterly cold that they did not mercifully bleed to death but just lay there in hopeless misery. For six days one of our men, shot through both legs, lay out in no-man's-land, which was periodically swept by rain, hail, snow, machine-gun fire, and shrapnel from both sides. Each night Germans from a nearby shell hole crept out to give him a warm drink, every drop of which they must have longed for themselves as their plight was as bad as that of the British.

Endpiece

'Whatever is before me and whatever life brings, I must always be a better man for having known these things and lived with such men.'

Private Thomas Hope

Opposite: A study in resilience: Captain George Birnie, photographer and medical officer, attached 8th East Surrey Regiment.

———————

The Battle of Cambrai was the last concerted action of the year. It was, in reality, a large-scale raid that germinated into a small-scale offensive. Indeed, so low key were the original plans that no one, in retrospect, could recall precisely when it was first mooted, only that, as an idea, it was discussed as the fighting for Passchendaele seethed away in the north.

The operation would be led by the tanks, keen to prove their worth after being stymied in the Ypres mud. They could be used in large numbers on firmer, relatively unspoilt and chalky ground, to punch their way through the Hindenburg Line and cause considerable localized mayhem amongst German troops who would not expect further attacks before winter. In harrying the enemy, the assault fitted in with the Allied objectives of 1917, but it was not a strategic assault to take territory of critical importance to the enemy. The town of Cambrai served as a communications and transport hub for the Germans but was not initially a target. Yet as the momentum for the attack grew, so did the objectives, and by mid-November a decision was reached that if early and rapid success was achieved, the cavalry could be used to encircle the town.

Such was the speed of planning that no heavyweight bombardment was included, rather a short hurricane assault on key positions would be the prelude to an infantry attack by six divisions, spearheaded by an Armada of 476 tanks, the greatest concentration of the war.

At 6.20 am on 20 November, in mist and drizzle, a 1,000 gun bombardment opened up, smashing enemy batteries and defences before the tanks rolled over the enemy's barbed wire, engaging trenches and machine-gun positions while the infantry followed, using the tanks as cover. The results were unexpected and spectacular. The Hindenburg Line was breached with comparative ease, allowing the cavalry to exploit the breakthrough.

Remnants 4th B. The Worcestershire Regiment. (29th Division) after "CAMBRAI" Battle. November 1917. Going back to rest.

4th B. The Worcestershire Regt. marching out of the battle area after "CAMBRAI" 1917, having suffered severe losses.

As the troops moved forward, one village after another fell, one division advancing 5 miles. There had been hold-ups, even failures along the way, but these appeared dwarfed by successes. The Germans were reeling. Even so, the cavalry had not exploited gaps in the enemy line to threaten Cambrai, and over a third of the deployed tanks were knocked out or had broken down by the end of the day; important strategic positions were still in enemy hands.

The danger, as had so often been the case in 1917, was that momentum would be lost, giving the Germans time to recover. The failure to push on ensured the British would get caught up in localized fighting once again and a worrying salient in the enemy line had been created. Momentum slowed, and the window for wider strategic success closed as the Germans regrouped and rushed men up from their reserve. Heavy snow fell, hampering the movement of British troops and supplies, while the infrastructure of roads and tracks fell apart under the constant movement of tanks, limbers and guns.

Then, just as the British looked to shut down the offensive, the Germans counter-attacked the salient made in their lines, recapturing most of the ground lost on 30 November. British troops fell back in confusion; it seemed likely that large numbers of men would be cut off and surrounded. It took the involvement of the Guards Division to help restore order and to hold the line. The fighting first subsided and then officially ended on 4 December.

The year's four offensives had cost Britain and her Empire around 450,000 casualties, or around 2,700 casualties, on average, each fighting day, and that figure excludes the attritional losses in merely holding the line. The Germans had been brought close to battlefield exhaustion and, but for the terrible weather, the year might have ended differently, perhaps even with victory as Haig had so often mooted. We shall never know. The revolution in Russia changed the tide of war once again, for Russia's withdrawal from the war permitted Germany to switch a million troops from the Eastern to the Western Front and to launch its own bid to win the war the following spring. Some of the men whose testimonies appear in this book would be in France and Belgium to hold the British line, men like Driver Aubrey Smith and Sapper Albert Martin. Others were already dead, like Lieutenant William Bloor, killed by a shell explosion in January 1918. And then there were those, like Lieutenant George Brown and Company Quarter Master Sergeant William Andrews, who would be home for good; Brown was wounded and subsequently discharged. Both men had been through the very worst conditions that war on the Western Front could manufacture.

Lieutenant
George Brown,
9th The Suffolk
Regiment

My fighting days are over.... Of course, I should never really have come out, but seeing the chance I took it, and shall always be thankful that I did. For in these months I have had years of educational value, and have gained experience that will be useful to me throughout my life. To have learnt at first hand of war from which all romance has been stripped is indeed a gain, apart from the knowledge that danger brings and, greatest gift perhaps of all, the knowledge of human character. Well, no knowledge comes without payment, and I shall pay, for years to come, by a fractured dislocation of the shoulder and the constant ache of synovitis and rheumatism which such an injury will bring – and yet it has been worth it.

CQMS William
Andrews, 1/4th
The Black
Watch (Royal
Highlanders)

I call them the haunting years, for nothing in our time will haunt us like the war. Our dead comrades live on in our thoughts, appealingly, as if afraid to be forgotten. Peace came, but not at once for those who survived. The war pressed down on some of us like a doom for years after the last shot was fired.

I was luckier than most, but three years as an infantryman in France had worn me down. For some years after the war, like many, many others who had been there a long time, I woke almost every night in terror from a nightmare of suffocation by gas, or by being trapped by a bombardment from which I ran this way and that, or of fighting a bayonet duel with a gigantic Prussian Guardsman.

The specialists told me the best thing I could do was to forget the war, and build up with hearty feeding – porridge, apples with their skins, potatoes with their jackets, oatmeal cakes, wholemeal bread.

The advice on diet jumped with my humour. I craved for things rich and greasy and feeding. When I was coming home from the trenches on leave it was always sausages and eggs and tomatoes fried together that I longed for most. And one of the happiest moments of the peace for me was when we were at last allowed to go to a dairy and drink a glass of milk straight off. The specialists approved heartily.

But the other part of the specialists' advice, to forget the war: how was I to do that? How could any of us? By what effort of will could I blot out the memory of those years of flame and death, and life in trenches....

And then there was teenager Private Thomas Hope. His war was over, too: he was wounded in early December while carrying an urgent message across the open. His sojourn at the front had lasted less than five months, but in 1917, the most demanding year of all those fought, that had felt like a lifetime.

8 December: If I raise my head a little I can just see from the rear of the ambulance lorry the long winding road unfolding itself like a mysterious grey ribbon, guns, limbers, ammunition columns and parties of infantry, all going the same way 'up to the front'.

Private Thomas Hope, 1/5th The King's (Liverpool Regiment)

But the day for which I have longed and prayed has arrived. I am going down the line, away from it all, and yet a strange feeling mars my happiness. It is something almost beyond my ability to explain. I am leaving this manmade hell. That occasions my joy and also my sorrow, my joy at escaping from the shadow of death so lightly, my sorrow at losing all the things that shadow gave me.

No sunset was ever so entrancingly beautiful as the one the evening before an attack, no dawn so bewitching as the one that came with Zero hour. Scudding clouds and drenching rain, how exhilarating and refreshing when marching to a fire and a roof.

Did hot tea ever taste so much like wine as that first mouthful after hours of fighting? Was there ever a place like home when you might never see it again? What friendship so strong and above the strain of everyday life as that formed in a shell hole with death hovering around?

These are the things that shadow has given me, and though I may be leaving them behind, I must never forget them.

And those staunch comrades I'll never see again on this earth. Mac, who rests peacefully in a little cemetery on a gentle Picardy slope. Webby, who has no known grave, whose restless spirit must ever haunt the waterlogged flats of Flanders, prowling unseen over rain-soaked ridges and hovering in the valleys at dawn with the morning mist as its shroud, seeking, always seeking, the resting place that was denied its earthly form. Streaky, Naylor, Taffy, old Bellchamber, and all those others I knew whose very names spell 'The Salient' to me.

Whatever is before me and whatever life brings, I must always be a better man for having known these things and lived with such men.

Perhaps I have nothing to be sorry for; death had passed me by as I always had a feeling it would, and a new chapter is opening out before me. I must make it my second 'Great Adventure', and like the old grey-haired padre, I'll put my life and trust in God's hands, and He will carry me through.

A captured German sign, presumably in front of a barbed wire pen for British prisoners: 'It is forbidden to throw away or destroy military passbooks, identity discs or packets, epaulettes and so on. Infringements will be severely punished.'

Acknowledgements

I would like to say thank you to all at Pen & Sword Books who have been very helpful and supportive. Jonathan Wright is always extremely kind and has given generously of his time, when I know he has many other commitments: thank you, Jonathan. I would also like to thank Charles Hewitt for supporting this book. I am grateful for the kind and friendly help of the professional team at Pen & Sword: Tara Moran (marketing) and Heather Williams (production), who have both worked exceptionally hard to bring *The Road To Passchendaele* to print. I would also like to thank Jon Wilkinson for the cover design, and Dom Allen for the maps, as well as expressing my gratitude to Linne Matthews for astute and intelligent editing. Mat Blurton has once again pulled the rabbit from the hat with his superb layout design, and my thanks also go to Katie Noble.

Once again, I would like to note the kind help of my good friend Fiona Gell in Special Collections, Leeds University. The support of the Archive is always generously given, for which I am very grateful. I always enjoy my visits to the archive and the help of Fiona and her colleagues is second to none. My thanks too to Richard Davies, who is always helpful and offers his usual sage insights into the collection. Thank you all.

As always, I am indebted to my agent, Jane Turnbull. She has looked after me for many years and her professionalism is much appreciated. Once again, thank you, Jane.

My continued thanks to my family: to my mother, Joan van Emden, who has turned her great experience of the language towards this book and has made it all the better for her dedicated care and attention. My thanks again go to my wife, Anna, who is always supportive, and to Ben, our son, who may yet inherit the bug for WW1!

I am grateful as always to the following people for permission to reproduce photographs, extracts from diaries, letters or memoirs: Michael and Ann Brock for permission to use photographs from the album of Lieutenant Patrick Koekkoek; Richard Hills, for letting me borrow yet more images from the collection taken by his grandfather, Huborn Godfrey; Ian Collins for the images taken by his father, Norman Collins. I am grateful to Michael LoCicero, the author of the excellent *A Moonlight Massacre* (Helion, 2014) for his support and kindness and for permission to use the image (p.354) from his own collection. Thanks also to Paul Hewitt at Battlefield Design.

My gratitude for help and advice also goes to Julian Pooley of the Surrey History Centre, Jeremy Banning, Peter Barton, Jon Cooksey, Stephen Barker, Bob Smethurst and Taff Gillingham.

I have sought to obtain permission, whenever possible, to use all the illustrations and quotations in this book. When this has not been possible, I would like to extend an apology and would be glad to hear from copyright holders.

Sources and Permissions

Published Memoirs

Andrews, William L., *Haunting Years*, Hutchinson & Co, 1933

Bidder, Harold, *Three Chevrons*, John Lane, The Bodley Head, 1919

Bion, Wilfred, *The Long Weekend, 1897–1919*, Fleetwood Press, 1982

Bloor, William, *War Diary of Captain William Henry Bloor, RFA*, Ben Johnson & Co Printers, 1919

Bucher, Georg, *In the Line, 1914–1918*, The Naval & Military Press, 2005

Buxton, Andrew, *The Rifle Brigade, A Memoir*, Robert Scott, 1918

Collins, Norman, *Last Man Standing*, Pen & Sword Books, 2002

Creighton, Oswin, *Letters of Oswin Creighton, C.F.*, Longmans, Green & Co, 1920

Cuddeford, Douglas, *And all for What?*, Heath Cranton, 1933

Davis, A.H., *Extracts from the Diaries of a Tommy*, Cecil Palmer, 1932

Erberle, Victor, *My Sapper Adventure*, Pitman Publishing, 1973

Feilding, Rowland, *War Letters to a Wife*, The Medici Society, 1929

Floyd, Thomas Hope, *At Ypres with Best-Dunkley*, John Lane, 1920

Foley, G. A., *On Active Service*, privately published, 1920

Fraser-Tytler, Neil, *Field Guns in France*, The Naval & Military Press, 2003

Fuller, Sydney, *War Diary*, privately published, undated

Gibbs, Stormont, *From the Somme to the Armistice*, William Kimber, 1986

Greenwell, Graham, *An Infant in Arms, War Letters of a Company Officer 1914–1918*, Lovat Dickson & Thompson, 1935

Henderson, Keith, *Letters to Helen*, Chatto & Windus, 1917

Hope, Thomas, *The Winding Road Unfolds*, Putnam, 1937

Houseman, Lawrence, *War Letter of Fallen Englishmen*, Victor Gollancz, 1930 (incl letters from Lieutenant Henry Jones, Lieutenant Harry Lawson)

Luard, K.E., *Unknown Warriors*, Chatto & Windus, 1930

Mainwaring, G.B. (real name George Brown), *If We Return, Letters of a Soldier of Kitchener's Army*, John Lane Company, 1918

Martin, Albert, *Sapper Martin, The Secret Great War Diary*, Bloomsbury Publishing, 2009

Parry, Harold, *In Memoriam*, Privately Published, 1917

Pollard, A.O., *Memoirs of a Fire-Eater*, Naval & Military Press, 2005

Quigley, Hugh, *Passchendaele and the Somme*, Methuen & Co Ltd, 1928

Read, I.L. (Dick), *Of Those we Loved*, The Pentland Press, 1994

Rorie, David, *A Medico's Luck in the War*, Naval & Military Press, 2003

Russell, Henry, *Slaves of the War Lords*, The Naval & Military Press, 2009

Smith, Aubrey, *Four Years on the Western Front*, Odhams Press, 1922

Talbot-Kelly, R.B., *A Subaltern's Odyssey*, William Kimber, 1980

Thomas, Alan, *A Life Apart*, Victor Gollancz, 1968

Trounce, Harry, *Fighting the Boche Underground*, C. Scribner's Sons, 1918

Watson, W.H.L., *A Company of Tanks*, William Blackwood & Sons, 1920

Witkop, Philipp, Dr, German Students' War Letters, Methuen & Co, 1929 (including letters of Gerhard Gurtler)

Published Books

Barton, Peter (with Jeremy Banning), *Arras*, Constable, 2010

Barton, Peter, *Passchendaele*, Constable, 2007

LoCicero, Michael, *A Moonlight Massacre*, Helion, 2014

Nicholls, Jonathan, *Cheerful Sacrifice*, Leo Cooper, 1990

Unpublished Memoirs

Private George Culpitt, 10th Royal Welsh Fusiliers. By kind permission of Alan Culpitt

Archives

The National Archives

WO95/2385: Diary belonging to Major Bertram Brewin

Imperial War Museum, London

Lieutenant Edward C. Allfree. Ref: Documents 6976

Private Percy Clare. Ref: 15030

Second Lieutenant John W. Gamble. Ref: Documents 12003

Captain Lawrence Gameson. Ref: Documents 612

Sergeant Rupert S. Whiteman. Ref: Documents 3476

Lieutenant Arthur S. Worman. Ref: Documents 11819

The Liddle Archive, Special Collections, Leeds University Library, Leeds

By kind permission: Special Collections, Leeds University

Major George Wade – GS 1660

Photographs

All pictures are taken from the author's private collection unless otherwise stated.

Imperial War Museum, London

By kind permission of the picture library of the Imperial War Museum: pp.8–9, HU17544, p.14, HU17506, p.34, Q17528, p.37, Q17515, p.42, Q17531, p.57, Q17623, p.73, HU96217, p.78, HU96195, p.110, Q17575, p.112, HU96202, p.124, HU96188, pp.132–4, HU95899, p.170, Q17647, pp.220–2, Q56263, p.223, HU87971, pp.228–9, Q17646, pp.262–3 Q17652, p.264, Q17639, p.269, Q56255, p.298, Q56242, p.300, HU87970, pp.312–13, Q56253, p.316, HU87969, p.320, Q17648, p.321, Q56261, p.324, Q17445, p.327, Q56241, p.329, Q17650, p.340, Q17654, pp.347–8, Q56244, p.355, Q56249.

The Liddle Archive, Special Collections, Leeds University Library, Leeds

By kind permission of Special Collections, Leeds University:

Photographs by Lieutenant R.C. Perry: Ref. GS 1813. Half-title page, frontispiece, contents page, p.155, p.165, p.167, p.172, p.173, p.175, p.178, p.180, p.183, p.303, p.308, p.336, p.353.

Photographs of Lieutenant JD Todd:
Ref. GS 1607, p.294, p.331.

The National Army Museum, Chelsea, London
By kind permission of the picture library of The National Army Museum: Album of the 4th Worcestershire Regiment: NAM 1997-12-75-67 nos. 103600 and 103601, p.364.

Surrey History Centre, Woking, Surrey
By kind permission of the Surrey History Centre:
Photographs taken by Captain Birnie, 'Record of six months in 8th Battalion East Surrey Regiment', complied by Lt Lovell: Ref ESR/25/LOVE/1, p.225, p.266, p.270, p.271, p.273, p.276, p.286, p.289, p.291, p.292, p.295, p.303, p.362.

Photographs of Captain H.B. Secretan MC, 2nd Queen's Royal West Surrey Regiment: QRWS/30/SECR/1, pp.46–7, p.127, p.142, p.159, p.339.

Photographs of Lieutenant Patrick Koekkoek, Royal Engineers
By kind permission of Ann and Michael Brock: title page, p.27.

Photographs of Sergeant Huborn Godfrey, 215 Siege Battery, RGA
By kind permission of Richard Hills: p.19, p.23, p.50 p.52, pp.60–1, p.68, p.75, p.80, p.85, p.87, p.89, p.103, pp.106–107, p.144, pp.150–1, p.164.

Photographs of Second Lieutenant Norman Collins, 1/4th Seaforth Highlanders
By kind permission of Ian Collins: p.2, p.82, p.97, p.108, p.137, p.140, p.146, p.148, p.188, p.190, p.191, p.192, p.195, p.196, p.198, p.309.

Index

A NOTE ON THE AUTHOR

Richard van Emden has interviewed more than 270 veterans of the Great War and has written seventeen books on the subject including *The Trench* and *The Last Fighting Tommy*, both of which were top ten bestsellers. He has also worked on more than a dozen television programmes on the Great War, including the award-winning *Roses of No Man's Land*, *Britain's Boy Soldiers*, *A Poem for Harry*, *War Horse: the Real Story*, *Teenage Tommies* with Fergal Keane and most recently, *Hidden Histories: WW1's Forgotten Photographs*. He lives in London.

———

Gallipoli

Tommy's War

Meeting the Enemy

The Quick and the Dead

Tommy's Ark

Sapper Martin: The Secret Great War Diary of Jack Martin

The Soldier's War

Famous 1914–1918

The Last Fighting Tommy (with Harry Patch)

Boy Soldiers of the Great War

Britain's Last Tommies

All Quiet on the Home Front (with Steve Humphries)

Last Man Standing

The Trench

Prisoners of the Kaiser

Veterans: The Last Survivors of the Great War

Tickled to Death to Go (reprinted in 2014 as *Teenage Tommy*)

The Somme